Ageing with Smartphones
in Urban Italy

Ageing with Smartphones in Urban Italy

Care and community in Milan and beyond

Shireen Walton

First published in 2021 by
UCL Press
University College London
Gower Street
London WC1E 6BT

Available to download free: www.uclpress.co.uk

Text © Author, 2021
Images © Author and copyright holders named in captions, 2021

The author has asserted her rights under the Copyright, Designs and Patents Act 1988 to be identified as the author of this work.

A CIP catalogue record for this book is available from the British Library.

This book is published under a Creative Commons Attribution-Non-commercial Non-derivative 4.0 International licence (CC BY-NC-ND 4.0). This licence allows you to share, copy, distribute and transmit the work for personal and non-commercial use provided author and publisher attribution is clearly stated. Attribution should include the following information:

Walton, S. 2021. *Ageing with Smartphones in Urban Italy: Care and community in Milan and beyond*. London: UCL Press. https://doi.org/10.14324/111.9781787359710

Further details about Creative Commons licences are available at
http://creativecommons.org/licenses/

Any third-party material in this book is published under the book's Creative Commons licence unless indicated otherwise in the credit line to the material. If you would like to reuse any third-party material not covered by the book's Creative Commons licence, you will need to obtain permission directly from the copyright holder.

ISBN: 978-1-78735-973-4 (Hbk.)
ISBN: 978-1-78735-972-7 (Pbk.)
ISBN: 978-1-78735-971-0 (PDF)
ISBN: 978-1-78735-974-1 (epub)
ISBN: 978-1-78735-975-8 (mobi)
DOI: https://doi.org/10.14324/111.9781787359710

Contents

Chapter summaries — vi
List of figures — xiii
Series Foreword — xvi
Acknowledgements — xviii

1. Introduction — 1
2. Experiences of ageing: policies, perceptions and practices — 21
3. Everyday life, activities and activisms — 43
4. Social relations: social availability — 61
5. Smartphones: constant companions — 81
6. Health and care in digital times — 107
7. Coming of age with smartphones — 129
8. Life purpose: narratives of ageing — 142
9. Conclusion: threading together — 161

Bibliography — 171
Index — 182

Chapter summaries

This book is a fabric woven with the threads of multiple voices, ages and experiences. The resulting narrative is a combination of intersecting elements that make up the experience of age as, above all, the experience of living with and through many types of change. The northeasterly inner-city neighbourhood in Milan's zone 2, which in recent years has been termed 'NoLo' (North of Piazzale Loreto), is the physical setting of the volume, while much of the ethnography also took place in digital spaces and places that extend to the rest of Milan and, as the title of the book suggests, to much of the world *beyond*.

As outlined in the Series Foreword, this book forms part of a series based on the Anthropology of Smartphones and Smart Ageing (ASSA) project. *Ageing with Smartphones in Urban Italy* is not specifically a study of digital technologies among urban seniors in Italy. It approaches the subjects of ageing, smartphones and the urban Italian context in a broad anthropological frame, drawing on the holistic benefits of long-term urban and digital ethnography in order to examine the experiences of a wide range of people, of different ages and backgrounds, and how their lives play out amid multiple scales. These scales include multiple social contexts within the neighbourhood of NoLo, in the broader urban environment of Milan, across the country, and transnationally and digitally online in a changing Italy, Europe and world. A main focus of the book is the experience of midlife and older age, reflecting the ASSA project's collective research objectives and interest in studying ageing and technologies among older populations. However, this book also examines the lives of younger adults in Italy as a complementary perspective, discussing how individuals and groups invariably experience age and generation as an identity marker, alongside gender, sexuality, class and race. A range of categories and classifications are shown to impact upon individuals' sense of self, subjectivity and well-being at different points in their life, including where they feel they belong as they grow older or 'come of age' within – and beyond – the national context of Italy. The smartphone, as will be illustrated throughout the volume, has prominence in this figuring-out of life and the self, through the individual and collective forms of expression that the book examines.

The book is set within a broader global moment of rapid technological innovation, which, coupled with digital, urban and smart city developments in the city of Milan in recent years, has brought about a number of changes in how people live, communicate, work and retire. At the same time, ageing also involves experiencing a number of significant physiological changes, to and within the body, that affect how people live, view themselves and regard others. The book highlights how the smartphone device that accompanies people in their daily lives becomes embedded in wider practical, emotional and existential questions that in turn shape the embodied experience of life and the passing of time in this context. The smartphone, in this particular, anthropological account of ageing in a neighbourhood in Milan, is shown to be a tool for life, and for the multiple and creative ways in which research participants seek to tackle the various challenges and contradictions they experience and feel, or what I refer to as the 'ethical entanglements' of life's course.

Key findings

One of the core findings of the book relates to how categories of age are evolving in the light of wider changes in human sociality, mobility and aspiration in the digital era, and this is the focus of **chapters 1 and 2**. Research participants across the middle and older age groups expressed that they did not generally feel their age. Age may be associated with specific categories or expectations of being 'old' that might reflect normative ideas about being a grandparent, being at home or experiencing frailty, but ageing itself was part of a broader phenomenon, of experiencing life and its many changes. Official categories of age of course have specific implications in Italy as elsewhere; for example, the official retirement and pension age (currently 67) and the receipt of social support benefits apply to older adults, while for the children of citizens born in another country, who can apply for Italian citizenship only after the age of 18, age is a distinct political and legal marker. The book argues that it is important to acknowledge and deconstruct the top-down categories of age and separate them from the broader and subjective experiences of people in their everyday lives, including situating age and ageing within a broader framework of social and political justice concerning inequalities and discriminations throughout society. The experience of (older) age in a social sense is therefore differentiated from the experience of frailty, as a significant scholarship over many decades on the anthropology of age and ageing across the globe has highlighted,[1] and which is consistent with evidence from other fieldsites in the ASSA project, such as Ireland and Brazil, where people expressed similar distinctions.

In NoLo, Milan, initiatives aimed at older people (*anziani*), such as 'active ageing' or retirement groups, did not necessarily appeal to research participants who were retired. This was particularly seen among women, many of whom had experienced new forms of social agency through retirement, or generally in older age through volunteering, public service and neighbourhood activities, which constitute the focus of **chapter 3**. This chapter discusses how people in their sixties and seventies are very present and active in the public sphere in Milan, undertaking volunteering and a range of activities within the neighbourhood of NoLo, from allotment clubs, sewing groups and choirs to charities, church groups and cultural NGOs that work with migrants, asylum seekers and refugees. Social (and political) engagement in everyday life reflected people's moral and social outlooks through altruistic activities, and charity and social work: through these engagements people experienced an ethical engagement and a sense of purpose, and daily life in retirement had structure, routine and meaning. These public forms of participation were enhanced by WhatsApp and social media participation and interactions. The range of activities presented in **chapter 3** highlights the significance of cross-generational and cross-cultural social participation across the neighbourhood and in the experience of ageing with smartphones in this context.

At the same time, sociality has its limits. The theme of monitoring one's social life is something I pick up in **chapter 4**, which is built upon a theoretical framework I call 'social availability'. Social availability as a theoretical concept describes how people modulate their social participation or 'availability' to others via a range of mechanisms, from closing window shutters at certain times of the day to obtain some shelter, perhaps from sunlight or cold weather, or from the obligation to be social, to the smartphone version of this, such as exiting an app or purposely being seen as 'offline'. The issue here is about individuals' sense of autonomy and privacy in the social contexts of their lives, and how time for oneself is carved out and enjoyed amid broader social and care responsibilities, off- and online, and locally, transregionally or transnationally. Wanting to be variously socially 'available' or 'unavailable' can be about individual desires for social and private time, which may also reflect concerns about surveillance and privacy that arise from smartphone use and the sharing of personal data. However, it also relates to wider factors, such as economic necessity and social roles and responsibilities, that shape who can be available in various instances; for example, one may repeatedly be unable to go to or be late for choir because of uneven working hours or care responsibilities, but can stay connected and catch up on daily chit-chat via the WhatsApp group.

To put these practices into context, **chapter 4** discusses traditions and social roles that emerge from different regions across Italy – including kinship models or ideas concerning the family and the home – before exploring how these ideas and practices have been shifting over time, and how they take on new forms and wider meanings in the light of wider social, economic and technological change and transformations. The smartphone is discussed in this chapter as a prominent instrument for modulating sociality, and for navigating what a number of research participants called their '*equilibrio*', their equilibrium or balance, between social and private life and offline and online time, which people generally felt they wanted to – or *should* – control, but were sometimes unable to.

Chapter 5 zooms in on the smartphone as a material object of everyday life, teasing out some of the contradictions, affordances and problems it poses for people, such as guilt about how they spend – or 'waste' (*sprecare*) – so much time on it, versus how useful (*utile*) they find it as a 'companion' (*mi fa compagnia*). Smartphone addiction is shown to be a prominent theme in public discourse in Italy, and the chapter unpacks a range of these discourses in the light of the many ways people use smartphones in their daily lives and relationships. These include connecting with family, friends and community, organising schedules, work and finances, and navigating bureaucracy, citizenship and health. Case studies throughout the chapter illustrate how the smartphone can be understood within the broader constellations of practices through which people in midlife and in older age are engaged in crafting their lives.

Chapter 6 anchors the theme of ageing with smartphones in the field of health and care. The chapter provides an overview of the national and regional healthcare systems in Italy (and in the region of Lombardy in particular), illustrating how these systems have been and are currently experimenting with digital health innovation 'from above'. This discussion forms the backdrop to understanding how individuals are concurrently practising their own forms of digital health and care 'from below' in their daily lives, with and beyond smartphones, which, as I highlight in the chapter, has a range of implications for care, social relationships and wellbeing. For smartphone users, googling for health and using WhatsApp to communicate with and care for others, for instance, was not a wholly separate or distinct activity. Rather, it was enmeshed within the broader uses and moral evaluations of the phone that are mapped in **chapter 5**, and tied in with health and wellbeing practices derived from broader contexts, including family, regional and cultural traditions. The uptake and use of digital avenues for health information reflect issues discussed in the chapter such as unequal digital access, language barriers, and types of discrimination, which form part of the range of factors affecting the experience and equity of healthcare in Italy, and is part of the larger story of ageing with smartphones in the contemporary context.

In **chapter 7**, the theme of ageing is expanded by complementing the experiences of older people with those of younger people. The focus here is on younger adult children of whom one or both parents is from another country, the so-called 'second generation' in Italy, and their experiences of the meaning and significance of age, identity and citizenship.[2] The first half of the chapter explores this theme with research participants in their twenties, and the implications of discourses about 'new Italians' on the lives and subjectivities of research participants in Milan and across Italian society, whereby minority citizens and communities have been and continue to be constructed as Italy's and Europe's 'others' by discriminatory practices of inclusion and exclusion.[3] The latter section of the chapter broadens the discussion into an examination of identity and belonging in Italy among members of the Hazara community in Milan in their thirties who are originally from Afghanistan; some of them had come to Italy as refugees and had become resident in and citizens of Italy within the previous ten years. The chapter explores these younger people's pushes for social and political justice and human rights in Afghanistan and globally, through forms of activism, film-making and poetry. The examination of smartphone practices in this chapter looks beyond the claims of smartphone addiction, egoism or 'anti-social behaviour' that a number of the media reports and political narratives considered in **chapter 6** have directed at youth in Italy. Instead the chapter highlights dimensions such as popular culture, social justice, activism and identity practices, which also invariably resist or transcend notions of national identity based on a 'fictive ethnicity' or uncomplicated belonging.[4] Identities may instead be rhizomatic[5] explorations, in which, as many scholars working on transnationalism,[6] translocality[7] and urban environments have highlighted,[8] the city and urban neighbourhoods, schools and public spaces – to which I add an emphasis on smartphones and social media – play a significant part.

Chapter 8, 'Narratives of ageing', brings the core strands of the book together, by illustrating how *Ageing with Smartphones in Urban Italy* forms part of far larger, multigenerational and cross-cultural stories about how people narrate and shape their life experiences in and through the multiple contexts they inhabit, off- and online. Among the ideas explored in this chapter are the 'ethical entanglements' that people experience throughout life as they encounter various complexities and contradictions. These complexities include exploring ways of developing as an individual and maintaining belonging to place, a society, a culture or a family, or how to forgive yourself, make the best of things and develop narratives of self-justification when you are far from ageing and dying parents. The smartphone is centre stage in all of these ethical entanglements because it is deeply entangled with the person, their social networks and their socio-spatial geographies of work, life and care. In many ways the smartphone forms a kind of 'existential object', a particular type of human-technological hybrid object that people incorporate into their lives, relationships and subjectivities, and shapes the possibilities of what people might become with and through it, including how and 'where' they live.[9]

The intimate link between the individual and the smartphone outlined in **chapter 8** points to the notion, highlighted in the conclusion of **chapter 9**, of the smartphone as a 'constant companion' in the contemporary world. The book concludes by suggesting that ageing with smartphones in this urban Italian context is perhaps above all about living – with ambiguity and contradiction, with curiosity and change – in relation to the transforming world, to changing selves and to shifting classifications of and relationships with 'others'. In this sense, understanding people's relationships with technology and with change as they become older provides an anthropological window onto evolving experiences and expectations, scales and temporalities of being human in an age of rapid technological development and socio-political, economic and environmental change.

Notes

1. See Sokolovsky 2020a, 2020b.
2. Cohen 2009.
3. See El-Tayeb 2011.
4. Etienne Balibar (2002) uses the term 'fictive ethnicity' to describe the imagined notion of a nation-state community as a unit.

5. The term 'rhizomatic' derives from the concept of 'rhizome', a theoretical notion used by Deleuze and Guattari (1987) to describe multiplicities, interconnections and fluidity. 'Rhizomatic' is used in social sciences work on belonging and identity, in which, instead of being seen as fixed or defined by normative rules or procedures, these aspects are regarded as being in motion, and in the process of becoming.
6. Transnationalism is a key concept in social sciences to describe the multiple ties and interactions linking people or institutions across the borders of nation states. See numerous works in this field of study by Nina Glick Schiller (Glick Schiller et al. 1992; Glick Schiller 2014), Steven Vertovec (2009) and others.
7. Translocality is a concept used in social science that builds on insights from transnationalism (see note 6) and describes socio-spatial dynamics and processes of simultaneity and identity formation that transcend boundaries, including but extending beyond those of nation states. See Greiner and Sakdapolrak 2013, 374.
8. Soysal 2000; Balibar 2004; El Tayeb 2011.
9. For more on this idea of the smartphone as 'Transportal Home', see the ASSA project's collective volume, *The Global Smartphone* (Miller et al. 2021).

List of figures

1.1	Map of Italy showing the location of Milan. Created by Georgiana Murariu.	3
1.2	Photo of the Bosco Verticale in Milan, taken in 2019. https://commons.wikimedia.org/wiki/File:Bosco_Verticale_Milano.jpg. CC-BY-SA-4.0.	4
1.3	Map of Milan showing the nine municipalities. https://en.wikipedia.org/wiki/Municipalities_of_Milan#/media/File:Milan,_administrative_divisions_-_Nmbrs_-_colored.svg. Public domain.	6
1.4	Piazzale Loreto. Photo by Shireen Walton.	7
1.5	Painted mural at Parco Trotter, Milan: 'In my school no one is a foreigner'. Photo by Shireen Walton.	9
1.6	Popular hang-out spots in the neighbourhood. Photo by Shireen Walton.	10
1.7	Film: *Introduction to the neighbourhood fieldsite*. Available at http://bit.ly/introtonolo.	11
1.8	A street in the neighbourhood. Photo by Shireen Walton.	13
1.9	Film: *Urban Digital Ethnography*. Available at http://bit.ly/urbandigitalethno.	14
2.1	Film: *Short film portrait*. Available at http://bit.ly/filmportrait1.	34
3.1	Film: *One day in NoLo*. Available at http://bit.ly/onedayinnolo.	46
3.2	Community allotment in NoLo. Photo by Shireen Walton.	49
3.3	*Corso di cucito* (sewing course). Photo by Shireen Walton.	53
3.4	Street parade along Via Padova, Milan, celebrating diversity. Photo by Shireen Walton.	57
4.1	Window shutters on the *ringhiera* apartments. Photo by Shireen Walton.	62
4.2	*Ringhiera* apartments. Photo by Shireen Walton.	73

5.1	The Milan metro. Photo by Shireen Walton.	81
5.2	A typical kind of meta-commentary on the ubiquity of smartphone use today, shared on WhatsApp and other social media platforms via smartphones. Screengrab by Shireen Walton.	82
5.3	Film: *My smartphone*. Available at http://bit.ly/italymysmartphone.	85
5.4	A widely shared social media post that falsely depicted Libyan migrants as being ready to 'set sail to Italy'. Source: Twitter. Screengrab by Shireen Walton.	88
5.5	An infographic illustrating smartphone use in NoLo, based on data collected in the field. The sample was 30 participants. Created by Georgiana Murariu.	91
5.6	An infographic illustrating the use of different devices in NoLo, based on data collected in the field. The sample was 30 participants. Created by Georgiana Murariu.	92
5.7	An infographic illustrating the most used apps on participants' phones in NoLo, based on data collected in the field. The sample was 30 participants. Created by Georgiana Murariu.	92
5.8	An infographic illustrating the most used travel apps in NoLo, based on data collected in the field. The sample was 30 participants. Created by Georgiana Murariu.	93
5.9	An infographic illustrating the most used health apps in NoLo, based on data collected in the field. The sample was 30 participants. Created by Georgiana Murariu.	94
5.10	Watching an online cooking tutorial on the smartphone. Photo by Shireen Walton.	94
5.11	A greetings meme in NoLo. The text reads: 'Hello/good morning full of hugs'. Screengrab by Shireen Walton.	99
5.12	A meme sent in NoLo. The text reads: 'Tell the truth, you were waiting for my good morning!!!'. Screengrab by Shireen Walton.	100
5.13	Meme sent among friends. The text reads: 'Good morning'. Screengrab by Shireen Walton.	100
5.14	This device, halfway between a landline and an internet-enabled smartphone, was assembled by research participant Elisa. Photo by Shireen Walton.	103

6.1	Infographic illustrating Roberta's use of health apps, based on ethnographic data collected during fieldwork. Created by Georgiana Murariu.	114
6.2	Information posters in the area, directed at women's health. Photo by Shireen Walton.	120
8.1	Film: *Short film portrait 2*. Available at http://bit.ly/filmportrait2.	149
9.1	Objects and materials at the sewing group at the Centro Multiculturale. *Fascia per capelli* ('headband'). Photo by Shireen Walton.	162

Series Foreword

This book series is based on a project called 'The Anthropology of Smartphones and Smart Ageing', or ASSA. This project focused on the experiences of ageing among a demographic who generally do not regard themselves as either young or elderly. We were particularly interested in the use and consequence of smartphones for this age group, as these devices are today a global and increasingly ubiquitous technology that had previously been associated with youth. We also wanted to consider how the smartphone has impacted upon the health of people in this age group and to see whether we could contribute to this field by reporting on the ways in which people have adopted smartphones as a means of improving their welfare.

The project consists of 11 researchers working in 10 fieldsites across 9 countries as follows: Alfonso Otaegui (Santiago, Chile); Charlotte Hawkins (Kampala, Uganda); Daniel Miller (Cuan, Ireland); Laila Abed Rabho and Maya de Vries (al-Quds [East Jerusalem]); Laura Haapio-Kirk (Kōchi and Kyoto, Japan); Marília Duque (Bento, São Paulo, Brazil); Patrick Awondo (Yaoundé, Cameroon); Pauline Garvey (Dublin, Ireland); Shireen Walton (NoLo, Milan, Italy) and Xinyuan Wang (Shanghai, China). Several of the names used for these fieldsites are pseudonyms.

Most of the researchers were based at the Department of Anthropology, University College London. The exceptions are Alfonso Otaegui at the Pontificia Universidad Católica de Chile, Pauline Garvey at Maynooth University, the National University of Ireland, Maynooth, Marília Duque at Escola Superior de Propaganda e Marketing (ESPM) in São Paulo, Laila Abed Rabho, an independent scholar, and Maya de Vries, based at the Hebrew University of Jerusalem. The ethnographic research was conducted simultaneously, other than that of al-Quds which started and ended later.

This series comprises a comparative book about the use and consequences of smartphones called *The Global Smartphone*. In addition we intend to publish an edited collection presenting our work in the area of mHealth. There will also be nine monographs representing our ethnographic research, with the two Irish fieldsites combined within a single volume. These ethnographic monographs will all have the same chapter headings, with the exception of chapter 7 – a repetition that will enable readers to consider our work comparatively.

The project has been highly collaborative and comparative from the beginning. We have been blogging since its inception at https://blogs.ucl.ac.uk/assa/. Our main project website can be found at https://www.ucl.ac.uk/anthropology/assa/, where further information about the project may be found. The core of this website is translated into the languages of our fieldsites. The comparative book and several of the monographs will also appear in translation. As far as possible, all our work is available without cost, under a Creative Commons licence. The narrative is intended to be accessible to a wide audience, while more detailed discussion of academics and references are to be found in the endnotes. We have included films within the digital version of these book; almost all are less than three minutes long. We hope they will help to convey more of our fieldsites and allow you to hear directly from some of our research participants. If you are reading this in eBook format, simply click on each film to watch them on our website. If you are reading a hard copy of this book, the URLs for each film are provided in each caption so you can view them when you have internet access.

Acknowledgements

This book is the product of my research as a Postdoctoral Research Fellow at UCL Anthropology between 2017 and 2020. It is part of the Anthropology of Smartphones and Smart Ageing (ASSA) project, funded by the European Research Council (ERC) under the European Union's Horizon 2020 research and innovation programme (grant agreement no. 740472), to which I am grateful for the generous financial support. I wish to thank my colleagues at UCL Anthropology for years of insightful conversation, and the department for being such an inspirational academic home. I express my particular thanks to Professor Daniel Miller, for supporting me throughout this research and writing journey: his experience, energy and enthusiasm have been and continue to be inspiring. I would like to thank Georgiana Murariu for all her support and work on the manuscript, Ben Collier for editing the films, and all of the ASSA team members – Laila Abed Rabho, Patrick Awondo, Maya de Vries, Marília Duque, Pauline Garvey, Laura Haapio-Kirk, Charlotte Hawkins, Alfonso Otaegui and Xinyuan Wang – for their friendship, feedback and advice throughout the fieldwork and the writing of this book have been invaluable.

This book would not have been possible without the support, help and kindness of the people I met in Milan. They are the heart and soul of the book. I express my heartfelt thanks and appreciation to the neighbours I spent time with, the families I lived with, the bar and café owners I chatted with daily and the many research collaborators and participants who assisted and took part in my research. I am deeply grateful to the many friends and research participants who feature anonymously in the book and who participated in the short films: I cannot name them all here, but I thank them for generously sharing their time and stories with me, in different contexts and languages, as we explored the core themes of this book together. I would also like to thank Professoressa Carla Facchini and colleagues at the University of Milano-Bicocca for supporting my research as a Visiting Fellow in the Department of Sociology and Social Research, Lorenzo Caglioni for his friendship and support since the earliest days of my fieldwork in Milan, Piera and her family for their incredible generosity and friendship, and friends in the sewing group and the choir, and all who helped me and supported the research in countless ways across NoLo, Milan, and Italy. I am very grateful to the staff of UCL Press, Glynis Baguley who copy-edited the volume, and to the anonymous reviewers of this book for their insightful feedback and encouragement on the manuscript. All gaps in my understanding and errors in this book, of course, remain my responsibility.

Finally, I am deeply thankful to all of my family for supporting my work and movements in and between the UK and Italy, and for their lifelong love, support and inspiration, without which this book would not have been possible: to Michele for journeying with me throughout; to my mother, Simin, Chris, my brother Robin, and my beloved grandparents Ali and Mali, for all of their love and encouragement, and for our precious conversations. I would also like to thank Florin and David, Laura, friends, family and colleagues in Oxford, London, Italy and across the world, for their kindness, support and encouragement, which remain so invaluable and so much appreciated.

1
Introduction

Italy is a country in south-central Europe, marked by the Alps in the north and long coastlines on the Mediterranean Sea. The population is currently around 60 million,[1] and is the second-oldest in the world after Japan, approximately 23 per cent of the population being over the age of 65.[2] The median age of the population in 2015 was 46,[3] higher than any other European country except Germany (also 46), compared with the median of 41.6 in Europe. Population density is very uneven in the country, with almost half of the population residing in the industrial north, particularly in areas such as the Po Valley. Since the 1980s population growth has flattened: people are living longer and couples rarely have more than one child because of increasing economic pressures and work and movement patterns. The birth rate is currently 1.32 children per woman, which is among the lowest in Europe.[4]

Movement and mobilities

From the nineteenth century, during the Industrial Revolution in Europe, and until the 1960s, Italy experienced mass emigration, which has led to a vast Italian diaspora worldwide. Following the Second World War, the region of Lombardy, and in particular the city of Milan, saw two main periods of mass migration that require specific consideration in forming the basis for understanding the socio-demographic make-up of Milan today. The first period saw the internal migration of people moving to the northern regions and urban centres from the countryside and other regions of Italy in search of work. This has been considered both a cause and a consequence of the post-war economic boom, or 'miracle', as it has become known.[5] Later, from the 1980s, people from abroad increasingly came to Italy in search of work and better socio-economic prospects: individuals and groups have come from a range of countries, predominantly parts of North Africa and southeast Europe, in the context of economic growth and relatively low immigration controls.[6] Today, there are an estimated five million foreign-born citizens in Italy, which amounts to roughly 8.3 per cent of the population.[7]

The economic crisis of 2008 led to another period of rapid population change. The following years saw 1.5 million younger Italians move abroad,[8] which has had implications for the economy and society, as well as for relationships, family communications and care – themes that are examined throughout this book. High youth unemployment rates (27.8 per cent in 2019 – the third highest in the EU after Greece and Spain)[9] and the high cost of rent contribute to many younger people in Italy today living at their parental home into their thirties.[10]

In addition to these demographic changes, Italy has a prospering telecoms market, with a smartphone penetration rate of 58 per cent,[11] one of the highest in Europe. Government investment in recent years aimed at developing the fibre broadband sector nationwide has played a significant role in growing this market, and in developing 5G services in cities across the country. Digital communications have steadily altered the socio-economic fabric of the country, affecting particularly the experience of ageing and care.

The convergence of these changes and more constitutes the backdrop to this volume about ageing with smartphones in urban Italy.

Introduction to Milan

Milan is a city in the northern region of Lombardy (see Fig. 1.1) that has long been an important industrial hub within Italy and Europe. The city currently has a population of around 1.3 million in the municipality, while the surrounding metropolitan administrative area has a population of around 3.2 million.[12] It is the second-largest city in Italy after Rome (2.8 million). Milan underwent profound socio-economic and demographic changes in the post-war period of the economic boom years, including significant population movement within Italy[13] as people came to the city from the surrounding countryside and other northern regions, and then from southern Italy, to work, before settling and begetting future generations in the city.[14]

Milan today is a very different city from the Milan that many older adults I met remember from their youth. The city is strewn with former factories, many of which have been converted into co-working hubs, art

Figure 1.1 Map of Italy showing the location of Milan. Created by Georgiana Murariu.

galleries and educational establishments. Notably, the Milano-Bicocca university, which hosted me as a Visiting Researcher during my research in Milan, presents an impressive architectural structure, converted from the old Pirelli factory in the northeast of the city. Many older people today live by themselves or with their spouses, and many young people who left in the economic crash of 2008 are still living outside Italy and in other European cities. More than 45 per cent of households are single-person,[15] while many families are dispersed across the country and the world, and are in the business of working out how to be present and participate in each other's lives to varying degrees, in person or virtually.

The demography of Milan has undergone significant change with respect to ageing and migration patterns. Between 2003 and 2013 the total population grew by roughly 15 per cent, and although there has been a decrease in young Italian adults, this has been offset by an increase in older adults, children and citizens born abroad.[16] Today, in the city, around 260,000 citizens come from different parts of the world, making up roughly 19 per cent of the total municipal population.[17] According to official census figures, citizens born abroad are mostly from the Philippines, Egypt, China, Peru, Sri Lanka, Romania, Ecuador, Ukraine, Bangladesh, and other countries in the Middle East and in other parts of East and South Asia.[18]

Milan is known as one of the fashion capitals of the world and for its historical and contemporary reputations in the fields of design, architecture, food and glamour, from the iconic La Scala opera house, opened in 1778, the 1950s Pirelli Tower, which is a feature in post-war Italian neorealist cinema, and the Bosco Verticale ('vertical forest') building completed in 2014 (see Fig. 1.2), to the Milan Fashion and Design weeks and, since 2018, the annual Milan Digital Week, which reflects the city's active shift towards becoming a leading centre of digital innovation in the country.[19]

Because of a concentration of high-income groups in the city and its role in the tertiary sector (e.g. fashion, design, finance and publishing),

Figure 1.2 Photo of the Bosco Verticale in Milan, taken in 2019. https://commons.wikimedia.org/wiki/File:Bosco_Verticale_Milano.jpg. CC-BY-SA-4.0.

Milan is the metropolitan area with the highest average income in Italy. Despite the challenging economic climate in Italy, the city has in recent years undergone a kind of renaissance, typified by the 2015 World Expo that took place in and around the city, the second in its history.[20] The city has seen a lot of investment typified by new structures such as the Porta Nuova complex, an area of newly built skyscrapers, designer buildings, fashion houses, shopping malls, gyms and bespoke eateries in the mid-north of the city that brings capital, labour and tourism (domestic and international) to the city.

In addition to its reputation as a fashion and design capital, Milan has been widely recognised as an innovator of urban smartness and a leading 'smart city'. Since around 2010 the notion of the smart city has developed, building on earlier ideas of the digital or networked city.[21] It broadly denotes the increasing embedding of technologies into the infrastructures of cities around the globe.[22] Roberta Cocco, the Councillor for Digital Transformation and Civic Services of the municipality of Milan, proposed a specific agenda for digital development in the city comprised of four pillars: 1) digital infrastructure (including Wi-Fi, 5G and broadband), 2) digital services for citizens (regarding public administration and bureaucracy), 3) digital education (supporting digital literacy in order to access digital services and 4) digital skills (promoting these within the municipality and with cross-sector partners to boost employment and careers).[23] Cocco views Milan as a 'model of experimentation' with regard to technological urban innovation, and there is a consensus within the municipality and across the city that other Italian cities will follow suit. These developments in digital innovation in Milan will be referred to in chapters that specifically examine the presence of smartphones in daily life and digital health and care practices, in city, regional, national and transnational contexts.

Introduction to the fieldsite

My ethnographic research took place in a neighbourhood in Milan's zone 2 in the northeast of the city. The neighbourhood is or has been called 'Pasteur', 'Via Padova' and 'NoLo', reflecting particular historical periods, associations, ideas and preferences. Sometimes the terms are used interchangeably, as I will discuss later in the chapter. Zone 2 connects Milan's principal metropolitan area (zone 1) with its industrial and residential peripheral zones (see Fig. 1.3). The northeastern area of Milan contains the administrative and industrial districts 2, 8 and 9, which are known

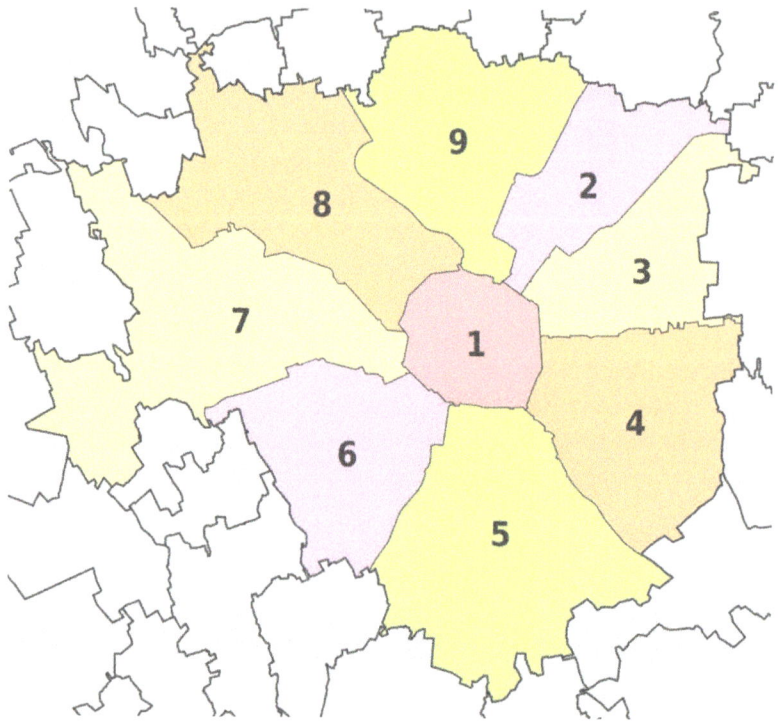

Figure 1.3 Map of Milan showing the nine municipalities. https://en.wikipedia.org/wiki/Municipalities_of_Milan#/media/File:Milan,_administrative_divisions_-_Nmbrs_-_colored.svg. Public domain.

as *zone di decentramento* (decentralisation areas). Some of the neighbourhoods in these districts were autonomous municipalities until the early twentieth century. In the 1920s these areas were annexed by the municipality of Milan and have since been incorporated into the wider city sprawl. Zone 2 is intersected by transport lines that connect it with the city, to the suburbs and beyond. The area has a diverse urban landscape and population, having undergone dramatic development in the second half of the twentieth century, before which the northeastern districts of the city were heavily industrial. In the years after the Second World War, zone 2 became a hub for people from outside Milan who came there to work and live, first from other parts of Italy and later from abroad. Until the 1970s, zone 2 was predominantly a working-class neighbourhood,[24] with a mix of recent migrants and settled communities, including different kinds of labourers.[25] In more recent years the area has undergone slow but significant gentrification because of an increasing middle-class presence in an area seen as a more affordable part of the city. Following the arrival of international migrants from the 1980s and 1990s onwards, the urban fabric has evolved, becoming increasingly socially diverse. Today 30 per cent of the residents in zone 2 are from other countries, which is the highest percentage among the Milan districts, compared with an average of 16 per cent of foreign-born citizens in Milan as a whole.[26]

Piazzale Loreto is the main geographical entry point to zone 2. Once a piazza and now a roundabout, it is a major landmark and thoroughfare in the city, distinguishing the commercial and tourist centre of the city from the wider administrative districts. Although the name Loreto refers to the roundabout/piazza (see Fig. 1.4), it is also used in a wider sense to mean the surrounding areas. The piazzale itself holds historical significance, being the location where the body of the fascist dictator Mussolini was publicly hung from the roof of a petrol station on 29 April 1945, after he was captured and killed by the partisan resistance in the nearby province of Como. Today, Loreto is typified by a mix of commercial and administrative features that include looming advertising billboards and 'office space to let' signs.

The main hub of my fieldwork was the area just north of the Loreto roundabout northeast of the city centre. The neighbourhood of Pasteur/Via Padova/NoLo is where this book is principally set, and where I lived

Figure 1.4 Piazzale Loreto. Photo by Shireen Walton.

during the research. However, wider sites across the city and country also inform the research, since I was studying not just the physical setting but also socio-economic and digital networks. I refer to the fieldsite throughout the volume as 'NoLo', reflecting the widespread use of this term by many of the people who live there, including the people who participated in the research. The area is slowly gentrifying, and has been coming to the attention of the media, academics, artists and writers,[27] youth and popular culture. Media and political discourses have represented the area in various ways, as a multi-ethnic neighbourhood, sometimes suggesting that it incorporates insecurity and urban violence, while community actors continue to challenge such representations and combat stereotypes,[28] which will be explored in chapter 3.

The neighbourhood has a range of architectural styles. At the southwestern end, nearer to Loreto and the centre of the city, there is a mixture of nineteenth-century apartment buildings, known as *palazzi*, early twentieth-century typically Italian structures in which families and older people live, the *case di ringhiera* apartment buildings with long balconies and single housing units facing an inner central courtyard that are typical of industrial, working-class Milan, and more modern buildings. Towards the northeastern end of Via Padova there are more post-war high-rise apartment blocks. Walking up Via Padova from Piazzale Loreto for a few hundred metres, one encounters banks and business buildings, with parked scooters and cars, along with numerous takeaway places, restaurants, eateries and cafés, as well as electronics shops.

The diversity seen across the neighbourhood recalls the notion of 'super-diversity' discussed by the anthropologist Steven Vertovec to highlight the 'multiplication of significant variables that affect where, how and with whom people live',[29] which includes conceiving of 'diversity' not only in terms of ethnicity.[30] The term 'hyper-diversity' has also been used in specific relation to Milan and the area of zone 2, highlighting 'not only ... diversity in ethnic, demographic and socioeconomic terms, but also ... the differences that exist with respect to lifestyles, attitudes and activities'.[31] Individuals have very different daily and life routines, between public and private practices and mobility patterns that might be neighbourhood-bound, and also extend across the city (and beyond) through 'multi-scalar networks'.[32]

Digital smartphone practices feed into distinctive experiences of everyday life online, as offline. In NoLo, there can be moments and spaces in which to experience or perform 'Peruvianness', for example at group hang-outs in the parks, at barbecues and at buffet lunches in the many Peruvian restaurants in the area, while developing one's relationship to the Italian urban context and to a range of identity markers based on diverse urban social formations and groups, such as being a 'yogi' (a person who practises and is proficient in yoga) or a horticulturalist.

Still, matters of identity loom large in Milan. Many people are depicted as – or feel themselves to be, in one way or another – outsiders or foreigners in the city or the country. Conversations between people meeting for the first time may be marked by the question 'Where are you from?' In some cases this may be the casual utterance of, say, a curious neighbour, while in other contexts the question may be positioned or received as a more political issue connected to ideas about 'Italianness' and belonging: regional identities remain strong in Milan. A host of groups and organisations across the neighbourhood demonstrate and promote respect for the co-existence of people's diverse backgrounds, in recognition of the journeys that have brought people to this place over time from across Italy and the world. One of the state primary and middle schools in the neighbourhood visibly declares this ethos with a prominently positioned painted mural adjacent to the school's main entrance that reads 'In my school no one is a foreigner' (Fig. 1.5). There is a deep historical dimension to practices and logics of foreignness and otherness within the Italian context, which concerns the history of unification, regional identities and conflicts, mobility patterns and different encounters with

Figure 1.5 Painted mural at Parco Trotter, Milan: 'In my school no one is a foreigner'. Photo by Shireen Walton.

integration, discrimination and racism over time. Research participants across NoLo would share their experiences of these themes, which had variously shaped their lives, and so notions of identity and belonging form part of the narrative about ageing presented in this book.

The area has witnessed gentrification in recent years, and there is an increasing presence of young people, including those who through clothing and visual and material culture reflect aspects of urban cultural consumption and practice associated with the category of 'hipster'[33] and are part of the story of the urban and socio-economic transformation of the area. Several hang-out spots, such as the bars and eateries around Via Padova and the parallel roads running to the west, including nearby Viale Monza and Via Giulio e Corrado Venini, have been opened by younger people in the last few years, and these places are full of people coming to eat, drink and socialise, in line with the Italian *aperitivo* ritual, which consists of a drink and a bite to eat – sometimes closer to a full meal – usually from around 6 p.m. A number of these bars are also social spaces, hosting photography exhibitions, live music performances or theatre productions. A hub of this younger vibe is Piazza Morbegno, where, nightly, groups spread out into the street drinking beer and cocktails, and hang out after work or university (see Fig. 1.6).

Figure 1.6 Popular hang-out spots in the neighbourhood. Photo by Shireen Walton.

Figure 1.7 Film: *Introduction to the neighbourhood fieldsite*. Available at http://bit.ly/introtonolo.

All of this makes for a multigenerational and multicultural urban setting, where diverse lives are lived in close proximity, which I reflect upon in the short film that introduces the neighbourhood fieldsite (Fig. 1.7). This setting is reflected in the multigenerational focus of the book, which seeks to highlight the distinctive experiences in individual lives, and the urban and digital domains of commonality people share by being in NoLo together, either physically or virtually.

NoLo: what's in a name?

The concept of NoLo has developed since 2016, when residents of the geographical neighbourhood came together around a Facebook group, NoLo Social District.[34] This follows the concept of the 'Social Street' in Italy, which originated in Bologna in 2013[35] and was developed among residents in a Bologna neighbourhood who created a Facebook group to promote socialising between residents of the area, to build relationships, exchange needs, share expertise and knowledge, facilitate collaboration and foster social interaction 'from virtual to real life'.[36] Because of this origin, the Social Street group, and its NoLo counterpart which followed suit, remain closed Facebook groups. Individuals have to ask to join by answering a few questions about where they live in the area, and the area itself. The Social Street has spread across Italy and the founders have established a 'how-to' guide for other city communities to follow. The model operates by sociality and word of mouth; there is no financial investment, only, as the central platform states, a 'willingness to interact with your neighbours'.

I arrived in NoLo in 2018, when the concept was becoming known but was still relatively new, and therefore the unfolding of this concept accompanies the story of my research. I saw how many social areas increasingly adopted the NoLo brand. Radio NoLo, for instance, is a neighbourhood radio station that has become popular across Milan. The GiraNoLo-themed neighbourhood walking tour group of the area also became established (*girare* means to take a turn or short walk), and NoLo4Kids is a community group for parents of young children that undertakes group activities and meet-ups. Annual events such as NoLo Pride are prominent points in the neighbourhood calendar, alongside the recently established NoLo fringe theatre festival and the SanNoLo music festival, playing on the national Sanremo music festival.

During my fieldwork I was able to live in and study the development of the neighbourhood amid the wider development of the city. Debates about the name of the area refer to discussion in the neighbourhood's history regarding its gentrification, and to critiques of neoliberalism directed at Milan's moves to become a leading European smart city.[37] I came to know many of NoLo's chief advocates, participants and designers, as well as other members of the population, including a small selection of older adults who preferred to call the neighbourhood Pasteur or Via Padova.

As an anthropologist, I employ the term NoLo as an ethnographic category;[38] in other words, it reflects how the term was employed by people I spent time with in the field.

Methodology: urban digital ethnography

My research was carried out within the geographical place and social spaces of the neighbourhood of NoLo described above, where I lived and carried out ethnographic research for 16 months (see Fig. 1.8). The research was conducted mostly in the Italian language, as well as in Persian when I conversed with Hazāragi-speaking members of the Hazara community in Milan. One of the central principles of long-term ethnography is participant observation, a method of social research involving immersion in the daily lives of the groups and individuals within the context one is exploring. It involved collaborative discussions with research participants and friends, concerning the themes of life, age and social and technological change. In NoLo I undertook a range of

Figure 1.8 A street in the neighbourhood. Photo by Shireen Walton.

activities through which I came to meet and get to know people, hang out with them and experience with them the different aspects and textures of daily life in multiple settings. These activities included volunteering in the community, joining a multicultural women's centre and 'social space' as part of an NGO that carries out social activities (including a women's sewing group) and provides support for women in the area, joining a multigenerational women's choir and attending social events, such as shared dinners at the community allotments and Saturday morning community breakfasts in NoLo where people bring food and drink to share. In the diverse neighbourhood urban setting, I adapted with care to the different contexts I became involved in, in order to be in and traverse different spaces appropriately. During my time in Milan I also frequented, and supported events at, a restaurant that doubled as a cultural centre and which is located beyond NoLo, to the north of the city, learned how to cook Sicilian and Egyptian foods and sweets, was a teaching assistant in Italian language classes at a cultural NGO and lived in a diversely populated apartment block, a *casa di ringhiera*, in the fieldsite. All of this added up to a rich and immersive way of sharing time and stories with people in more intimate registers.

In addition to the 'hanging out' of ethnography, I carried out 30 in-depth semi-structured interviews with research participants in the neighbourhood on the themes of ageing and care, health, relationships and the life course. Most of these longer 'life story' interviews were carried out in people's homes over coffee, as well as in public places such as cafés and parks, on walks, at restaurants and in takeaway eateries. All of these interviews entailed a focus on the smartphone in the lives of people between the ages of 45 and 80, including narratives about the smartphone – how people view it and use it, and how it shapes their daily lives and practices. I also observed the smartphone as a material object, observing how people adorn it with stickers, or photographs of grandchildren stuck on with tape, how they personalise their screensavers, and engage with their photos and apps. I was curious as to why one person had arranged the placing of their apps in a colour order, while someone else did it in order of those most used, why another person did not care, and how someone else ran their business via an app and scheduled their daily life via WhatsApp. These interviews form the basis of the discussion of smartphones and apps in chapter 5, and some of them are reflected in the short films that are embedded throughout this volume.

The smartphone as object of research was directly implicated in the research methodology. It both formed an object of study (what I was exploring) and contained within it multiple site(s) of study. 'Following the thing' with the smartphone took me where I needed to go, or was drawn into through the research and through my engagement with the people I came to know, including offline in the neighbourhood and across Milan, and online to WhatsApp conversations, Google Maps, bespoke

Figure 1.9 Film: *Urban Digital Ethnography*. Available at http://bit.ly/urbandigitalethno.

apps, photo archives on smartphones and geographical locations.[39] Incidentally, spending a number of evenings in my apartment in NoLo on WhatsApp was a significant part of how I engaged with urban digital ethnography[40] – both sited in place *and* virtually augmented; I was present over many months of research (and continuing to be connected) with research participants and friends, both offline and online, in various social contexts, languages and 'affective economies' across the distributed fieldsite of NoLo.[41] In the short film above (Fig. 1.9), I discuss living in the neighbourhood, and how I carried out my research.

The approach

In this book I have aspired to a particular way of thinking and writing, just as I had aspired to a certain way of researching ageing with smartphones in NoLo. I discuss the overarching approach here, starting from the research framework of a neighbourhood or community ethnography and the scope, scales and limitations of the research. Neighbourhood ethnographies were prominent approaches in urban ethnography in the 1990s, seen in diaspora and migration studies, and in studies of multiculturalism and 'superdiversity' in particular. However, a problem of neighbourhood ethnography, similar to the one pointed out in critiques of the concept of community in anthropological studies, is its potential methodological logic,[42] in which focusing on certain groups within a specific area may imply a certain distinction or detachment of the lives, networks and experiences of individuals and groups apart from broader social contexts, namely the rest of the city, society and the world. Approaches to place as fixed in time and space have long been regarded as outmoded by anthropologists, among whom a significant scholarship highlights, for example, how places, as contexts of human experience, are, as anthropologist Christopher Tilley has put it, 'constructed in movement, memory, encounter and association' and encompass 'far more than location'.[43] Furthermore, Ayşe Çağlar and Nina Glick Schiller, writing about urban ethnographic research, emphasise a focus on 'multi-scalar' economic and social networks that traverse parts of cities, transnationally and globally.[44] Inspired by these approaches to place, space and the city, while also foregrounding the neighbourhood and its related (and wider) *digital* environments as a locus of social life and ethnographic enquiry, my research investigated the social economic and digital networks that emanated from within NoLo and also traversed spaces of the city of Milan, and which operated transnationally. Therefore, although I was physically based in NoLo, my research was not reducible to or contained by the geographical space, but was rooted in a number of networked social fields in motion.[45]

This book employs a concept of the social that considers how urban social life can be built through and on 'domains of commonality'[46] that are invariably witnessed both in urban spaces[47] and in digital environments, from parks, schools and apartment buildings, to social media and smartphone apps that pertain to wider offline city-based sociality, and to broader, transnational socialities. In particular, the book foregrounds the experiences of individuals and groups with whom I became connected via participant observation, offline and online, over the course of 16 months, including a number of people I came to know as friends, and neighbours, individuals, couples and families I met through volunteering activities and other forms of participation in the neighbourhood in which I lived. My approach, in entering the field, was to keep the ethnographic frame wide, in order to participate and observe, and over time to experience, explore and think collectively with people about how they experienced their daily lives, online and offline. This being so, I did not focus my research or writing on a particular social or ethnic group.[48] The aim, rather, was to carry out research with a range of people and their transnational social and digital networks, and to try to understand their particular and collective experiences, while also excavating various logics of distinction and exclusion that invariably work to classify selves and others in different ways and contexts.[49]

As mentioned earlier in this chapter, notions about Italians (*Italiani*) and foreigners (*stranieri*) are widespread in Italy, in discourses ranging from political and policy narratives to daily chit-chat, and accordingly the construction and employment of categories of persons, and within and between different age groups, became a core component in the research and writing of this book, as it relates also to intergenerational relationships and narratives of ageing and socio-cultural change and continuity. A person from another region of Italy can feel, or be regarded as, a kind of outsider to Milan, while someone from a rural context might be discriminated against by urban dwellers, as was often seen in the post-war period. At other times, people from distinct regions might be viewed as, or self-identify as, *Italiani*, in contradistinction to migrants and citizens born in different countries, or they may feel a shared but differentiated foreignness based on being outsiders to Milan.[50] Encountering these moveable identity distinctions during fieldwork in Italy pointed me towards the frameworks, histories and exclusionary logics by which identity categories are constructed over time and in the present, including ethnonationalist notions of 'Italianness' as white European.

The examples and case studies that are positioned throughout the book aim to reflect, on the one hand, the diversity of the experiences of the people I conducted research with and among in Milan, and, on the other, their shared concerns, experiences and practices. Such occurrences range from the experiences of displacement and ruptures in life that accompany different biographical journeys involving movements and migration, to various instances of feeling social and cultural disjuncture in Milan, and to how one can feel intimacy and distance at once through the smartphone and its geolocative and emotion-locative capacities, to how sociality – however desired, shared and enjoyed – does not erase the needs, desires and hopes of individuals. Accordingly, these are some of the main themes of this book.

The people

The people you will meet in this book are friends and people I was fortunate to spend time with, get to know and share stories with in Milan and online. They are from a broad range of backgrounds and socio-economic contexts from across Italy, including Sicily and Apulia in the south, and from countries including Egypt, Peru, the Philippines and Afghanistan. People who had moved to Italy from abroad had done so at various points in their lives and under different circumstances, which are discussed throughout the book in relation to individual case studies and biographical journeys. The majority of the research participants had been living in Italy/Milan for approximately ten years and had acquired residency or citizenship. The age range in my study was generally between 40 and 85, while chapter 7 specifically looks at the experiences of younger people, including the so-called 'second generation' of young people in their twenties and Hazara research participants from Afghanistan in their thirties. The names of the research participants are pseudonyms, and some details have been changed or omitted for the purposes of anonymity. The Hazara film-maker, journalist and poets whose works are discussed in chapter 7 are referred to by their real names in relation to these works.

Understanding people's experiences of and discussions about age and ageing, whether as younger adults, approaching midlife or in older age, involved an emphasis on biography and narrative; this is reflected in the book as a whole and culminates in the penultimate chapter (chapter 8), which is subtitled 'Narratives of ageing'. What connects a number of the people featured in the book, at different stages in their life, is that, first, they now live in Milan, and, secondly, most of them demonstrate preoccupations with care, time, social relationships and economic circumstances. All shared experiences of navigating questions of 'belonging' in different ways throughout their lives, all described a number of ethical dilemmas in life that they had sought to work through via various means, and all used smartphones regularly in their daily lives. Research participants generally aspired towards personal development and a better future for subsequent generations, and these aspirations were met with uncertainties of multiple kinds and scales. In NoLo, as we shall see throughout the book, the smartphone accompanies people in their daily lives, through larger periods of rupture and uncertainty throughout life and amid the uncertainty and moral anxieties of the age, and concerning the future, in which, as some pointed out more than others, digital technologies and smartphones are deeply implicated as the age of surveillance capitalism unfolds.[51]

The ultimate aim of this volume about ageing with smartphones in contemporary urban Italy – in line with the Anthropology of Smartphones and Smart Ageing research project as a whole – is to illustrate the humanity of people amid technological change, as well as the technologies, infrastructures and practices that are involved in personal and social transformations in ageing, as the digital age unfolds.

Notes

1. Tuttitalia 2020b.
2. Tuttitalia 2020c.
3. See Hall et al. 2019, 29.
4. Johnson 2020.
5. Foot 2008.
6. There are exceptions to the changing socio-demographics of the city that fall outside these general timeframes of immigration patterns to Italy, such as the Chinese communities in Milan present since the 1930s, the Somalian refugees of the early 1970s and the growth of Milan's Jewish community. See Foot 2001, 39.
7. Such official census figures exclude undocumented migrants and refugees.
8. See Romei 2017.
9. See Eurostat 2019a.
10. See Eurostat 2017b.
11. Sources from 2018 global statistical reports on smartphone usage: Newzoo 2017; Statista Research Department 2016; Poushter 2016.
12. Comune di Milano 2018.
13. Foot 1997, 185.
14. On the social history of Milan in the post-war period see Foot 2001 and Foot 1997.
15. Barberis et al. 2017, 27.
16. Barberis et al. 2017, 27.
17. Tuttitalia 2020a.
18. Tuttitalia 2020a.

19. The inauguration of Milan Digital Week concept coincided with my fieldwork in 2018–19. See Milano Digital Week 2020.
20. The Milan International world fair, *L'Esposizione Internazionale del Sempione*, was held in 1906.
21. Datta 2019.
22. Academic literature on the smart city from the social sciences that has emerged over the last decade is prevalent in the fields of urban and human geography. See for instance the work of Ayona Datta on smart cities and digital urban transformations in India, and Gillian Rose on smart cities and the (visual-digital) production of knowledge. The smart-city concept can best be understood as a constellation of features and potentials made up of big data, algorithmic governance and automated urban management, as well as citizens' active engagements with technologies. Critical social science scholarship has argued that the smart city represents a 'techno-utopian fantasy' (Datta 2019), bringing together two neoliberal urban visions: that ICTs will drive economic growth and urban prosperity, and that they can make urban governance more efficient and equitable. Broader research has highlighted the acute contradictions within smart urbanism, including its very different expressions across the global North and South and digital divides (Luque-Ayala and Marvin 2015).
23. See a transcript of an interview with Roberta Cocco at Morning Future 2019.
24. Agustoni and Alietti 2014.
25. Agustoni and Alietti 2014.
26. Barberis et al. 2017.
27. In her novel, *Milano, fin qui tutto bene* ('Milan, so far so good'), the Indian-Italian writer Gabriella Kuruvilla (2012) describes daily life in Via Padova. Kuruvilla paints a picture of the area in an ethnographically rich manner, detailing the lives of the people she knew and spent time with.
28. Verga 2016.
29. Vertovec 2007, 1025.
30. Among the variables that affect where, how and with whom people live that Steven Vertovec highlights are 'differential legal statuses and their concomitant conditions, divergent labour market experiences, discrete configurations of gender and age, patterns of spatial distribution, and mixed local area responses by service providers and residents. The dynamic interaction of these variables is what is meant by "super-diversity"' (Vertovec 2007, 1025). See also Vertovec 2016.
31. Barberis et al. 2017, 12.
32. 'Multi-scalar' as used here is a methodological perspective drawn from contemporary urban anthropological scholarship that highlights the move beyond fixed notions of urban communities, and ethnic categories as units of study and analysis, to examining the complex, plural, heterogeneous, multidirectional relations and ties between groups in an urban environment. See Çağlar and Glick Schiller 2015.
33. The concept of 'hipster' is defined in a range of ways in different contexts, including in sociology and studies of contemporary urban subcultures. In an article discussing this topic, Janna Michael has suggested: 'The hipster can be seen as the ideal type of a trendy person: he or she is on top of current trends, owning vintage items before their remake appears in mainstream clothing chains, inhabiting the trendiest areas of urban centres' (2015, 164). Elements that have popularly come to characterise the hipster subculture may include the wearing of vintage or non-mainstream clothes, full beards, stylised moustaches and vintage make-up (Maly and Varis 2016). Lorenzo Caglioni (2020), on the basis of ethnographic research in London and Milan, defines the hipster subculture in terms of commitment to certain ethical values and practices, such as engaging with sustainable materials and produce (including clothing and food). This engagement, and the sustainable materials and produce, reflect this generation's experience of cultural and material crisis. Caglioni writes about a 'crisis generation' of people born in the 1980s and the 1990s, for whom the hipster can be seen as embodying economic, social, political and cultural change.
34. For more discussion on the founding of the NoLo Social District Facebook group see, for example, Di Iorio 2020.
35. See Social Street 2020.
36. 'Residents of Fondazza Street' Facebook page.
37. During my fieldwork, I witnessed a number of resistance practices such as protests, banners, graffiti and gatherings among groups, including students in their twenties and thirties,

protesting against the neoliberalisation of the city of Milan. These resistance practices contested Milan's budding reputation as a smart city and a centre of the Italian gig economy.
38. This 'in-field' or 'in-*voce*' approach represents what is known in anthropology as the emic perspective. The distinction between the emic and the etic perspectives is that the former presents the voices of research participants in 'the field', and the latter the anthropologist's voice or analysis.
39. Here, the smartphone represents a methodological insight for contemporary (digital) anthropology. As an object of material culture that one attends to, follows, stays with, listens to, the smartphone represents what I have elsewhere called a 'place-object', an object – either a technology such as a smartphone, or a digital photograph – that takes the researcher where they need to go for research. The object puts the researcher into a 'place' (a place-object) for social research. This can be a spectrum of spaces, physical, social or digital. See Walton 2020.
40. Urban digital ethnography, or 'digital urban ethnography' (Lane 2019), builds on scholarship that highlights the interrelatedness of urban life and digital media and communications. See for example Georgiou 2013.
41. 'Affective economies' is a term used by Sara Ahmed to describe how emotions do things, such as align individuals with communities – or bodily space with social space – through the very intensity of their attachments. See Ahmed 2004a.
42. See Çağlar and Glick Schiller 2018, 136 on the potential theoretical and methodological problems associated with neighbourhood research.
43. Tilley 1994, 15.
44. For more information on multi-scalar urban ethnographic research, see Çağlar and Glick Schiller 2018.
45. Levitt and Schiller 2004.
46. Çağlar and Glick Schiller 2018, 128.
47. See Pink 2012.
48. During the course of my ethnography I also worked along more collective lines in various group contexts within, for example, Egyptian, Sicilian and Hazara communities, which is also reflected in the book.
49. My research approach has been inspired by ideas about moving 'beyond methodological nationalism' (Wimmer and Glick Schiller 2002; Amelina, Negiz, Faist and Glick Schiller 2012) and 'methodological de-nationalism' (Anderson 2019) in contemporary urban and transnational research. These approaches in cross-border studies query the citizen/migrant distinction and the predetermined construction of 'others' seen in national frameworks.
50. For further discussion concerning themes and issues in contemporary Mediterranean anthropology see Ben-Yehoyada, Cabot et al. 2020.
51. See Zuboff 2019.

2
Experiences of ageing: policies, perceptions and practices

> It's as if you're in the last carriage of the last part of the last journey but you don't realise it – you feel twenty years younger than you actually are and the journey has been ongoing and so on it continues. I would say that ... age passes you; you enter it, like a train into a mountain tunnel, and you don't realise when you're at your station, you don't want to stop or get off, and you wonder – 'There must be some mistake, this isn't *me* ... *is it?*'
>
> (Ava, aged 84)

Introduction: (how) does age matter?

Ageing involves matters of experience and practice, definition and discourse. In the Italian context a number of terms are used to describe older people. Over-65s can be described as *senior*, while over-75s may be termed *anziani*. In an ageing population such as Italy's, categories of age stem from national and European policymaking, socio-cultural norms and media discourses, as well as popular culture and commercial industries. Several research participants felt that they were expected to perform a certain kind of societal role, or look or dress in a certain way that did not necessarily reflect their self-perception or their practices. Many people who were reasonably healthy did not feel their actual age; nor did many consider themselves 'old', which was a label reflecting a certain category of elder they associated with features such as grey hair, physical frailty or being housebound. As Ava, quoted at the start of the chapter, said, 'you feel twenty years younger than you are', as she wondered 'This isn't *me* ... *is it?*' I wondered why this was. Why did older adults in NoLo feel younger than their age – why, and why *now*? Smartphone ownership and use were widespread and varied among research participants. Some people in their sixties and seventies who are mobile, digitally and physically active, and have sufficient economic means, had experienced a sense of rejuvenation in or near retirement, as they discovered new capacities, soaked up the information on the internet and learned new things and, through various forms of social and digital participation in a socially buzzing neighbourhood, by and large kept themselves 'young'. More broadly, the social category of age and the diverse experience of ageing with smartphones is complicated further as it intersects with how life itself, its inequalities, opportunities and contradictions, are experienced, on- and offline.

At the same time as the experience and social categories of age are shifting, official categories of age also matter. They matter in a number of ways, social, legal and bureaucratic, which have a number of concrete implications. Categories of age are relevant to how people are classified (within both regional and national administrations) as senior citizens entitled to various benefits, from transport and entertainment discounts to health and care support, at specific ages, and on reaching retirement age (currently 67), when citizens are eligible to receive an old-age pension (*pensione di vecchiaia*) from the state.[1] Age classifications also matter among younger generations in Italy: young people whose parents were born in another country are excluded from applying for Italian citizenship until the age of 18. Putting my research participants' experiences of ageing into context requires, first, outlining how ageing has been defined and categorised in the country in recent decades, across a range of sectors, and then exploring what people in NoLo made of these classifications, as well as considering what the classifications revealed about the experience of ageing with smartphones at this time and in this context.

Ageing actively in focus

'Active ageing' policies in Europe and 'successful aging' movements in the US emerged in the 1980s and 1990s and have evolved over time in different national settings.

These agendas broadly aimed to encourage people to exercise control over the ageing process and stave off the experience of decline and frailty through a range of 'active' practices, such as physical and mental activity, engagement with others, a good diet and even cosmetic surgery and medication. Social scientists have since challenged the assumptions upon which these movements were based, in which ageing was posited as a highly individualised and personal choice, enhanced by help from the pharmaceutical and cosmetic industries. Anthropologist Sarah Lamb, for example, has argued that a significant problem with 'successful aging' frameworks is that any sign of 'unsuccessful' ageing – such as the onset of dementia or deafness, dependence upon others, even too many wrinkles – is seen and felt as a personal failure rather than as a change beyond individual control.[2] This assumption can reinforce the ageism that notions of 'successful ageing' purport to resist, potentially increasing anxiety about aspects of ageing, including physical decline and death.[3]

The focus on active ageing from the 1990s within the European Union, and its more recent incarnations such as the 2007 campaign 'EU: Ageing well in the information society',[4] have deeper historical roots in the Italian context, where distinctions between autonomy and self-responsibility on the one hand and dependency on the other can be observed within the national healthcare system, the *Servizio sanitario nazionale* (SSN). As Barbara Pieta's work in Italy shows, public health reforms in the 1970s had formally distinguished between an individual being self-sufficient (*autosufficiente*) and not self-sufficient (*non autosufficiente*), giving rise to a legal classification in Italy and an ensuing public narrative that categorised older persons according to their perceived physical (and cognitive) capabilities.[5] Within this binary distinction, self-sufficiency (*autosufficienza*) characterised a type of older person that not only did not require support but was also an enterprising and 'useful' citizen. *Non autosufficienti* within this framework were considered the opposite, dependent individuals who required the services of care homes or day-care centres.[6]

Notwithstanding critiques of policies that imagine citizens in terms of utility, in a different sense, and from an ethnographic perspective, ideas about being useful are important to people in a number of ways, including in older age, as people search for narratives and practices to define a sense of 'purpose' in later life. For example, a number of research participants would talk about how it was important to be useful and helpful to others through volunteering in the community or grandparenting. Here a moral upbringing based on religious teachings, normative ideas about being good and virtuous through charitable service and other outlooks formed part of how people I met described or imagined their roles in their middle and later years. Notably, it was in terms of utility (*utilità*) that the smartphone was widely talked about, as we shall see in chapter 5, in which people explain that it was something that 'served' them, as a very useful thing to have and use in daily life: the use of WhatsApp groups for scheduling, organising and participating, for example, lent itself to these wider ways of being useful.

Returning to active ageing, the concept today remains a multidimensional panacea to the implied 'problem' of old age and frailty, on the basis of several factors, including physical functionality, lifestyle, urban environment and social inclusion.[7] In 2015, the World Health Organization report on ageing and health defined active ageing as 'the process of optimizing opportunities for health, participation and security in order to enhance quality of life as people age' and healthy ageing as 'the process of developing and maintaining the functional ability that enables well-being in older age'.[8] This report underlined the role of public health strategies, and the development of health and social organisations in particular, in maintaining health among older adults today and in the future. In Italy a current emphasis in the discourse on ageing policy is on the acquisition and sharing of skills, including digital literacy, among older adults, which form one of the main ways in which ageing is seen as a push towards enjoying life through what has been termed 'active welfare'. This concept is defined by Auser, a leading nationwide NGO in the field of ageing, as an 'integrated system of subjects and public and private interventions, where, through informal networks, the state, the third sector and individual citizens work to build the social welfare of people, thus strengthening the concept of community and of social cohesion'.[9]

Social welfare was a key concern across NoLo. A significant range of activities, initiated by community organisations and NGOs, multicultural centres and charities, provided social support and legal advice for a range of people in the area, including asylum seekers, refugees and migrants, while allotment clubs, sewing groups and yoga classes made up the wider picture of healthy ageing (*invecchiamento sano*) within the community based on active social lives. Among women and men in their sixties and seventies, participation and volunteering in these activities were widespread and seen as valuable; they contrasted with the language and policies that such people saw as targeting *anziani* (older people) along 'active' lines – policies that some felt did not apply to them with their already busy lives. Among such people, there was a reluctance to participate in initiatives specifically designed for older people, such as the University of the Third Age; they expressed preferences for the kind of cross-generational and cross-cultural socialities to be found within the community, if one knew where to look and, indeed, how to get involved. As Adela, aged 73, a retired volunteer in many of the community organisations, put it, 'I'm too busy to be old – I've no time to die!'

In addition to ageing frameworks in Italy, a certain rebranding of ageing is currently taking place, as seen in Milan, that links older adults with digital technologies and social media as a form of empowerment.

An organisation in Milan dedicated to the 'third age' that I came to know about during my research, the Grey Panthers, aims to be a resource for the 'grey age' through promoting information sharing, dialogue and, particularly, digital and smartphone literacy and social solidarity. The organisation has been particularly active during the Covid-19 pandemic throughout 2020 in offering weekly online tutorials in how to use Zoom, WhatsApp, Skype and other platforms to enable older people to stay connected during the pandemic and amid the regional and nationwide lockdowns in Italy.[10]

Stigmas surrounding older age have come more and more into public awareness in recent years in Italy through increased access to information and talking more openly about issues. In her ethnographic study of a senior care centre in northeast Italy, Barbara Pieta has shown how older adults can be referred to differently in such places beyond categories of *anziani* (the elderly). Here, older adults were referred to as the 'differently young', as a strategy of 'stigma management'.[11]

Despite visible shifts in narratives and stigmas about ageing in institutional settings in Italy, prevailing discourses in the public domain to do with what ageing is and looks like are still markers against which older adults measure themselves. Consider Bernadetta, aged 70. Bernadetta conceives of her life as in decline, in terms of embodied conditions such as aches and pains and wider health issues. She also became more philosophical about this during a long discussion we had in an interview one summer afternoon in 2018 as we took coffee together around the table in her apartment kitchen. Bernadetta talked about her childhood in the nearby countryside outside Milan, her life, her family, her care responsibilities and at length about the loss of power she had experienced in older age, which she felt was about *reacting* as opposed to acting to shape her life actively as she felt she had done in her younger years:

> When you're old, you aren't designing anything new any more. You're not active, or creating things anew, but you're mostly reacting to things as they happen to you and people around you – visits, joys, pains, physical ailments, deaths ... but even these reactions change over time, they can become less intense. Less ... less active.

Bernadetta described the sense of passivity she felt at this stage of her life, calling herself 'old' (*vecchia*) and, in her words, feeling that she was more *re*active than 'active', her choice of adjective chiming with the aforementioned policy ideal of 'active ageing'. Despite how she described herself, getting to know Bernadetta over some months I observed that she leads a socially and physically active life, from day to day. She is mostly responsible for maintaining her and her husband's household, including the shopping and cooking, as he is less physically active, and two or three times a week she cycles from her house to volunteer at local community activities, including teaching Italian to women from other countries at a local NGO and lending a hand at the community association, where we first met.

Through engaging with the community in these ways, Bernadetta is continuing to create things by sharing her time, presence and skills with others, such as by teaching Italian and knitting to children who attended social clubs and societies with their parents. The fact that she did not see herself as an active person highlights the significance of the prevailing discourses in the public domain against which people measure themselves. Bernadetta is neither particularly old nor frail. However, she appears to have internalised a number of narratives about what it should mean or feel like to be old, so that she felt she was no longer creating or adding anything to the life around her. Bernadetta's example reveals how the widespread policy and societal emphasis about what one ought to do accompanies people in middle and older age and can come to shape how they perceive themselves.

Ageing and care

The theme of expectations surrounding ageing brought up in Bernadetta's example leads to the question of normativity and models for ageing in regional contexts across Italy, which I will now discuss briefly. The site of older age and cross-generational care across Italy has traditionally been the family (*la famiglia*) and the family home (*la casa*), which relates to the wider symbolic significance of *la casa* and *la famiglia* in Italian society more generally (see also chapter 4).[12] The ideal for ageing in Italy, in both rural or urban settings, has long been to stay in one's home as long as possible, something that had been hard fought for, for example, by women, for whom being in charge of one's own household and not sharing its administration with one's mother or mother-in-law came to be regarded as important marks of autonomy. For reasons of personal pride, defending autonomy and not wanting to burden others, individuals and married couples in urban contexts generally tended to take care of themselves and each other in older age for as long as was feasible, not wanting to either burden family members or rely on external (to the family) care. The ideal would be to explore all options for family care before considering anything else. In elderly married couples, many men have traditionally relied on care given by their wives in the home, though the reverse scenario has been less widely reported: if elderly women were not self-sufficient, a child – usually a daughter – would typically take up primary care responsibilities.[13] Older women I met in NoLo could still be head of the home in their eighties, performing all the household chores alone and keeping things clean and in order, whether they lived with a spouse or alone. The removal of that valued social status was viewed as a significant personal loss, even a form of social death,[14] by some elderly Italian women; the loss of the site of the home signalled an acute loss of a sense of personhood.[15] The concept of home remains prominent in notions of wellbeing across Italy, both for people who live alone and others, and across ages. Thus, *la domiciliarità*, or home care for the elderly (known as 'ageing in place' in English), is considered part of the dignity of life in later years, which can be threatened by health problems, lack of economic resources or limited family care; its loss may require the use of retirement homes, which, as I discuss later in this chapter, occupy a somewhat fraught position within family contexts across Italy.

Care responsibilities

Care for parents is particularly prominent among adult daughters in Italy, which reflects normative gender models and expectations that traditionally have placed women (especially mothers and grandmothers) as carers and keepers of the family.[16] Middle-aged and older Italian men in NoLo showed mixed views on care in older age, and often these depended on material and financial considerations and their existing marital and other family relations. Where a married couple had been together for decades, for instance, a common presumption was that they would continue to care for each other in the home for as long as possible, along with receiving care from any children, if they were able to supply it. For other male research participants with different family experiences, including divorced men in their sixties, alternative ideas were emerging for care in later years, which coincides with the rise of smartphones and mobile health in Italy that will be looked at specifically in chapter 6.

A particular phenomenon concerning care concerns the 'sandwich generation'.[17] This well-established concept refers to persons, often in midlife, living between, or 'sandwiched' by, caring for ageing parents and their children simultaneously. In Europe, including Italy, academic research has highlighted the sandwich generation as a health concern, as well as a socio-economic one. This is particularly the case for women, whose role as primary care givers stems from entrenched societal and familial expectations.[18] For example, this 'in-between' or bridge-like status can affect the (mental) health of women carers (usually daughters)[19] by causing anxiety and depression, because of the emotional strain, lack of personal time, financial burdens and general conflict created by carrying out multiple care roles.[20] Because of cross-regional and transnational migration, these issues are complicated by forms of care diversifying across time and space, incurring physical remoteness but also, in some cases, new-found digital intimacies.

The following example illustrates some of the expectations surrounding in-family care between women, especially among mothers and daughters in 'sandwich' and other types of care set-ups. The experiences of Carla, aged 48, are an example of the 'sandwich generation'. She is married with two children. Her parents, originally from another region of Italy, live a few streets away. In order to care for her elderly parents personally, seeing them every day, she works part-time and locally. Her parents are a big part of her children's upbringing. Describing her decision to reduce her working hours to care for her parents and children simultaneously, she explained that it was 'a choice I undertook gladly'. But at the same time, Carla feels overwhelmed now and again by the multiple care responsibilities she carries, 'upwards' and 'downwards' between parents and children. She feels her life is fulfilling, and feels nurtured by the strength of the relationships she cares about and sustains, both in her family and in the community. But Carla, for her own part, has 'not much time' for herself. Moments salvaged for herself during the day are given to listening to music on YouTube on her smartphone in the kitchen while she cooks dinner and a meditation app that she has tried out before bed and is finding quite soothing; she also finds breaks from exclusive family sociality within the wider community, in which she is active during the day, both on- and offline. She has introduced her mother into this wider community, for example to a *nonne* (grandmothers) group who have a WhatsApp group and go out for dinner once a month. Carla hopes that her later years will bring more time for herself and for pursuing hobbies and interests when the children are grown up, but for now she is occupied in the flows of life, approaching midlife with multiple and multidirectional care practices. The smartphone here is an object for organising daily life, but it also provides a place or space she can go to in order to be quietly with herself or to foster her individual interests, such as music and meditation.

In another example, we see a delicate care relationship between Elena, aged 53, and her 80-year-old mother, Maria. Maria lives alone following the death of her husband, Elena's father. Elena, who is married without children, works full-time. Maria has a range of physical mobility issues, meaning that she is largely housebound. She does not accept help from care workers (*badanti*), because, she says, she feels such help would encroach on her sense of autonomy in her home. The bulk of the caring responsibilities are carried out by Elena, who does not have siblings. Maria does not have a smartphone, and Elena calls the house phone up to three times a day from work to check in. Elena provides weekly shopping and carries out basic household chores. Elena herself, meanwhile, faces a range of personal challenges of her own, including anxiety brought about by employment cuts at work.

Maria and Elena's close and nigh on co-dependent relationship reveals that what makes ageing so complex and intense a social experience is how the physical conditions of ageing bring about the modulating of roles, without altogether subverting or eradicating existing ones. 'At a certain point,' Elena explains, 'you swap – daughters become mothers and vice versa.' The relationship, in reality, is not quite so clear-cut. Instead, the mother–daughter relationship thickens and intensifies as denial of change sets in. Maria appears to be very much still *la mamma* in charge of the family home, while Elena effectively 'project manages' her mother's care. Never explicitly acknowledged between the two women is how ageing has modulated their relationship.

Elena's situation as a carer is not uncommon in Italy and elsewhere, which leads to the next point about midlife and care roles. Assessing the social roles performed by 60-year-old adult children in Milan, sociologist Carla Facchini writes:

> Sixty-year-olds are a central resource for children regarding the care of their grandchildren, contributing in a decisive way to the possibility for women to remain in the labour market after the birth of their children, and despite the scarcity of part-time work and limited children's services that cover different care needs. However, the role of 60-year-olds is equally important – and growing – in the care of elderly parents.[21]

The present generation of people in their fifties and sixties appear to live their lives within this kind of highly active and multidimensional care framework, some with extra care help, some without. Let us consider the case of Rosella, who is 57. Rosella is not married, has no children and lives by herself. She was born in Milan, as her parents had moved to Milan for work from different regions of Italy in the 1960s. She has worked since she was 18. Rosella's father, to whom she was very close, died when she was young. Her mother, Loredana, who is in her eighties, continues to live in the apartment Rosella grew up in. Her brother, Filippo, has a wife and his own family in another region in northern Italy, where he works full-time and runs his own business. When Loredana was diagnosed with cancer, Rosella oversaw and organised her mother's care, while maintaining a very busy working life. More recently, Rosella has experienced a range of health problems of her own, but still works part-time. 'Work is life,' she explains, hinting that continuing to work despite illness offers something of a distraction and a purpose. With the acceptance of her mother, Rosella employed a care worker, Teresa, 30, from Peru, to live in and care for her mother full-time. The situation is working out well for the family, as Teresa and Rosella's roles support the family care set-up that they have established for Loredana.

In families across Italy, as happens in other places, such as Ireland, at least one adult 'sacrificial child' who did not end up marrying performs the role of primary carer, remaining at home to care for ageing parents, as has been noted by scholars.[22] Rosella in Milan today undertakes this role of unmarried adult child carer, or rather care manager, supplemented by WhatsApp-facilitated family communications. At the same time, the live-in professional carer complements Rosella's role by carrying out the actual care for her mother in her home. Rosella's brother Filippo, meanwhile, sends some money to help sustain the set-up from afar. While women such as Carla and Elena are able to attend to their mother's or parents' care needs themselves, others, such as Rosella and her brother, make different decisions about the care of *genitori* (parents) and *parenti* (relatives), which may or may not involve *badanti*, depending on the availability of financial resources and the family's or individuals' attitudes towards care labour. The *badante* framework is a significant feature of the contemporary landscape of ageing and care in Italy and requires further discussion.

Badanti (care workers)

In recent decades *badanti* (singular *badante*), or care workers, have constituted a significant form of elderly care not provided by a family member.[23] *Badanti* are paid care workers who also undertake the role of housekeeper, and often live in the home of the individual(s) they are caring for. The Italian word *badare*, which means to 'look after' or 'watch over', has become synonymous with care giving for the elderly.[24] Many *badante* in Italy come from countries such as Romania, Ukraine, Poland, Ecuador, Poland, Moldova and Peru, and are often between the ages of 25 and 45.[25] A majority of *badante* are women.[26]

Badanti who live in the homes of those they are caring for generally work long hours and attend to the individuals' everyday personal needs, including cooking meals and, if required, helping them to eat, bathing and dressing them and accompanying them on walks, managing medication schedules and cleaning the house. The idea, though individual cases entail their own problems and paradoxes, is that employing a *badante* makes possible the ideal of ageing in place, at home,[27] and so sustaining a sense of personal agency, while the younger, middle-aged family members are also able to continue with their lives to varying degrees without significant practical disruption. The advantages conferred on Italian families by the *badante* care industry have been widely acknowledged in academic and policy reports, which show that migrant carers help Italian families to maintain semblances of traditional in-family care.[28] For their part, migrant carers occupy a tenuous position in Italian society.[29] Seemingly indispensable to the ageing and care industry, they may experience more favourable immigration policies than other migrant groups, but they are faced with conditions of uncertainty and precarity, many having entered Italy on tourist or student visas. Some *badanti* remain in Italy if applications for work permits have not been successful, at the behest of their employer but with potentially no legal protection. The employer or employer's family is often required to assist the *badante*'s request to stay by officially applying for the regularisation of their care by the migrant worker, which can incur a fee and be more expensive than if the care remained informal.[30]

Badante care in Italy should therefore be understood in a broader social and political context. Middle-aged Italian research participants in NoLo demonstrated a mixed response to the idea of *badanti*, ranging from employing them and forming close bonds with them to seeing them as occupying a tenuous presence in the care sector but being useful. But what happens when, for financial or other reasons, intra-family caretaking or care management is not an option for elderly family members? In the following section I turn to a more institutional field of care, namely retirement and care homes, and some of the social stigmas surrounding them in Italy.

Case di riposo, case di cura (retirement and care homes)

Retirement or nursing homes (*case di riposo*) emerged in Italy in the 1970s in the wake of socio-economic change brought about by urbanisation, mobilities and changing lifestyle patterns and family structures, which had modulated patterns and practices of care.[31] Hospices and care homes (state-run and private) provide assistance and a permanent residence to older adults who suffer physical or cognitive decline or have severe health conditions. State day-care centres are a more recent development in Italy: these are institutions that employ care workers for older adults who cannot be fully independent, providing assistance to those who suffer from physical or cognitive decline. Care workers may also who visit people's homes, and enable 'ageing in place' for people with conditions such as dementia who, despite their condition, are still able to live at home.[32]

Nursing homes have a mixed status in family discourses. While they are used by some, there is the potential for their use to signal abandonment of the elderly individual by the family. *Genitori* (parents) and *nonni* (grandparents) hope, by and large, to remain in their own homes until their deaths. Mixed or negative attitudes towards care homes are not exclusive to Italy.[33] Among some research participants there was a sense that care homes were a negative reference point for being older, and this view influenced how some people envisaged, or feared for, their own futures. Caterina, for example, recounted the case of her uncle, Franco, who had passed away in his late seventies in a *casa di riposo* in another region:

> He was ill, he was depressed there, and was in a poor physical condition generally. I will never forget how overjoyed he became when people came to see him. It was as if one half-hour visit could keep him filled with joy for several months.

Concerns about the future loom large for people like Caterina whose own futures remain bound up with economic anxiety. For some people, such concerns can contribute to a greater emphasis on living in the present and on occupying time and space that smartphone practices play a part in, as subsequent chapters will further illustrate.

In another example Loretta, in her seventies, recalled that when her father died her mother had suffered from anxiety and depression, and had come to live with her and her family in Milan. Loretta had struggled to attend to her mother's care needs while raising her children and maintaining a full-time job, and after long periods of thought and difficult conversations, the family agreed that Loretta's mother should move to a care home in Milan, where she lived until she passed away. Though this had been the most practical option for the family at the time, the difficulty of the decision has stayed with Loretta.

Midlife and retirement: time, desire, freedom and money

Discussions about retirement with research participants in NoLo threw up a number of different attitudes and experiences, hopes and concerns – concerns about money, time and different ideas about freedom. Of the research participants in NoLo who had taken retirement in their forties or fifties, some have taken on second careers, such as Roberto, a retired engineer-turned-schoolteacher, or were heavily involved with grandparenting, or community volunteering. Many Italian middle-aged research participants in NoLo are at present immersed in exploring the boundaries of their own freedoms – freedoms that typify this generation as they break away, to various extents, from their parents' more conservative moulds, navigate inherited expectations about their identities, lifestyles and choices, and – if they are in a social and economic position to have the choice – are asking themselves, 'What should I do with all this freedom and time?' In the 1990s people could retire as early as 45, given the fact that many individuals began working as early as 16 in the 1960s. By 2003 the official retirement age was 60 for women and 65 for men, though the average age was around 57 since earlier legislation had guaranteed retirement at 57 after 30 years of employment. The total expenditure on the pension system is the second-highest in the EU, at 16.5 per cent of GDP.[34] People talked a lot about the devastating economic situation in Italy after the 2008 economic crash, which for many had made the idea of retiring seem nigh on impossible, particularly if sufficient structures of in-family or *badante* care were not in place. For some older adults, retirement offered opportunities for social participation in the community. Let us consider a few examples of how retirement was envisaged and experienced differently among a number of research participants beginning with the following film, made with a friend in NoLo.

Figure 2.1   Film: *Short film portrait*. Available at http://bit.ly/filmportrait1.

Time and freedom

Mario, who is in his mid-sixties, is from a region in central Italy. He moved to Milan as a child in the 1960s with his parents, who had come here to work. He is an active member of the local community. He is retired and is active in the community allotments, and is passionate about the development of green spaces in the city, to which he has devoted weekends, holidays and evenings over many years. Mario and others have been instrumental in restructuring and revitalising the image of the community allotments as a social space. They host regular events and gatherings, and nature-related events such as collecting the first honey of the season from the bees they keep, as well as cultivating new crops and harvesting seasonal produce with other volunteers. This inner-city green space is one that Mario deeply enjoys today in retirement.

In the past a prominent aspiration among middle-class people who worked in or near Milan was to leave the industrial cities to retire in the mountains, or by the sea. Today investment in the city, its green spaces and its urban socialities makes retiring in inner-city neighbourhoods such as NoLo an attractive option for people who have invested, over many years, in literally growing a space to retire in and which, crucially, younger generations can also enjoy and partake in. Mario described this preference for life in the neighbourhood in retirement thus: 'What good is being by the sea if you're alone?!' The allotment role is a form of work to Mario, but a welcome one that has comfortably bridged the gap between working life and retirement. Retirement for Mario is therefore regarded as an opportunity to carry on being useful in the city, and doing things he cares about within the local community and beyond.

Mario's emphasis on the continuity between working life and retirement is common among research participants in NoLo, where being useful, engaged and active is seen as a virtue and as part of a healthy and fulfilled life (see chapters 4 and 8). Here, in contrast to findings from research at other ASSA fieldsites, such as Marília Duque's in Brazil or Pauline Garvey and Daniel Miller's in Ireland, where retirement leisure can be seen as the repudiation of previous work, Mario and others in NoLo show an attitude towards retirement that lies somewhere in the middle, between enough continuity and enough change. Mario, surrounded by wildlife and nature in the city, feels that part of him is kept young by his engagements with nature and a buzzing social life, and, like others in their sixties, does not particularly feel his age. Economic circumstances clearly play a significant role in how retirement is envisaged and practised and how age – ensconced in life more broadly – is experienced. On a seemingly different ageing trajectory, for example, was Cristina, aged 50.

Money, time and financial precarity

Cristina was born in Milan to parents who had moved from a region in southern Italy in the 1960s for work. Cristina has a son with a former partner and lives with her son and her cat. She worked full-time as a secretary in a PR company in town for many years, but because of a recent company reorganisation had recently been made redundant. Speaking about her experiences, Cristina highlighted ageism as a problem in the Italian workplace: 'It's not easy being my age and without work. There's a lot of discrimination in the workplace. You're old by fifty, you're easy to let go of. You're also not as favoured as you used to be', implying a systemic sexism in the workplace whereby, for a woman, being younger would help one to gain employment. A number of the people in their fifties I came to know during the course of my fieldwork had lost their jobs, and were struggling economically and experiencing anxiety as a result. Retirement, in these cases, was not something they could envisage, eager as they were to find new employment and carry on working well into their later years.

Currently unemployed and at home during the day, Cristina experiences a kind of freedom, of time – time she did not have when she worked full-time, often doing overtime, in the city, but that she does not necessarily want now, concerned as she is at not earning an income. This freedom is certainly a poisoned chalice without financial security. In the past Buddhism had helped Cristina in processes of self-reflection following the death of her parents a few years ago, and today through a mindfulness app she tries to practise principles of acceptance and patience in her life, mired as it is in financial uncertainty and emotional sadness regarding the loss of her parents, the felt absence of her son, who is growing up and has his own life, and the loss of her job. Cristina raised a broader theme in my research, about meaning and purpose in life, one I will return to in chapter 8 when I explore how people figure out how to live with potentially more time if they live longer, and with the possibility of expanding information and relationships through digital communications and smartphones. As Cristina put it, 'I have freedom – especially now that I'm without work – but I've nothing really meaningful to do … and not much money to do it!' For Cristina, without plans for travelling, moving house or anything that required spending money, the digital world and the gig economy had filled a certain void. They opened up an array of opportunities for seeking temporary or regular income, such as renting out her spare room easily on Airbnb, and undertaking casual work in the catering industry, found through a range of job-seeking and sharing platforms, alongside tentatively exploring new relationships through dating apps. In the face of structural challenges, relationship breakdowns or losses and lack of secure or permanent employment, the smartphone, and the virtual worlds it can connect a person to, can fill roles in people's lives in middle age as they figure out how to live, work and socialise while adapting to change.

The question of who gets to retire, on a state pension or otherwise, remains closely linked to social, economic and political factors. The critical conversation about ageing and retirement in Italy needs to extend to all sectors of an ever-evolving society, including the experiences of those whose work patterns, care infrastructures and social participations do not necessarily follow a simple or mainstream image of retirement. With many people currently undertaking temporary or casual work and living in rented shared accommodation, and with caring being experienced and practised in a range of contexts, including transnationally and online, important questions remain about how social care and welfare will reflect, and operate along, socially inclusive lines. These issues are intimately connected to the rise of mobile health, smartphone practices and citizens' experiences of social, economic and digital inequalities within the unfolding 'smart city' of Milan (see, for example, chapter 6 on digital health and social and economic divides). In the light of these wider concerns, the concluding section of this chapter highlights the experience of ageing in NoLo in an age of multi-sited and transnational care which forms a central part of the framework of this book.

The bridge generation

As a wealth of scholarship on transnationalism and transnational families has highlighted,[35] many people across the world today in midlife are living and ageing away from their countries of origin and from close family, living globally distributed digital social and working lives in multiple places and spaces. Walking down the street or in the supermarket in NoLo, one might be video-calling on WhatsApp a relative in Lima, Cairo or Palermo to catch up on family news, while organising one's children's school schedules or one's work commitments via WhatsApp and Facebook groups that extend across the neighbourhood or the city. Managing kin relations and responsibilities within and between cities, cross-regionally and transnationally, is a hallmark of contemporary urban life in the digital age all over the world, and we see these distributed practices clearly in and across Milan. In the Italian context, studies of present-day second-generation Italian émigrés[36] have highlighted how intergenerational care is maintained transnationally among Italian adult children living abroad in Europe and beyond. Of their parents' generation, many had also moved, either internally across Italy to cities such as Milan or abroad to places such as Australia or the US. Today both generations can be involved in navigating 'Care Transcending Distance'.[37] Social research in Italy has shown that Italian labour migrants and their families are learning how to manage continuity and changes in care practices, such as practices and narratives about combining motherhood and work.[38] Sociologist Elisabetta Zontini's research with Italian migrants has suggested that, despite the tensions that sometimes occur between parents and children, reciprocal bonds across generations remain very strong: children provide care for their ageing parents and at the same time receive various forms of support from them.[39] Individuals and families I came to know in NoLo were engaged in a variety of intergenerational care practices at a distance, as examples throughout the book illustrate. The smartphone, and digital technologies and infrastructures, today play a prominent role in these relationships and practices.

Among research participants in NoLo who had migrated from other countries, experiences of having left family, and in many cases older parents, play a prominent role in their daily life, and can affect their sense of wellbeing, place and presence. Noor is in her early fifties and was born and grew up in Egypt. She has been living with her family in Italy for over a decade, having moved to pursue 'a freer life' and better socio-economic opportunities. Noor was a schoolteacher in her hometown in Egypt, and in Milan she is a teacher and engages in social work across the community. Ageing for Noor was predominantly associated with life experience: 'It is the journeys we have undertaken, our sufferings, our resilience, that make us who and what we are. Your age is a marker of these things.' With an emphasis on the life course, Noor talked about (living in) the present, something that her work and social activities in the community and online via WhatsApp groups and Facebook keep her busy with. The past could, at times, be troubling to revisit, with its regrets and trails of difficult choices made.

There was an emphasis in Noor's narrative on putting up with life's challenges, choices made, carrying on and muddling through in midlife the best one can. In speaking about the future, Noor spoke, above all, about the health and happiness of her children, through which she defines her own success and her happiness. 'I work and live for my family to get ahead in their lives – it is their future that matters. They are growing up here, they know the culture, the language, better than me. Their future is what matters.' Noor speaks about her life as a kind of generational bridge, from her life in Egypt to the one in Italy that she has been actively crafting and cultivating and which she hoped to enjoy over time with her children and potential grandchildren. Noor's vision of the future was of being together with her children and reciprocal in-family care.

Like those of many other people I met and know whose families live physically far away, Noor's emotional attachments spanned time and space. Among the most significant sources of pain for Noor was having been far from her elderly parents, the predicament of reconciling *where* she ought to be with where she is. These issues concerning place would arise via social media viewed on her smartphone, spaces in which memories and emotions were conjured through viewing old, digitised photographs[40] and current images of her family and her natal home, a place she retains many precious attachments to, including through her children and their various attachments, curiosities and desires to connect with aspects of her culture and with family in Egypt. Noor is keen to nurture her children's sense of their Egyptian identity by speaking Arabic at home alongside Italian, cooking Egyptian food and participating throughout the year in cross-cultural events in the neighbourhood, at which she proudly shares cultural aspects of and offerings from 'her country'.

Noor's experiences highlight a significant global theme in the contemporary experience of ageing, that is, conveying the challenges of reconciling place, belonging, aspiration, work and care while being physically distant from close kin, including elderly parents. The ethical entanglements experienced by individuals within their multidirectional and transnational care webs form a significant part of the ethnographical details that make up the experience of ageing as, as we have seen, a feeling of multiple emplacements and displacements, of being at once in and out of place, of a complex synergy between humans, geographies and technologies that is a hallmark of the contemporary experience of ageing. Noor, along with many other research participants, had faced the ethical dilemma of 'Where should I be?' with regard to family commitments. However, these feelings of personal conflict were overcome by her will to provide the best for her children and to support them. For Noor life includes both blessings and sacrifices. The gains entail the losses; she also highlighted 'God's will' in the greater flows of life.

Earlier in this chapter I discussed the 'sandwich generation' and its care roles and responsibilities. Further dynamics of this can be observed in the experience of Noor and other research participants who form a 'bridge generation', a transnational connection between care duties in multiple places and spaces, off- and online.[41] We will meet Noor again in chapter 7, when we look further at care practices and intergenerational relationships.

Conclusion: ageing at present

My research in NoLo highlighted a dissonance between, on the one hand, institutional categories of age and, on the other, the wider experience of age and how it is lived in the present moment of digital technology-facilitated communication practices.

Age, for a number of research participants in NoLo, was about the experiences and narratives surrounding their day-to-day lives, in relation to their experiences of sociality and autonomy, health and frailty, and care responsibilities, through all of which they subjectively conceived of their age as their sense of self, now, in the present. Active ageing policies for older adults which were centred on certain narratives or examples of activity and utility did not necessarily reflect or define how activity and social participation were practised or understood by my research participants. Moreover, as we saw with Bernadetta at the start of the chapter, individuals can internalise certain top-down narratives to project a negative judgement onto themselves as being, for example, not active enough, despite living relatively healthy and socially engaged lives in older age. Despite a number of people feeling younger, or not feeling 'old', women and men in their sixties to eighties in NoLo did say they felt 'old' where health and frailty were concerned, or if this became visible, such as in a brief glance in the mirror or a shop window where they momentarily viewed their body as smaller, frailer or older, or when they experienced sensations such as aches and pains, or felt their body to be slower and heavier, in addition to specific health conditions.[42]

Ageing, then, as a lived experience, explored though ethnographic research, throws into relief a range of intersectional issues, and is rooted in socio-economic context and in wider inequalities.[43] The case studies from NoLo presented in this chapter have highlighted that these discrepancies apply to people with varying degrees of digital technology in their lives, with and without family care in place, with and without the financial means to support care for parents, among those living physically far from close kin, and so on. The neighbourhood is a kind of microcosm of some of the challenges of ageing in contemporary urban contexts defined by work, by the busy demands of life and by distinctions in the desire or ability to plan for the future. While some enjoyed the new-found freedoms of retirement in NoLo, others, such as Cristina, felt that they could not afford to grow old or to retire; they rather had to carry on working to make ends meet, and could not envisage an end to this in the future 'unless a miracle happened'. Some people felt that reciprocal care within the family would be their model for ageing in future, as we saw with Noor and her image of ageing with her children. When people across society feel they cannot afford to think of the future or cannot envisage retiring, or not working, important social and political questions remain about inclusive older-adult care and the capacity to imagine one's place in society that should be the basis for ongoing critical and policy discussion. This is particularly significant in national contexts, in which minoriy communities are not included in national or mainstream imaginings, or in ethnonationalist narratives of the 'family' of the nation about who gets to *be here*, and to *become older here*.

The uncertainty about the future expressed by many of my participants in NoLo tied in with contemporary ideas about 'living in the present moment'. As we saw with Carla's use of YouTube videos and meditation apps, her smartphone practices constituted ways of carving out some 'me time' amid her multiple family and wider responsibilities. Contrary to critical claims that the smartphone detracts from individuals' 'being present' in social contexts, engaging with the smartphone is one way some participants stayed in the present moment as a mode of living and in some sense staving off thinking about the past or worrying about the future. Ageing with smartphones in this contemporary urban Italian context is about living in – and with – the present.

In sum, cases seen throughout this chapter highlight that ageing is not simply an idea or ideology that exists apart from people, bodies or technologies. Ageing as a human experience concerns the multidimensional and variously augmented experiences of living, at certain stages of life, rooted in multiple contexts, on- and offline. These practices, in turn, impact upon *who* people feel they are, and *where* they feel they are, as they enter their later years, an idea that recalls the tunnel metaphor seen in Ava's words which opened this chapter. The next chapter will build upon these insights by looking specifically at everyday life, rituals and routines, and the role that social life plays in the larger story of ageing with smartphones in Milan that is explored in this book.

Notes

1. Although the official retirement age is 67 in Italy, there are a number of exceptions to the pension scheme, such as 'early retirement' packages and other options, as laid out in European Commission 2020.
2. Lamb 2017.
3. Sarah Lamb describes how such policies can obscure 'socioeconomic inequalities just as it ["successful aging"] denies aging as a normal and even potentially meaningful part of the human life course' (Lamb 2020, 50).
4. See https://joinup.ec.europa.eu/collection/ehealth/document/eu-ageing-well-information-society. Accessed 13 November 2020.
5. Pieta 2020.
6. Pieta 2020.
7. World Health Organization 2020.
8. World Health Organization 2015, 225, 28.
9. See Auser / Associazione per l'invecchiamento attivo 2020. Accessed 26 January 2021. https://www.auser.it/wp-content/uploads/2020/10/Documenti-Congressuali-pubblicazione-per-congressi.pdf, p. 34. Author's translation.
10. Grey Panthers 2018.
11. Pieta 2020.
12. See also Weibel-Orlando 2009.
13. Facchini 2016.
14. The concept of social death has been used by a large number of scholars across disciplines. I employ the term here from Erving Goffman's (1961) concept of 'mortification of self': the series of experiences undermining a person's social identity, whereby a person may feel, because of a variety of institutional, biological, psychological or other reasons, socially 'dead'.
15. Erving Goffman (1961) describes a 'mortification of the self' that can occur through the removal of an individual from society.
16. For an example of normative notions of the grandmother see Vincent Lezzi's 2005 autobiographical novel, *More Coffee with Nonna: Stories of my Italian grandmother*.
17. See for example Chisholm 1999; Riley and Bowen 2005; Rubin and White-Means 2009.
18. Brenna and Novi 2015.
19. Amirkhanyan and Wolf 2006; Coe and Van Houtven 2009.
20. See Barnett et al. 1992.
21. See Facchini 2016. Author's translation.
22. For a discussion of the 'sacrificial child' in the Italian context, see Weibel-Orlando 2009.

23. Van Hooren 2010.
24. Nicolescu 2020.
25. For an anthropological discussion and overview of *badante* based on ethnographic research in southeast Italy see Nicolescu 2020.
26. A survey carried out by Iref, the Istituto di Ricerche Educative e Formative (2007; institute for educational and pedagogical research) found that only 13 per cent of all formally registered migrant domestic or care workers were male. See also Bettio et al. 2006.
27. See Istituto di Ricerche Educative e Formative (Iref) 2007.
28. Rugolotto et al. 2017.
29. Scrinzi 2007.
30. Nicolescu 2020.
31. Salvioli 2007.
32. For a discussion of care homes based on an ethnographic study in northern Italy, see Pieta 2020.
33. Sarah Lamb's work on ageing in India and in the US (2009) presents a parallel with the ideas discussed here regarding different narratives about care homes, ideas of family-based responsibility and the complexities of negotiating older adult care.
34. See Birot 2018.
35. On transnational families see for example Walsh and Näre 2016 and Bryceson 2019. In the Italian context see for example Baldassar 2007.
36. Zontini 2007.
37. Pols 2012.
38. Zontini 2007, 2015
39. Zontini 2007, 2015.
40. On digital photography, experience and space in transnational families see for example Prieto-Blanco 2016.
41. There is a sizeable anthropological literature on the topic of migration, care and digital networks; it is referred to mostly in the endnotes of chapter 8, which discusses this theme further.
42. Interview transcripts from research participants in NoLo: a man (81) and a woman (78).
43. For further critical discussion of inequalities within the experience of ageing in the US see Nussbaum and Levmore 2017.

3
Everyday life, activities and activisms

Introduction

As discussed in the previous chapter, as people grow older they face certain existential questions regarding themselves ('Who am I, at this age?'). Such questions pertain to the experience and perception of time (how to fill it, how to conceptualise one's use of it) and space/place ('Where should I be?'). Such questions form part of a figuring-out of how (best) to live. In this chapter, I break up these meta-questions (examined further in chapter 8) with an in-depth focus on the minutiae of everyday life, on mundane aspects such as the passing of time and how this is moralised in terms of what one ought to do, or not do, such as waste it. With this decidedly ethnographic approach, a phenomenon such as ageing can be examined, as anthropologist Veena Das's work on violence powerfully shows, not as 'an ascent into transcendence but through a descent into the everyday', and into the ordinary.[1] Moreover, if the smartphone is an object of everyday life, and forms a contemporary 'companion' to everyday life, which is one of the core arguments in this volume, then it is also directly implicated in the practices and activities of daily life. The passing of the minutes, the hours and the days with (and without) smartphones is, for many people, how living and ageing, in physical and virtual places, are embodied and experienced.

On this note, let us begin by looking at everyday phenomena such as the weather. The weather is a prominent feature of everyday chit-chat. I noticed how the weather often affected the moods and interactions of the people I came to know. It could be a source of commentary through which people made conversation and forged micro-bonds with each other in daily life or at the supermarket checkout. The weather in Milan could be 'too cold' (*troppo freddo!*), wet, damp and dark with winters 'lasting too long', or too dry, or hot and humid, lacking cool fresher air. At other times it was pleasant, fresh, with beautiful blue sky and sunshine, as when the Alps can be viewed on a clear winter day, seemingly positioned just at the end of the long boulevard Viale Monza, which cuts through the neighbourhood. In apartment buildings across the area people live with their fan heaters and dehumidifiers in winter and air conditioning and fans in summer, which, accordingly, are much-talked-about objects in everyday life. Among these everyday, seemingly mundane, objects, the smartphone takes up a prominent position, mediating time and space and the everyday experience of the day and of comfort.[2] Checking the weather via smartphones was one of the most common daily smartphone practices of research participants in NoLo. For example, Anna, a schoolteacher, often talks about the weather by saying 'Let's ask him, shall we?' She transforms the smartphone into her personal weatherman, a useful and friendly presence in her daily life. After all, forecasting the weather helps her to plan things, from her classes with the schoolchildren to what clothes and shoes to wear that day.

Seasonal rhythms

Time in NoLo is structured by the rituals and hours shaped by work, school, care duties, coffee, meal-times and socialising that make up an average day. To ask the time in Italian, one asks what the *hours* are (*'Che ore sono?'*). A broader marker of time in the neighbourhood is the *anno scolastico* (school year) from September to June. In the summer months, those that can and wish to visit family members in other regions leave the city, as they have done historically. Several iconic black-and-white photographic prints from the 1960s and 1970s that today float around Milan's flea and vintage markets, such as the ones down by the Navigli (the interconnected canal system) in the southwest of the city, depict scenes of people boarding trains at Milano Centrale station, heading back to Sicily, Apulia, Calabria and other regions for annual holidays,[3] while others head *al mare* (to the beach) or *nelle montagne* (into the mountains) towards Liguria and Piedmont for a few weeks. People who can afford to visit their children or family in other countries, such as Egypt, Morocco, Indonesia, Peru, the Philippines or China, do so. For those who cannot afford to take *le vacanze* (holidays) or who cannot take the long summer off, work and inner-city life continue amid the heat and the summer *umidità* (humidity). In July and August, daily life in NoLo takes on a somewhat altered pace, with younger children at home or out with their friends and families freestyling their time and commitments outside the usual more precise routines. Retired individuals and couples, families and friends may spend a few months away from the city, while bars and shops tend to close for a long weekend (*ponte di Ferragosto*) around, the public holiday called *Ferragosto* celebrated on 15 August.

In addition to seasonal changes, the year and social life in NoLo are broken up and demarcated by special days and periods, such as saints' days – which traditionally are as significant among Italian families as birthdays – Easter (*Pasqua*), Christmas (*Natale*), Eid al-Fitr and Ramadan. They are times of *festeggiare* (celebrating) with family and friends and within the community, online and offline. On these occasions, there can be big public or semi-public parties and gatherings across the neighbourhood, many of which I participated in during my fieldwork in NoLo in 2018–19. Key moments, which hold pride of place in Italian political and social memory, also play a big part in the yearly cycle. From 25 April (National Liberation Day, the anniversary of Italy's liberation from fascism and the Nazi occupation) to 1 May (International Workers' Day), schools, shops, bars and businesses are shut for public holidays. This is known as *fare il ponte* – literally 'to do the bridge' – which describes being off work on the Friday and Monday either side of a weekend. Mondays in the neighbourhood also have their own particular pace and rhythm. On Mondays, many bars and restaurants close – as is common across Italy, with the exception of large commercial city centres, since Sunday is a popular social day when consumption is high and things remain open, making the following day one of rest. At lunchtime a number of small businesses, bakeries and shops close for lunch. Some restaurants, having been open until 2.30 p.m., will close until 7.30 in the evening, when they reopen for business, adding to an urban village feel. In the evenings the area fills up with local residents: bar, shop and restaurant owners and workers from across Italy, and from Peru, Egypt, the Philippines, Bangladesh, Pakistan, Morocco and the Dominican Republic, between the ages of 20 and 60, work, hang out and chat. The residents of the neighbourhood's apartment buildings are a mix of individuals, couples, mixed groups of tenants and families living in close proximity.

Individual rituals and routines

Amid the wider rhythms of the day, month or year, individuals carve out their own timetables and practices in accordance with their care duties, responsibilities and wider obligations. The experience of time for some retired and older research participants in NoLo acted as a kind of moral and emotional barometer. Time was something that could be wasted, lost

Figure 3.1   Film: *One day in NoLo*. Available at http://bit.ly/onedayinnolo.

or, like the potentially time-warping experience of retirement itself, represent a kind of existential challenge. Time among older adults in retirement or later life was filled with care giving and receiving, with being with others and spending time with oneself. The film above (Fig. 3.1), made with a friend in NoLo, conveys the sense of a day in the neighbourhood.

Space and place

Inhabiting space in everyday life in the neighbourhood is a highly variegated experience and practice. As I got to know a range of individuals, couples, groups and families throughout my fieldwork, from a range of backgrounds and of different ages, I observed that a number of research participants felt varying levels of comfort and discomfort in different spaces across the neighbourhood. As was discussed in chapter 1, negative representations of the Via Padova area continue to appear in the Italian press and this image, as we shall see, impacts on how the neighbourhood can be seen and lived. Gabriela is a writer and journalist born in Milan to an Indian father and an Italian mother. In her 2012 novel, *Milano, fin qui tutto bene* ('Milan, so far so good'), which is set in and around Via Padova Kuruvilla includes portraits of the lives of a number of the people. Noting the changes the author witnessed in the area in the wake of a stabbing incident in 2010, she charts a move away from a lively, public-facing sociality at all times of the day and night to a climate of fear, anxiety and police surveillance associated with the social and political tensions of the times: 'It used to be that Via Padova was for everyone ... now it is only at certain times, and it is under control.' The Via Padova Kuruvilla charts is one that had ostensibly moved for a period, from 2010 onwards, towards one of closed doors, indoor cultures and fear: 'Via Padova has fallen ill,' Kuruvilla writes. 'Via Padova is not yet dead, but it has very little fun.'[4] Notwithstanding the picture painted by Kuruvilla at that time, a number of years later, and along with the ongoing development of the area, the neighbourhood buzzes with a sense of urban regeneration and renewal. At the same time, how public space is experienced and incorporated by individuals and groups is more subtle and complex on an everyday, ordinary level. For example, Alejandra, in her early forties, who lives with her family, describes their life as 'fairly quiet and closed'. 'We don't usually go out at night,' she tells me. 'We prefer not to.' While she is generally out during the day, at work, taking her child to and from school, and doing the shopping at the local supermarket, in the evenings the family are usually at home together. They watch television, she oversees her child's homework, and Alejandra and her husband may watch a film or a TV or online series together, or spend some time individually on their smartphones and tablets, reading the news, searching for things of interest and communicating with relatives across the world. Like many families, they usually spend the evenings after school and work at home, preparing and eating dinner and doing various things before bed. Alejandra has certain anxieties about city streets at night and prefers to participate in digital, virtual or televisual domains from the comfort of her own home. In such contexts and similar examples, smartphones and digital technologies allow forms of social participation from within the home.

While Alejandra is out and about during the day, but generally at home in the evenings, the opposite is true for Joel, who lives in a shared rented apartment. We meet at an Italian-language class run by volunteers. Joel came to Italy a few years ago from Lima, Peru, and has Italian residency. He works as a cleaner in a series of office blocks in the business district in town. His hours are often 6 p.m. to midnight, one or two o'clock in the morning from Monday to Friday, and he also works some mornings at different sites. Joel's Italian is upper-intermediate and he also speaks some English. He enjoys watching comedy shows and music videos in English on YouTube on his smartphone, seeing this as a helpful tool for learning languages, which he loves. Joel also uses his smartphone to communicate with friends and other Peruvians in Milan and with his family at home. His proficiency in Italian means that the teachers often involve him in helping the other students as a kind of informal language assistant, a role that Joel seems to enjoy. Joel enjoys improving his Italian-language abilities, but the social aspect of coming to class is its main appeal.

The volunteer teacher, Luca, aged 75, is a retired history teacher. He teaches Italian in order to 'keep active', to meet new people and participate in society and the local community. Luca is softly spoken and has a calm and warm presence. The students from a number of different countries appear to feel comfortable in his company, as he does in theirs. Italian classes in the morning are something Joel looks forward to, seeing Luca as something of an uncle figure. The convivial atmosphere and warmth of the heated classroom in winter add a pleasantness to the social experience. From time to time, Joel dozes off in class. In one instance, a couple of the younger students notice this and find it amusing. Luca handles the situation with care. He does not know Joel's precise working hours, but is aware that his schedule is demanding. Luca gently nudges Joel's elbow, offers him a reassuring half-smile and a wink, before saying something that pays a compliment to Joel's Italian proficiency, which means 'he can afford to doze off during learning about the future conditional tense', before gathering everyone together with '*Eccoci qua* [here we are]! Right, now, where were we …'. Luca is among many retired Italians engaged in volunteering, and many of these activities form a key part of their experience of living and ageing in the neighbourhood.

Activities

Aside from individual experiences, preferences and practices of everyday routines, activities in NoLo are wide-ranging and can be cross-generational – from sewing groups to exercise classes, language classes, film and book clubs, choirs, horticultural groups and bicycle clubs. Some social care enterprises and NGOs are aimed at specific groups, including migrants, refugees, asylum seekers, older adults, the young, families or individuals in need of social or medical support. Access to this information and to social participation can be unequal, haphazard and filtered through existing networks and social relationships, and can therefore have a limited reach to individuals, who do not necessarily know about the range of activities on offer. Here neighbourhood social media pages can be mechanisms for communication and advertising services and groups. I participated in a number of these activities throughout my fieldwork (16 months), and in this section I select four of them for discussion.

Environmentalism is one of the prominent means through which people in the neighbourhood express their values and concerns. Like

Figure 3.2 Community allotment in NoLo. Photo by Shireen Walton.

other things that people care about and share in, environmental concerns are expressed via WhatsApp, from details of neighbourhood marches and green protests to awareness videos about climate change and the importance of protecting children's futures, to campaigns to lobby the *Comune di Milano* to implement more bicycle routes and traffic-free zones in the city and in specific neighbourhoods.

During the period of my fieldwork Milan City Council, working with NGOs and community activists, had rolled out a scheme to implement a series of small gardens in central NoLo to help promote a greener neighbourhood, while temporarily pedestrianising a central area outside one of the main schools as an experiment to see how the space would be used differently by children, parents, the elderly and others in the community as a mini piazza (public square). These efforts were greeted with mixed responses by NoLo Facebook, Instagram and WhatsApp groups, where people routinely express their opinions, comment and rally round community issues.

In the light of this environmental activism, the community allotments have significant status as landscapes that represent the kind of ethical vision of the neighbourhood, the city and the future that a number of people partake in carving out and collectively enjoy (see Fig. 3.2). A small number of core allotment sites hold events throughout the year, from beekeeping lessons and tours (an annual event popular with the children of the neighbourhood) to large community 'bring-and-share' dinners where everyone brings something to eat or drink together, to live performances and exhibitions by local artists. Among retired and younger people, these are significant social spaces, particularly in the warmer months but also in winter, in which volunteers in the local allotments can be seen gathering around a small hut drinking coffee, playing cards, and running the organisational business together via WhatsApp and Facebook, including enlisting young volunteers. The younger volunteers are often university students or unemployed youth who are keen to get involved in developing green initiatives in the city.

An activity that has emerged in recent years as part of the regeneration of the neighbourhood is a walking tour initiative. This guided walking tour guide of the area, run by community volunteers, is made up of a mix of younger, middle-aged, retired and still-working people who participate in the tours, which are free. The initiative is aimed at public education and urban redevelopment, enabling residents of the neighbourhood and people from other parts of the city to come to the neighbourhood to learn about the area's history and architecture from local historians and community enthusiasts. Each monthly tour is organised according to a particular theme, such as the 'historic buildings' tour, which takes participants into old palazzo buildings that used to house, hide and smuggle out partisans in the resistance movement against Mussolini, or the 'Valentine's Day special' tour, centred on lesser-known love stories that took place in the neighbourhood. Participants are often from a range of ages, including individuals and couples in their late twenties and thirties, and groups of people in their forties, fifties and sixties. The tours tend to last a couple of hours. There is a central meeting point, where there is an introductory lecture, sometimes from a community historian, a local street artist or a university lecture, and a band made up of residents may take part in the walk. Permission to enter buildings is secured in advance and the idea, akin to that behind global city initiatives like open-door or open-house projects,[5] is to encourage exploration of the built environment and public participation in spaces which may usually be out of bounds, and where individuals learn about places through experience and by receiving contextual information. These initiatives are designed to be educational, and they also contribute to the urban regeneration of the area whereby residents of different parts of the city learn more about different neighbourhoods and areas.

A member of one of the walking tour groups told me about their interest in the activity and in the broader socio-political significance of fostering understanding about the neighbourhood as a kind of counter-narrative or corrective practice:

> People need to see what this neighbourhood is really about! This is real life here, how people live here, every day. Whenever this neighbourhood is in the press or the news it's for all the wrong reasons. ... We only hear about the violent incidents that happen. We have to show people what everyday life is all about here.

Participating in these tours, one gets the sense of pride the organisers feel towards their neighbourhood and the sharing of it in these ways. It is important to highlight the broader context in which such counter-efforts exist, and which partly fuels the tours and adds to the interest, in them and in the neighbourhood, that exists across Milan. Discourses about 'failed integration' and right-wing rhetoric against foreigners and migrants intensify what the group member quoted above outlined as the need to 'show' and 'exhibit' 'real life' in the area precisely in such 'everyday' terms.[6]

The walking tours are one indication of how much this community is aware of itself as a vibrant zone that is playing a part in the rejuvenation of the city of Milan, as the mayor, Giuseppe 'Beppe' Sala, has recently acknowledged; he was seen in a photograph posted on his Instagram page holding a NoLo fan scarf. A number of comments on Sala's Instagram page about his support of 'NoLo' and of the community at large point to ongoing divisions seen in attitudes towards the neighbourhood and its name. One user commented, 'How sad. ... NoLo is an excuse for not saying the direct Viale Padova and Loreto', while others responded with the opposite sentiment, with love hearts and the hashtag #NoLoforever! This is but one instance in which the neighbourhood is shown to be enmeshed in wider issues and divisions across Italian society.[7]

A *Centro multiculturale* (multicultural centre) plays a prominent role in community life in the neighbourhood. The centre forms part of a local non-profit organisation established to support the community life of the school with which it is associated. The Centro is run by community volunteers and teachers; it was envisioned and operates, year in, year out, as a social space (*spazio socialità*) that, during the time I lived in Milan, ran weekly in term-time. For a couple of hours during the afternoon a number of women, including mothers of children at the school and others in the neighbourhood, come here to meet and socialise, to undertake a number of social and educational activities, and to drink sweet tea and eat home-baked goods from traditional recipes and various cultural traditions.

Among the range of activities run at the Centro are Italian-language classes, a weekly sewing group, Zumba classes and a weekly open drop-in meeting with various programmes offering social support and information concerning a variety of aspects pertaining to life in Italy, such as medical facilities and healthcare. The make-up of the Centro sees women from a range of ages, ethnicities and backgrounds, including countries such as Egypt, Peru, Indonesia, Pakistan and Tanzania. Helping to run the group are a mix of middle-aged and older Italian women who volunteer as Italian-language teachers, sewing instructors and exercise class instructors, shifting between roles as facilitators, teachers and participants. Something that one hears people talking about proudly in this context is '*essere insieme e fare cose insieme*' (to be together and do/make things together).

These groups present a lively social environment, both at the physical site and in the WhatsApp group spaces. In the physical space, Arabic and Italian can be heard together amid laughter, banter and affectionate joking. Ringtones break through the sounds of voices: one smartphone ringtone is the sound of the Islamic call to prayer, another a contemporary Egyptian rap song. Some of the women bring infants along, nursing them, drinking cups of sugary black tea and feeding the toddlers with biscuits, home-made or bought by everyone from shops on nearby Via Padova.

Organisations such as the Centro are co-operative initiatives that involve and serve their participants in different ways. While younger migrant women attend in order to learn practical skills like the Italian language and to socialise with other women and younger mothers, older Italians share craft-based practices such as needlework and sewing (see Fig. 3.3), participating in a sense of fulfilment and engagement through friendships formed and nurtured.

A volunteer in her early seventies explained that she enjoys the dynamic environment and the energy of the group. 'It keeps me energised – it gives me a good feeling, like life is dynamic and flowing.' Coming to the Centro twice a week is something she looks forward to. Another woman in her early seventies explained that the joy of the group is about the social relations that are made and nurtured, including through the activities. She draws on her different language skills and her interests in education and society, which afford her some continuity with her previous work and are what she enjoys doing. These activities complement the values of those who co-run the space and are part of cultivating the kind

Figure 3.3 *Corso di cucito* (sewing course). Photo by Shireen Walton.

of community and society that the participants believe in and want to live in. Dahlia explains that the Social Space afternoons at the Centro are a significant event in her week. 'It is something special for us to be together here. Many mothers are at home alone all day with young children. It can get terribly lonely. Here, there is a chance for people to meet and be together, practise a skill, and share our time and develop our Italian!' For Mariana, in her forties, with children at the local school, the sewing group is 'a special thing'. It is a chance to be with other women during the day, to share time and learn and exchange skills. Mariana enjoys the company of the women from different backgrounds; the meeting doubles as an enjoyable occasion to make nice and useful things in good company: everyday shopping bags, skirts, hats and scarves in winter, that can be sold at the local markets or at a school fair. Over some months of attending weekly courses sewing skills begin to flourish, and a number of the women who participate and support the group become good friends in the community, maintaining relationships via WhatsApp.

Smartphones play a significant role in the contemporary sociality seen in a number of women's social spaces in the area. WhatsApp groups are melting pots of affect and emotion, expressed through a range of multimedia forms such as sharing photographs of activities undertaken together and of things they have made, from knitted items to jewellery and handbags that they will go on to sell at the local handicraft market. Festive days, such as Christmas and Eid, along with International Women's Day, birthdays, and key dates in the Italian calendar such as Liberation Day (25 April) and International Workers' Day (1 May), see a flurry of activity in the group chat: photographs, memes, videos, emojis and written messages and voice messages in Italian and Arabic circulate frequently on these days in particular, and every now and then on other days. WhatsApp groups facilitate a certain continuation of the relationships formed in these community spaces, which develop in the online setting in other ways than in the offline one, where some individuals might feel shy or inhibited, for instance about speaking Italian, and may be less sociable than in the online environment, in which they may use the forms and practices they like to express emotion and affection and to build and maintain relationships.

At the same time as togetherness is desired, appreciated and valued in social spaces across the community, in different settings there are rules and etiquettes, and quarrels when certain codes are broken. On occasion, in educational and volunteering sites across the city, tensions occur. For instance, if, in an Italian-language class, a group of individuals break into their native language, volunteers might convey frustration and disapproval; speaking Italian is a core part of the remit of particular projects and groups that provide support for navigating Italian language, society and bureaucracy. The use of smartphones in Italian classes may be met with particular disapproval, since it is seen as a potential distraction or deflection from the goal. Google Translate may be disapproved of, although it can be a helpful tool that people use in their day-to-day lives outside the class. Signs are often placed in Italian-language classrooms indicating that the use of smartphones is not permitted.

Tensions that can be experienced in volunteering contexts across the city are reflected in studies that highlight the fine thread that the altruistic practices of volunteers hang upon in contemporary Italy,[8] and particularly in the region of Lombardy. Lombardy has an active voluntary and NGO sector, which relies on the voluntary participation of individuals who maintain these initiatives and groups.[9] Social participation and togetherness should therefore not be romanticised without acknowledging the pragmatics, policies, practices and narratives of 'integration' that underlie or undercut how people perform and experience this being together.[10] Without being reduced to either their politics or their policy, these groups can, at a human level, offer joyful occasions for socialising, education and friendship across generational and cultural lines.[11]

Choirs (*cori*), including women's choirs, are a prominent activity in NoLo. One choir that performs across Milan has a base in the neighbourhood and rehearses weekly in a local school. It consists of around 30 women of different ages and backgrounds. The group learn and rehearse with the choir leader, a professional singer and performer, and publicly perform regional folk songs in dialect, songs from other countries in different languages, and familiar classics such as the 'Ciao bella' song, known throughout Italy and associated with Liberation Day and anti-fascism; this last is often heard, sung or played live by bands in the resistance marches and demonstrations that take place throughout the year in the neighbourhood. The choir, like the sewing group, provides an important and powerful form of cross-generational social connection among women in the neighbourhood. For a number of the older women and retirees who participate, the choir is an arena in which they express themselves and find friendship and solidarity, in a period of life that may be fraught with change and uncertainty.

Singing is an activity that a number of older women I met in NoLo enjoyed. Giovanna, in her late sixties, is a retired secondary schoolteacher and lives with her husband. She had found the adjustment to full-time retirement difficult, and missed the sociality of her professional role and the buzz of school life. One day, a former colleague suggested that she should come along to one of the local choir practices. Hesitant at first, Giovanna gave it a try. She soon found the group to be vibrant and friendly, and she stayed.

While they met only weekly, there was a constant buzz among the more than 40 participants in the choir WhatsApp group, from people sharing photos, videos, song lyrics and emojis full of hearts, flowers, shooting stars, laughs, tears and hugs. The group also became a political social space, as one of the choir members stated, 'The piazza is our natural environment!' The women's group and its activity have given Giovanna something of a new lease of life, as she has increasingly committed to this expressive dimension, in relation to both the singing and the politics. Retirement began to feel like something she could participate in and shape, carving out spaces for herself and her need for sociality, as well as broadening her social and political horizons as she approaches her seventies. Through the choir, and with the help of the smartphone, Giovanna has expanded her social life and participation in these ways. The stream of messages that flows on the group and the immersive and affective atmosphere it generates provide comfort, and access to and presence in these spaces.[12] With her phone buzzing with sociality, as her life did before retirement, she can feel less alone in daily life.

Older women are visible, present and active in many areas of the NoLo community. They grew up and 'came of age' during the 1970s, amid the feminist movements and social changes of the time. In the 1960s in Italy, forms of sociability for men were connected to the workplace. For example, social and historical research has shown that during the postwar 'boom years' male workers gained in effect a 'second family' through co-worker sociability, by, for example, eating together and being together for so long each day. It has also shown the extent to which, for instance, working for a company would penetrate the lives of individuals.[13] Today women of many ages and backgrounds in the neighbourhood feel they gain 'second families' through the groups they participate in within the public sphere, such as local associations, choirs, sewing groups, walking groups and grandmothers' groups. These groups enable their members to extend their care for others in the community, and form the backbone of much of the care that is provided in and for the community, by people who, to varying degrees, offline and online, take part in public life.

The examples presented above aim to convey the kinds of social activities seen in NoLo today, which are pursued by many middle-aged and older adults. Notably, many of these groups have socially and politically engaged outlooks that link to values observed within the community at the individual and the more collective levels, from wanting to cultivate a greener city and neighbourhood, to sharing skills and time across generational and cultural lines, or participating in anti-racism marches, joining choirs that perform on such marches and engaging in activism on different scales and fronts.

Being together *online* and *offline*

In this final section of the chapter, I highlight the role that social media plays in the neighbourhood. While chapter 5 will look specifically at WhatsApp, here I discuss how Facebook has become a community tool. As mentioned in chapter 1, the NoLo Social District Facebook page and its founders have been instrumental in crafting the concept of 'NoLo'. The private Facebook group currently has more than ten thousand members.[14] Membership is accepted by volunteer community administrators: applicants have to answer a few questions about the area and explain that they live there. Accordingly, it was not until I moved to NoLo that I became part of this group. The related Via Padova Facebook groups also have established community Facebook pages, but they have fewer members: the 'Via Padova Viva Social District' group, another closed, private group, has 3,747 members, and 'Via Padova – Via del Mondo' has 898.[15] The relatively high number in the NoLo group reflects the conscious development of 'NoLo' as a social district, connected through social media, as discussed in chapter 1 and throughout the book.

Facebook provides a digital community space for some people to share opportunities to be together, online, extending relational time together, to express solidarity with values and causes, and to find out more about events and gatherings in the neighbourhood. An example of the latter could be to arrange and advertise convening in a public space on one Saturday afternoon to stand side by side, holding hands to form a 4-kilometre-long *catena umana* ('human chain') in favour of solidarity and anti-racism, to celebrate the diversity and unity present in the neighbourhood, and to contest the negative media and political representations of this part of the city (see Fig. 3.4).[16] On many weekends, and during the week, all year round, declarations of solidarity, social justice and inclusivity can be seen in various events. Celebrations of Pride and International Workers' Day, and environmental awareness campaigns, are key features of neighbourhood activism and activity.

In online groups the offline development of 'community spirit' is enhanced by its cultivation within digital social spaces. On the NoLo Facebook page, people express willingness to offer their time or a helping hand to one another. For example, a research participant in her late

Figure 3.4   Street parade along Via Padova, Milan, celebrating diversity. Photo by Shireen Walton.

EVERYDAY LIFE, ACTIVITIES AND ACTIVISMS

fifties found it remarkable that, if someone gets ill or needs help with something and posts this to the group, there will be 20–30 responses from people offering them help, from buying basic groceries to picking up medicines. Many people who use Facebook in these ways have been creating a digital space for their community, a kind of digital allotment space, echoing the importance of the physical community allotments. The spirit of togetherness seen in these contexts is a long way from the divisive politics of the neighbourhood, city and country, and on the web at large; the altruism present across the neighbourhood roots itself and grows as a social organism via networked practices,[17] and these practices play out within the broader digital and data economies of Facebook, WhatsApp and technology companies.[18]

Conclusion

This chapter has set out to illustrate how everyday life in NoLo is experienced, in a phenomenological and a social sense as an evolving space of urban living and ageing. Examining ageing here has been about how people pass the time, how they spend their days and nights, and engage in daily practices, alongside ideas about how people felt, or had come to feel useful (*sentirsi utile*) and active (*attiva/o*) as individuals and as part of collectives. Individuals, empowered or disenfranchised by and within the various sites of the neighbourhood and whose daily routines were shaped by socio-economic activities, occupy place and space in different ways, from morning to night. Sites such as Italian-language classes or the multicultural centre can be spaces where these different routines, rhythms and experiences converge and sometimes overlap.

As this chapter and a number of the films accompanying the book seek to illustrate, the neighbourhood is a key character in people's lives, and so was a prominent character to emerge from the ethnographic research and into this book. Despite the negative perceptions of and discourses about NoLo and Via Padova expressed by different groups, and notwithstanding the tensions and clashes that exist or occur between people who live here and elsewhere, there are numerous examples of spaces of cross-generational and cross-cultural contact that the people involved feel are helpful and useful in different ways. These spaces form a significant part of the story of ageing with smartphones in this urban context. At the same time, socio-economic inequalities, biases, judgements and perceptions are manifest within the community. It is developing a self-image as a kind of 'island'[19] (*'un'isola'*, as I had heard it called by some people in NoLo) of inclusivity at a political moment in Italy of widespread xenophobia and racism, and of populisms that capitalise on exclusionary logics of 'us and them' and go against the green, open and diverse vision for society that many residents within and beyond the neighbourhood seek to develop.

The transformation of everyday life and social participation seen through digital forms of communication via smartphones has connected many people, but these connections do not transcend, and nor do they erase, existing socio-economic inequalities, or eradicate loneliness and isolation, which continue to be significant issues in older age across Italy, and are experienced by many people in NoLo; these will be discussed in chapter 4. What the digital has brought to many people's lives, as has been a focus in this chapter, is a range of avenues for social participation that affect how the neighbourhood sees itself and how individuals living there see themselves within it. As a woman aged 55 said, it's as though social media and smartphones had 'switched on all the lights' in this neighbourhood and brought many people into contact with each other, particularly here referring to the moment that 'NoLo' as an idea – as a 'Social Street' (as discussed in chapter 1) – was born. The role played by the community *online* through social avenues such as Facebook and WhatsApp is paramount for cultivating the kinds of inclusive spaces people want to develop and live in, which are made up of what many in the community view as the essential 'nutrients' of social care and participation, with the smartphone serving as a contemporary 'gardening' instrument.

Notes

1. Das 2007, 62.
2. See Miller 2008.
3. See for example https://milano.repubblica.it/cronaca/2011/08/13/foto/ferragosto_anni_70_alla_centrale_scatta_l_assalto_al_treno_per_il_sud-20395035/1/. Accessed 15 November 2020.
4. Kuruvilla 2012.
5. See for example https://www.openhouseworldwide.org. Accessed 15 November 2020.
6. On the NoLo–Via Padova distinction and my use of each and both see chapter 1.
7. 'Symbolic violence' is a theoretical term coined by Pierre Bourdieu (1988) that broadly denotes non-physical forms of violence that manifest in how power is differentiated between social groups.
8. Anthropologist Cristina Giordano (2014) addresses these kinds of cross-cultural, generational and ethical tensions in her long-term ethnographic research in Turin. Giordano's work describes complex relationships and logics of care between Catholic nuns and female migrants from Eastern Europe, North Africa and sub-Saharan Africa and critically examines, among a host of issues, the project of integration in Italy.
9. Writing about volunteerism in Lombardy, on the basis of ethnographic research Andrea Muehlebach (2013, 462) highlights the structural problems and power inequalities that exist within the volunteer industry in Italy.

10. For further discussion of integration in contemporary Italy see Giordano 2014.
11. For further context on tensions faced by migrants in contemporary Italy, see Giuffrida 2018.
12. On affect and the emotions, see Ahmed 2004a, 2004b.
13. Writing about the 'second families' that factory employees experienced in the 1960s in Milan, historian John Foot discusses a Bovisa-based telecommunications company in the 1960s, which celebrated employees' length of service with the company, birthdays and the births of children with gifts such as prams and financial contributions. Foot 1995, 332–3.
14. The group had 10,634 members in January 2021.
15. These numbers are from January 2021.
16. In February 2018, just before the March general election, the leader of the right-wing 'Brothers of Italy' party Giorgia Meloni organised a march along Via Padova, parading a 300-metre-long Italian flag, purporting to 'reclaim' the city. This was met with an array of flags from people from all over the world, from the neighbourhood and the city more widely, who lined the pavement of Via Padova expressing messages of defiance and solidarity, which, as discussed in chapter 1, are prominent social and political messages seen across the neighbourhood. See Regina 2018.
17. The point made here about the significance of Facebook and community is written up as an ASSA blog post co-written by Daniel Miller and Shireen Walton which compares the Irish and Italian fieldsites: https://blogs.ucl.ac.uk/assa/2018/06/28/whats-the-opposite-of-facebook-err-its-still-facebook-by-daniel-miller-and-shireen-walton/. Accessed 16 November 2020.
18. See Zuboff 2019. For further discussion on the theme of smartphones, social media and data and surveillance, see Miller et al., chapter 9.
19. The extent to which some research participants in NoLo see the neighbourhood as an 'island' in the greater context of Milan and Italy also influences how the neighbourhood positions itself socially and politically in line with ideas associated with the 'Social Street' concept discussed in chapter 1, a concept that began in Bologna in 2013.

4
Social relations: social availability

Introduction

In Italian, the word *disponibile* means 'available'. People often ask each other if they are available to go somewhere or to do something, online or offline. In this chapter I employ the concept of availability in a theoretical sense, and as an analytical strategy for examining social relations in which 'being available' to people is practised, and negotiated, in line with broader ideas about privacy, autonomy and the relationship between the two. The smartphone can be an instrument for modulating forms and levels of sociality between intense amounts of engagement, or for seeking what a number of participants called their *equilibrio* (balance) in social and personal life.

To introduce the theme of the chapter on social availability, consider an ethnographic observation regarding the characteristic window shutters seen in many apartment buildings in NoLo and across Italy, known as *persiane* (Fig. 4.1). These shutters are opened and closed in the morning and evening according to individuals' daily routines.

During the course of my research, I noticed that at times people would keep their shutters closed when they were inside their home. Sometimes this was to do with the heat, the light or the cold, but at other times it might be a subtle social act, of preserving privacy or signalling to neighbours or other potential visitors that they were either not at home or otherwise 'unavailable'. Anna, for instance, works full-time and is involved with grandparenting during the week. Leading a busy life in her sixties, Anna at times engages in small acts of salvaging time for herself. Sometimes she closes her window shutters when she is sitting in her apartment knitting, or watching the daily Catholic mass on a religious TV channel she likes to follow in the afternoons when at home alone, her smartphone next to her on the kitchen table on mute. Anna is 'signed off'

Figure 4.1 Window shutters on the *ringhiera* apartments. Photo by Shireen Walton.

from social life – phone muted and shutters closed – without explicitly stating her 'unavailability'.

This idiosyncratic example of 'shutters open, shutters closed' is less an established custom than a fieldwork anecdote. However, it is a metaphorical and material representation of the broader issues of sociality that I explore in this chapter concerning how individuals balance social participation and presence with privacy and autonomy, and how the smartphone figures in this, in later life. Though the fine line between sociality and autonomy is an established feature of social life, today this spectrum is augmented via smartphones, and WhatsApp and social media practices, as the smartphone is incorporated into how people live and manage their lives. At times one has – to keep the metaphor running – to keep the shutters 'closed' – or, in WhatsApp speak, be 'last seen today at …' in order to salvage some time away from social or professional roles and their various demands and performances. At other times, when one wants to engage, reach out and signal presence, the reverse is enacted: the shutters open or online status returns. At the same time engaging socially, for example with the smartphone, is not always something controlled by the agency or desires of the individual. One receives alerts, messages and notifications, which one might feel compelled to respond to instantly or might check out of habit, or one might be compelled to act in situations where contact and communication are particularly anticipated on a human and social or a wider level (consider Gloria in chapter 8, who takes the smartphone with her everywhere, waiting to hear from her partner, who currently lives in another country for work). The smartphone as technical object occupies a place within a broader nexus of human and technological/infrastructural action and engagement.[1]

Before I examine the theme of social availability and its sites (from the home, family and social groups, to the neighbourhood and beyond through the smartphone), I map out some of the frameworks in which social life is traditionally understood in the Italian context, beginning with ideas of the home and the family. Then I discuss how these frameworks have been shifting over time in the light of wider societal transformations, stemming from urbanisation, economic and socio-technological change and evolving kinship patterns, which have a number of implications for the experience of ageing with smartphones today, as people confront questions such as financial difficulty, what to do with free time or how to be with loved ones across distance.

Kinships and social practices: traditional and contemporary perspectives

In rural and agricultural contexts across Italy during the nineteenth century, multigenerational families often lived in one house. It was common for three generations of a family to share living space in a large farmhouse provided by the landlord who owned the land the family farmed.[2] Sons and daughters who married might move away from these households into new homes but, traditionally, as scholars have noted, at least one adult 'sacrificial child', who had not married, would remain in the household to take care of ageing parents, as was discussed in chapter 2.[3] Over time this multigenerational co-operative household model gave way to other models, such as that of the nuclear family consisting of parents and their children living in their own house, as was widely seen in cities.[4] In urban Italy, particularly in working-class industrial Milan, family life has undergone various transformations, though family experiences in the city were never uniform and it remains hard to generalise about this. Within neighbourhoods in Milan, the type and make-up of families were so varied as to differ from house to house and street to street. John Foot, writing about the social history of Milan, has noted that there were significant differences between different blocks of houses within the city, and in the industrialising context of working-class neighbourhoods in the 1960s that he writes about there were almost no single-person households.[5] Migrants from other parts of Italy had brought, at the same time or later, their (nuclear) families with them to Milan after the Second World War, while older relatives might be left in the rural regions of their origin, in Sicily or the south, to which workers and their families might return for holidays.

La famiglia (the family)

The family in Milan after the Second World War appeared to be at the epicentre of social and economic transformation, as well as being a site and keeper of tradition. With each post-war generation the Italian family household decreased in size and generational depth.[6] The nuclear family model, including heteronormative notions of 'nuclear' and of 'family', has seen change over the last few decades.[7] Same-sex civil unions were officially recognised in Italy in 2016, but without a mention of parental rights in the law same-sex parents and their children remain vulnerable in legal terms, and there remains an ongoing debate about same-sex parenting.[8] Discrimination against LGBTQ people persists, which is met with campaigns across the country for LGBTQ rights and social justice.

Milan is a vanguard of social change in Italy.[9] In the city, changing work, migration and lifestyle patterns over decades, diverse gender and sexual identities and sexual orientations, developing societal discourse about non-biological kinship and family, migration and movements, and the role of digital technologies in transnational family life all form part of contemporary urban life and social care. I particularly observed this in NoLo, where, as discussed in previous chapters, many individuals and groups, social spaces and initiatives seek to foster social justice and inclusion.

Casa (house/home)

The hub of the family in Italy has traditionally been the home (*la casa*). Today socio-economic, legal and demographic changes, along with digital transformations and the development of smart cities, have brought about changes to the sites of *casa*, including what and where it can be and become for whom. In cities such as Milan, including in neighbourhoods such as NoLo, social transformation over time has seen a large number of households in which many middle-aged and older adults live alone (see later in this chapter), as well as multi-ethnic, multigenerational and LGBTQ households, while the smartphone itself forms a kind of 'Transportal Home' for individuals who live out their lives between offline and online environments.[10]

To take an example in which *casa* reflects some of these shifts in socio-economic and labour patterns, particularly amid the challenges of midlife, consider Giulia, in her early fifties. Giulia had taken to the smart economy in Milan as a way of earning extra income. She enjoys cooking and hosting, and began to host dinner parties at her home through an app which had recently been developed in Milan and is centred on meeting in a particular place, such as a host's home, for a social event such as dinner and networking. Sometimes these meet-ups have a particular theme, such as a language night at which the aim is to speak another language for the duration of the evening. The app draws on the social and cultural appeal of the home space, including the sociality surrounding food and eating together, to create an online-facilitated offline social event at someone's home in the urban context. Participants pay a fee to attend hosted events and are able to rate the events on the app, which is one way a host builds up their profile.

On one of these occasions, Giulia hosted a dinner event at her home with the help of a friend. Around 25 people between the ages of 20 and 50 were in attendance – a mix of young professionals, university students and people for whom Milan was still quite unknown, such as professionals who had moved from other parts of the country, or from elsewhere in Europe or the world. All were hoping to explore ways of socialising in the city, with the added appeal of doing so in a real home environment. The guests networked, chatted, ate and drank, and a few exchanged numbers to keep in contact. Through the smartphone and the app, Giulia is able to modify the degree to which she opens up her home, in other words to what extent it is made 'socially available' as opposed to when the space returns to being a private space for herself and her family. The smartphone as a container of platforms is thus a mechanism by which she modifies her social participation in the light of wider socio-economic factors.

If the family home can be transformed from a private space into a semi-public social networking space that also serves a social or economic purpose, how are other concepts evolving in the digital age, and what is the role of the smartphone in these changes? To consider this, let us consider the role of *la nonna* (the grandmother) in contemporary Italy.

Nonna (grandmother)

Grandmothers in Italy play significant roles in care giving within families, in the current socio-economic context. As a number of sociological studies have shown, grandparents in Italy provide practical, economic and social support to couples and individuals in a country with one of the lowest fertility rates in Europe, coupled with increased life expectancy, and in the wider socio-economic context in Italy, where working parents work long hours and the cost of living is high, not least the cost of childcare, which is not always available.[11] For these reasons, informal childcare provided by grandparents may be the only (feasible) option some parents have if they are to continue participating in the labour force.[12] According to a sociological study of grandparenting in Italy (2018), the most common age range for high involvement in childcare is 60–64 years, compared with younger grandparents or those over 75. When childcare is less intensive, grandparents are less likely to provide childcare only when they are older than 75.[13] Previous studies have stressed the prominence of women in caring roles in a variety of European countries, including Italy, and gender distinctions play a part in the differing roles, expectations and desires that grandfathers and grandmothers have with respect to care and family involvement.[14] The presence and the 'social – and economic – availability', to refer to the central theme of this chapter, of a grandmother (or grandfather) who lives nearby, is retired and is in good health, are very significant, and an important explanation for the use of informal childcare, especially when young children are involved.[15]

The resulting picture is one that sees older women with significant responsibilities in later life, balancing working lives, retirement and childcare provision, and many grandparents who provide this kind of care to grandchildren are older today than in earlier decades because of later retirement and greater life expectancy, coupled with their children having children later.[16] At the same time, although life expectancy is increasing, there remain many challenges in this potentially fragile model of care, in which the longer working lives of older people and health issues in older adults can call the feasibility and sustainability of these set-ups into question. Indeed, grandparenting roles with a high level of commitment can be challenging, and for some they impact on the freedoms of later life.[17] Grandparenting is also complicated by physical distance, which can be transregional or transnational.[18] A number of the women I met had moved from different cities or regions to be near their adult children in Milan, or already lived near them, and many were actively involved in grandparenting. The smartphone can be an important instrument in this: WhatsApp is used for arranging schedules and practical matters, for sharing photographs among families and friends, and for pursuing individual interests and activities. Smartphones are incorporated into many grandmothers' lives and duties, practices and desires.

Among grandparents who work, the likelihood that they will provide intensive childcare may be reduced, but studies of grandparenting in Italy have shown that grandmothers may be asked to help their adult children with childcare even if they are still working, as I found during my research in NoLo.[19] I came across many grandparents who were engaged in their families' lives in active and practical ways from their fifties into their eighties. For example, Nonna Lina's everyday life at 60 spans a spectrum of public and private participation, at home, at work and in the local community. Aside from her full-time job, one of her routine activities is to collect her granddaughter from primary school and bring her home for *la merenda* (a light afternoon snack) until her mother returns from work. Sometimes Lina, her daughter and granddaughter will eat dinner together if her son-in-law is out of town with work. Lina is an important figure in her granddaughter's life and is willingly on call for care, which mother and daughter organise through their WhatsApp chat.

Images and idealisations of *la nonna* are prominent inside and outside Italy. Evidence of this can be seen in a range of fields, from folklore traditions such as songs, poems and lullabies to memoirs, films, material culture and souvenirs. *Nonna* has been romanticised in nostalgic terms outside Italy, as part of the perceived purity and innocence of childhood. For example, in his 2005 autobiographical book, *More Coffee with Nonna*, Philadelphia-born author Vincent Iezzi reflects on his Catholic grandmother's migration to the US and her life in Philadelphia duringthe Second World War. The author describes her home as a 'slice of Italy', acknowledging and celebrating the impact she had on his childhood and life. The tone is one of adoration and idealisation, focusing on and celebrating Nonna's faith, piety and charity:

> She was a woman of customs and traditions. She followed the dictates of her traditions to live life close to God and His Church. … She followed the examples of her ancestors in sharing, caring, and loving others, always finding a bit of truth in everyone and in everything.[20]

The author insists that *his* Nonna is not merely a representative of a typical Italian grandmother, but a unique individual:

> No one cooked as she did, or sewed, crocheted or knitted as she did. No one understood other people as she did, and no one had the patience that she had. No one worked as hard or regretted as little as she did. No one was as grateful for the small things that came her way as she was. None of us saw and understood life as she did.[21]

This author's celebration of *his* Nonna is heightened by the author's family's experience of emigration. Here, the loss of homeland, cultures and traditions becomes manifest in the nostalgic sense of sacrifice, dignity and purity with which Nonna's virtues are endowed. This kind of adoration of a particular type of older womanhood often takes on saintly connotations within the social Catholic imagination, where the Italian mother evokes the paradigm of the Madonna.

The word *nonna*, meaning 'grandmother' in standard Italian, bears a loose similarity to *nanna* and *ninna*, words for 'sleep' in infant talk used in lullabies.[22] Indeed, part of Nonna's practical and symbolic power has been realised in infant-rearing practices such as lullabies, as well as in hearsay and folklore passed on to successive generations. In the following lullaby from Lazio (a region of central Italy that encompasses Rome), the grandmother figure rocks the child to sleep while the mother is out working in the fields. While mother fulfils the practical necessity of economic survival and sustenance, Nonna, here charged with the baby's care, remains the keeper of the family, or, literally, the 'guardian of the walls':

> Ninna nanna ninna nonna
> mother's out [working] and soon will return
> when she returns she'll bring
> breasts, full, full [of milk].
>
> Rock [my] heart rock [my] heart
> rock-a-bye sleep securely [sure]
> 'cause your grandma is guardian of the walls.[23]

While the mother casts herself and is cast by society as self-sacrificing – 'out working' – the guardianship role is transferred to the grandmother as carer of the child in the mother's absence because of the necessities of work, as well as in times of illness or crisis. This transfer of status from the mother out at work to the retired *Nonna* as a central carer is something we see increasingly today in the context of the socio-economic situation in Italy, with its intense demands of working life and child-rearing.

In the digital age, the celebration of Italian grandmothers has found creative expression in digital contexts, including entrepreneurial start-up initiatives across Italy; this was seen in an earlier example, in which an app had transformed the private home into a social network space in the urban environment. Grandmothers also feature in digital initiatives in line with the tourism industry in Italy. An example of this can be seen in the marketing of the experience of cooking with a real Italian *nonna* to tourists from abroad. In a number of initiatives, tourists from around the world can learn how to prepare typical Italian dishes, such as homemade pasta, gnocchi and cakes, before eating all together at the end of the class. Though such instances imply niche socio-economic participation, some Italian grandmothers have been championing the idea, seeing it as an opportunity for fun and for cross-cultural and cross-generational dialogue.

As a significant literature in the anthropology of tourism and mobilities has shown, tourist appetites for tradition are widespread. The appetite for observing traditional practices has often been thought of as a nostalgic product of modernity, as part of the broader tourist gaze.[24] That cooking with *Nonna* today is marketed as an 'authentic' experience on tours of Italy is significant in a country in which tourism is among the primary industries, accounting for roughly 13 per cent of the country's GDP.[25]

Furthermore, the figure of *Nonna* and her Madonna-like status have taken on a more politicised role, becoming inculcated in contemporary Italian politics. In August 2019, in the midst of the ongoing crisis concerning refugees in Italy and Europe, and against a political backdrop of far-right and anti-migrant and anti-refugee discourse emanating from then Interior Minister Matteo Salvini and his supporters, a photograph of three *Nonnas* from the town of Campoli del Monte Taburno near Naples went viral and attracted nationwide attention on Italian and global social media.

The photograph shows the three grandmothers holding three migrant children in their arms or on their laps, the moment being linked to a reception centre for migrants. The image was posted on a Campoli-linked Facebook group titled 'You're from Campoli if ...', and before long it had been shared on social media across the world, and picked up and disseminated by mainstream Italian newspapers such as *La Repubblica*. The left-leaning press positioned the image as 'a testimony that a better Italy exists',[26] implying that the message on social media that the photo evokes is one of inclusivity: 'This is the Italy I want', read another headline.²⁷

The attention the image gained online in the summer of 2019 amid the climate of right-wing sentiment that followed Salvini's hard-line policies towards migrants and refugees throughout 2018 and 2019, including closing the southern ports to ships carrying migrants and speaking openly and actively against immigration to Italy at rallies across the country and on his Twitter account. These acts had been met with hostility and resistance from the left and liberals across Italy. Against this backdrop, the image gained traction online, tapping into popular debates about 'Italianness' and notions of (southern Mediterranean) hospitality (*accoglienza*).²⁸, ²⁹ Here kinship categories, such as the figure of the (southern) *nonna*, are also meant to present certain sets of moral visions about types of people and what they are supposed to stand for – here older women as kind, hospitable and nurturing – that can be co-opted for political or personal profit (see also chapter 7 on citizenship debates).³⁰ The example highlights the political significance of instances in which older age and status become bound up with social and political themes, issues or agendas via social and mass media.

Vivere da sola/o (living alone)

A transformation in lifestyle models has been the rise in single-person households. In Italy, the proportion of single-person households is 31 per cent.³¹ Many of the people I met during my research lived by themselves. Of these, a number were women in their fifties to eighties. Reasons for single-person households are varied and link to a number of transformations over time. From my research, these included changing intra- and transnational work patterns, evolving social relationships, individual lifestyle patterns and choices, including ones other than nuclear family set-ups, the death of partners, and children and grandchildren living autonomously in other parts of Milan, Italy or the world. Moreover, divorce and separation have increased in Italy since divorce was legalised in the 1970s. However, in 2018 there were 1.5 divorces in Italy for every 1,000 inhabitants, which is lower than in other large European countries and among the lowest in the EU, alongside Malta, Ireland, Slovenia, Bulgaria, Croatia and Romania.³² A number of research participants were separated or divorced, which had implications for their care, health and wellbeing, and for social relationships later in life (see chapter 6 and other cases throughout the book).

In the social history of Milan, single-person households are a relatively new phenomenon. Writing about this topic in the context of the early 1960s in northeastern neighbourhoods of the city, John Foot notes that families in this context were largely nuclear; 80 per cent consisted of either two parents and their children or two parents alone.[33] Single-person households were almost non-existent and consisted of widows or widowers; in other households there were very few pensioners and large numbers of children. Family structures at that time and in that place were almost the complete opposite of what they are in Milan today, with a higher numbers of pensioners, fewer children and an increasing number of people living alone.

The prevalence of single-person households in Milan today reflects a broader trend across Italy, Europe and the world. Loneliness and isolation are core social and health concerns among older adults. Accordingly, loneliness and isolation are reflected in ageing-related policy discussions the world over and remain pressing concerns, particularly amid the Covid-19 pandemic and its impact upon older people living by themselves. My research highlighted how I found that it was important to question some common assumptions about people who live alone, for example that such people are alone in their lives. An ethnographic understanding of individuals' social networks, patterns of sociality and lifestyles can offer further perspectives on this issue. In the following example, of Clara and Claudia, we see how alternative models of care and kinship play a significant role in how care is enacted between middle-aged and older women, which brings us back to the chapter's theme of social availability and the lines between autonomy and togetherness.

Privacy and autonomy

Clara, in her late seventies, is widowed and lives alone in the apartment building she has lived in for 25 years. She has two children, who live with their families in other cities in Italy and who she sees infrequently because of their busy lives. On the one hand, such women live with a degree of isolation, particularly concerning the 'empty nest' feeling of the home space that Clara describes. Claudia, in her early fifties, lives in the apartment next to Clara's. She works full-time and also lives by herself. What started as a sharing of responsibility for watering each other's pot plants on the balcony of the floor on which they live blossomed into a friendship over the ten years the women have lived side by side. Claudia describes Clara as her 'go-to person' for many things:

If one day I was to have a fall, or pass out on the floor, it would be Clara who would notice first. She would notice my absence – my leaving for work in the morning, my coming home at night. ... Clara would often come round to check on me, and I on her. I've given her a key, of course. I also have hers.

The relationship between the two women constitutes a kind of mother–daughter one, one that has been crafted over time, supported by the social infrastructure of their neighbourly set-up, the *ringhiera* apartment building, which habitually brings the women together, and which can afford little privacy.

To go outside to water the plants on the balcony, for example, is invariably to encounter neighbours doing the same, or hanging out washing, or walking up and down the corridor speaking on their smartphones to get some personal space outside their apartment.[34] Outside the space itself, the women have nurtured a bond through reciprocal care giving and receiving and sustained goodwill. Clara does not have a smartphone, so this sociality plays out through in-person encounters as well as frequent calling via the house phone to check in and express care.[35] If Claudia is away for work or she has not seen Clara for a day or two, she will check in via the landline telephone.

Clara and Claudia are, in effect, each other's next of kin in Milan, a social kinship crafted within the urban context and the broader context of their lives and needs. Contrary to claims that living in settings like the *ringhiera* apartments leads to an 'enforced intimacy' deemed stifling or negative,[36] my own research findings revealed capacities for co-operation and mutual care, particularly between people who lived alone. In this respect, my experience chimes with related sociological ethnographic work on single-person households in Milan. In her 2015 monograph based on a study of 250 women above the age of 45 living alone in apartments in the city, the sociologist Graziella Civenti found that through a variety of ties and practices, women research participants established intricate care and exchange networks that carried out many of the social and economic functions traditionally performed within family structures.[37] By so doing, they were able to establish a functional sharing economy that is mutually sustaining and nurturing and is based on the premise of solidarity, mutual assistance and attending to common problems. These findings agree with the kinds of social and care practices I observed and participated in, living myself in a similar apartment building, a *casa di ringhiera*. In daily life, I was struck by the iconic architecture and forms of sociality I witnessed within the building, its corridors and its courtyard, and the *casa di ringhiera* I lived in incidentally became an important part of my experience of living in the neighbourhood.[38] This being so, I briefly describe and reflect upon the theme of the *casa di ringhiera*.

Built in the early twentieth century, apartment buildings in the neighbourhood, known as *palazzi*, including the *ringhiera* apartments of Milan, have housed generations of families, groups and individuals from different regions and other countries over the decades, first of the working and later the middle class.[39] These structures are in some sense iconic of Milan, and can be seen across the NoLo/Via Padova neighbourhood (see Fig. 4.2). Forms of sociability have been a key feature of them, in part because of their architectural design. The *ringhiera* structure consists of balconies grouped around a central *cortile* (courtyard). Apartments are either *monolocale* or *bilocale* (one- or two-roomed flats), and in earlier decades, after the Second World War, residents shared bathrooms, washing facilities and stairwells. A central aim of this housing was to economise on living space, accommodating the maximum number of families

Figure 4.2 *Ringhiera* apartments. Photo by Shireen Walton.

within the minimum possible space.[40] In the heightened intensity of these living arrangements in industrial and post-industrial Milan, where privacy was limited, the panopticon-like framework had created a certain awareness of the presence of others, which is, by and large, still present today, and can be said to be somewhat amplified by living with smartphones and digital technologies in an age of 'surveillance capitalism'.[41] In the description of *ringhiera* apartments in his book on Milan during the economic boom of the 1950s and 1960s, John Foot describes the blurring of private and public spaces in such buildings as follows: 'Ringhiera housing encouraged collective activity and minimized privacy. Every entrance and exit could be observed. Arguments were heard by everyone.'[42]

Despite the potential for voyeurism of the *ringhiera* and the intensity of the living arrangements, these spaces have positive social connections, such as friendships between neighbours.

However densely populated apartment blocks may be (as much urban studies scholarship has highlighted), living in proximity (or in fact being a member of Facebook or WhatsApp groups) does not automatically lead to sociability,[43] and Clara and Claudia's story should not be over-romanticised as a general portrait of Italian apartment living.[44] In NoLo today, where living arrangements are a mix of family-inherited property, social housing and privately owned or rented properties, and where we see a variety of residents living alongside one another, of different ages, ethnicities, cultures and backgrounds, sociability takes a number of forms and not all of them are socially harmonious.

In one building live Layla, aged 46, and Karim, in his fifties, and their four children. The family have lived here for 15 years: the young-adult children, having moved to Milan from Egypt at early ages, attended school in the city and speak Italian and Arabic fluently. Maximising space and obtaining some privacy has been a priority for this family and they have explored a range of creative ways to achieve this: a replacement door, and rooms with dividers for greater privacy for the family members. The family do not have Wi-Fi at home, and instead use mobile data on their smartphones; it often runs out, which requires topping up or borrowing each other's available data.

Each morning at 7 a.m. Layla heads off to work. Often at a similar time Karim returns home, since he works night shifts. Whenever their paths cross in this way on the long communal balcony outside their apartment, the two greet each other, exchange a few words and go their separate ways, he to bed, she to work. Their children, at their various paces, head to high school or to work. In the evenings the sound of dinner chit-chat, laughter, jokes or arguments penetrates the walls of the adjacent apartments. For Layla and Karim, approaching midlife, life can feel like a constant cycle of renewal, of losses and gains that neither they nor these housing structures in Milan are strangers to.

In times of personal or family crisis, including financial pressures, or other tensions throughout the course of a year, family members in different households across the neighbourhood quarrel and reconcile. At these moments, residents may come out onto the shared balconies or communal spaces, curious about the commotion, or peer from behind net curtains and shutters to catch a glimpse of a dispute, whispering and reporting sequences of events to relatives inside. Personal, economic and social tensions may therefore be witnessed semi-publicly, including in *case di ringhiera* buildings, partly because of the panopticon-like set-up.

In Luchino Visconti's seminal film set in post-war Milan during the economic boom, *Rocco e i suoi fratelli* (1960) (Rocco and his brothers), residents of the apartment building the family live in witness both the social elevation and the socio-economic hardships of the Parondi family, who had moved to Milan from Apulia in the south. Several scenes of the film convey the sociality of living in close proximity in apartment buildings, with whole households bearing witness to others' struggles and experiences. As I observed throughout my research, this accidental or otherwise witnessing of the semi-public plights of others can occur in housing contexts.[45] As this chapter highlights, these experiences form part of the bigger picture of how research participants experience and negotiate privacy and sociality in daily life, including with smartphones, which is a core theme in this book.

Public and private lives

Moving from the residential contexts of apartment buildings to the experiences of individuals, one sees how private versus more public-facing behaviours play out in older age and the kinds of spaces and places people feel comfortable inhabiting, including the kinds of relationships they may wish to cultivate. At one end of this spectrum is Bernadetta, aged 73, who is married with three grown-up children. Bernadetta never undertook official employment because she was caring for her children, one of whom has disabilities and requires full-time care. Alongside fulfilling her role as a mother, Bernadetta has been an active member of the local community, particularly in the charity sector. She has been involved in raising funds for charities devoted to supporting people with disabilities, and in refugee associations and groups supporting homeless people. Bernadetta has also taught Italian twice a week at a local school. Speaking with Bernadetta about her family history, looking at photo albums with her in her home, and at the scrapbook of newspaper cuttings she proudly shared with me, I learn that she was particularly close to her father, who was a partisan in Milan in the fight against Mussolini. The political situation and the resurgence of the far right in Italy made Bernadetta angry.

Under the breeze and buzz of an electric fan over coffee around her kitchen table one hot summer afternoon, Bernadetta recounted an incident to me. One morning, she had gone with a friend for a coffee in a local bar to catch up. They met at a fairly low-key bar which is frequented by locals, and took their coffee to a table in the corner of the bar. An Italian couple in their late seventies were at a table nearby in the centre of the room. On noticing Bernadetta's friend, who is a Roma, the man stood up, signalling to his wife to do the same. He looked displeased and, leaving the bar, mumbled under his breath that such people (Roma) had no place in Italy. He grabbed his wife by the arm and the two walked out, leaving their coffee half-drunk. Bernadetta, infuriated by this, had expressed her shame at the incident. Instances of racism and practices of social exclusion are not uncommon in Milan, Italy or Europe, and, as chapter 7 also highlights, many citizens are discriminated against and labelled 'others' regardless of their legal status within a national or EU context.[46]

Bernadetta has directed her care both inward to her family and outward to society throughout her life. Demonstrating a different level of sociality is Angela, in her early eighties. Throughout her life Angela has attended to her sons and, until his death, to her husband. Occupied by her family, its conflicts, gains and losses, she lives with the family's issues and talks about them from time to time with friends and confidants. *'E allora? Che devi fare?'* (And so? What can you do?') are phrases she uses often in conversation.. She attends church but is not particularly active in any of its social groups, nor in the community at large. Today she lives alone in the apartment she lived in with her late husband and leads a home-based life. One of her sons owns an apartment nearby and she sees him fairly regularly for lunches on Sundays and special occasions. The house phone, along with the television, is her main portal to the wider world. Angela does not engage much in politics or community groups. She is occupied more by her life at home, her daily routines, general chit-chat and gossip with neighbours. Once every fortnight or so she will have a coffee with a friend or two, women of similar age. She looks forward to this, and dresses up for the occasion: an elegant jacket, smart shoes, combed hair, a touch of make-up, jewellery and a squirt of musk perfume.

Bernadetta and Angela highlight how the line between how people engage in social life and living between more public and more private spheres reflects individuals' lives, backgrounds and experiences, along with their personalities and desires. The smartphone notably did not feature in either woman's life, which shows that the ways in which private and public activity is modulated remain a core feature of how many people live their life in older age with older technologies; landline house phones, televisions and radios, and window shutters all play their part in the everyday experiences of ageing, caring and wellbeing.

Conclusion

In this chapter we have seen how older adults experience and shape their social worlds and activities between levels and layers of autonomy, privacy and freedom. In our looking at how social relations and individuals' 'availability' and care for others and for themselves play out and are managed, examples have pointed to domains of commonality and shared experiences between people and to how these evolve at a more individual level in daily urban digital life in the neighbourhood. In some instances sociability exists within certain spaces; this may be within the architectural structures (such as the apartment buildings) or the digital infrastructures and platforms (the smartphone, the platform and the apps) that bring all kinds of people into proximal relationships with one another, as we saw in the mother–daughter relationship of Clara and Claudia, among members of a large, multigenerational family and between older women and widows living alone.[47] A core finding of my ethnographic research was the existence and social salience of networks of urban kinship or 'urban families', comprised of non-biological kinship, diverse identities and wider solidarities seen across the neighbourhood in a variety of physical and digital settings, from residential sites to public spaces and WhatsApp groups, which, as we saw in the previous chapter, also entailed cross-cultural and intergenerational relationships.

The chapter has highlighted a theoretical notion of social availability witnessed in this urban setting and its relevance to the study of ageing with smartphones. 'Sociability' has its own academic definitions in social science scholarship.[48] As a host of urban anthropologists, geographers and sociologists have shown, there are multiple forms of daily socialities in everyday life in cities, which enable potentially co-operative and harmonious sociabilities to develop, even in cases of acute difference or unequal social and economic capital.[49] This is the kind of sociability that we have seen in not only the urban but also the digital spaces of NoLo.[50] I have suggested that the concept can be broken down as a combination of the 'social' and the 'availability' of individuals who modulate their social relations (and their socio-economic activity), with and without smartphones, and which can be seen as reminiscent of older material practices like leaving one's window shutters open, closed or ajar. Social availability is experienced and performed via a variety of practices and within a range of physical urban and digital sites as people scale their sociality up and down in midlife and in older age in line with their preferences for and practices of autonomy and collectivity, and these practices reflect broader socio-economic factors, such as participation in the workplace, in society and in the home.[51]

The smartphone, for those who engage with it regularly, is centrally placed within this modulating, as will be further explored in the next chapter. It is physically portable but it can also move between domains of sociability and between physical public and private spheres, all the while mediating the notions of public and private that many research participants had found offered a positive addition to their experience of everyday life, and their capacity to modulate it to their needs or desires. As shown throughout the chapter, amid these digital practices, traditional sites such as the home, along with the figure of the grandmother or a neighbour, may maintain their social or traditional values, but they can also be repurposed in urban and digital contexts to respond to shifting social ideas and practices, economic circumstances and work demands.

Research participants demonstrated feelings of belonging and attachment to family, friends, and neighbours and peers within and beyond the community with whom they participated in activities and engaged in care, on- and offline. As a result, the neighbourhood and the city of Milan were places many people, older and younger, were proud to live in, and in which to cultivate both the neighbourhood and their individual and collective social lives.

Notes

1. For a contemporary anthropological discussion of the technical object see Coupaye 2020.
2. Kertzer and Saller 1991.
3. I employ this term as quoted by Joan Weibel-Orlando 2009, 537. Weibel-Orlando quotes from the anthropologist of ageing and ethnicity Andrei Simić, who used the term 'sacrificial child' in relation to 'successful aging' strategies and differing levels of responsibility among siblings for elderly parent care.
4. Weibel-Orlando 2009.
5. Foot 2008, 321.
6. Kertzer and Saller 1991.

7. A prominent stereotypical representation of an Italian nuclear family in popular culture outside Italy can be seen in the television advertising campaigns of the food products company Dolmio, which since the late 1980s have featured across North America, Western Europe, Australia and New Zealand, and have contributed to popular perceptions outside Italy about the traditional Italian family.
8. Selmi et al. 2019, 226.
9. Centro Risorse LGBTI 2017, cited in Selmi et al. 2019.
10. On the theory and concept of the Transportal Home see Miller et al. 2021.
11. Zamberletti et al. 2018.
12. Zamberletti et al. 2018, 274; Sarti 2010.
13. Zamberletti et al. 2018, 273.
14. Di Gessa et al. 2016.
15. Del Boca et al. 2005.
16. Leopold and Skopek 2015.
17. Continued and increasing reliance on informal, flexible and low-cost in-family childcare remains an important theme in policymaking in the context of social research on families, labour patterns, gender distinctions, and health and wellbeing, in Italy, the rest of Europe, and elsewhere.
18. On intergenerational relationships in transnational contexts, see Zontini 2010, 2015.
19. Zamberletti et al. 2018, 273.
20. Iezzi 2005, 2.
21. Iezzi 2005, 2.
22. Del Giudice 1988, 289.
23. As quoted in Del Giudice 1988, 282.
24. On tourism imaginaries, see for example Salazar and Graburn 2016.
25. See Statista Research Department 2020.
26. See the original report, Today.it reporters 2019.
27. See Camarda 2019.
28. For further insight and critical anthropological discussion of popular culture and notions of 'Italianness' see Favero 2017.
29. For further critical discussion of the concept, narratives and logics of hospitality in relation to immigration and Europe see Rosello 2001.
30. During the Covid-19 pandemic, a popular video went viral in early March 2020 that showed an Italian *nonna* giving advice on how to deal with the coronavirus and how to make the best of time spent at home under quarantine. Female care was linked with the crisis in this and a number of other ways during the pandemic in Italy during 2020, and memes, public art and visual culture tapped into national and global public imaginations of the Italian nation state as *la famiglia*. See the video at Al Jazeera 2020.
31. See Eurostat 2017a.
32. See Eurostat 2020.
33. Foot 1995, 322.
34. Fieldnotes from NoLo apartment blocks, 2018.
35. For an anthropological discussion on frequent calling as care see Ahlin 2020.
36. Saraceno 1991, 474–6.
37. Civenti 2015.
38. By writing about the *casa di ringhiera* from an ethnographic perspective I join a host of scholars, authors and film-makers interested in how social life plays out in these buildings. For example, in this chapter I refer to the film *Rocco e i suoi fratelli* (Rocco and his brothers) by Luchino Visconti, in which several scenes take place in *case di ringhiera* in the context of industrial, post-war Milan. See also the 2004 documentary film (and related essays and books) by John Foot, *Story of a House: Piazzale Lugano 22*, which is based on participant observation, oral history interviews and documentary research; it tells the story of a working-class apartment block. For a description of the film see https://www.ucl.ac.uk/place-and-memory/milan/bovisafilm.htm.
39. For a social-historical discussion of the *ringhiera* housing structures of Milan see Foot 2001, 9.
40. Foot 2001, 9.
41. On surveillance capitalism see Zuboff 2019.
42. Foot 2001, 9.
43. See Çağlar and Glick Schiller 2018.

44. Italian apartment living has acquired an international reputation for its intense sociability. During the Covid-19 pandemic of 2020, news and social media reported on the balcony and rooftop singing in apartment blocks in Milan and other cities that captured global media attention and made images and videos of contemporary Italian lockdown sociability go viral, positing it as a sign of positivity and hope based on the kind of solidarity and sociality that these apartment blocks and Italians have garnered a reputation for representing. See *The Guardian* 2020 and Taladrid 2020.
45. For further discussion of the film *Rocco e i suoi fratelli* in the context of the post-war social history of Milan, see Foot 1999. For more historical context and discussion of the *casa di ringhiera*, see also Foot 2001.
46. See Bridget Anderson 2019 on both the formal exclusions of non-citizenship and the multiple, and sometimes informal, exclusions within citizenship.
47. On proximal relationships, particularly between people with diverse backgrounds in city contexts, see Çağlar and Glick Schiller 2018, 134–5.
48. Sociologist Georg Simmel (1949) defined the concept of 'sociability' as relations derived from sets of commonalities.
49. See Çağlar and Glick Schiller 2018, 128–9.
50. For the sociologist Georg Simmel, daily life cuts through these more idealistic moments of co-operation, bringing broader realities such as inequalities to the fore. This notion of sociability, may be differentiated from the anthropological notion of sociality. According to Marilyn Strathern (1996, 66), sociality denotes the holistic field in which individuals are embedded in a 'matrix of relations with others'.
51. The concept of 'scalable sociality' in the context of social media is helpful here, in similarly describing how sociality is scaled up and down between levels of public and private engagements. See Miller et al. 2016.

5
Smartphones: constant companions

Introduction

Conducting research on smartphones in Italy, one commonly hears statements such as 'We are all addicted!', 'Just look at people on the metro these days – heads down, scrolling away, ignoring the real world', or 'At a party, no one speaks to anyone any more!', points that seem borne out by Fig. 5.1, taken on the Milan metro.

Figure 5.1 The Milan metro. Photo by Shireen Walton.

Figure 5.2 A typical kind of meta-commentary on the ubiquity of smartphone use today, shared on WhatsApp and other social media platforms via smartphones. Screengrab by Shireen Walton.

Narratives about smartphone addiction find particular prominence in, ironically, smartphone-circulated memes, cartoons and photos. People in their fifties and sixties in NoLo, as elsewhere, can circulate smartphone- and technology-themed memes as part of their broader meme-sharing practices. One such meme is pictured in Fig. 5.2; it purports to portray the extent of smartphone use today. In the image we see the purposeful juxtaposition of a historical image of a street scene from the early twentieth century, in which members of the public pause on the pavement to read the newspaper, and a more contemporary image, in which a group of younger individuals are standing equally motionless and engaged, but their attention is on their smartphones in their hands.

In Italy, smartphones are commonly spoken about in terms of the ages of the people who use them. Older people are often depicted in the media and in political debates as a vulnerable group that is susceptible to 'fake news', while young people, regarded as 'digital natives', can be presented as at risk of addiction or becoming enslaved by the device, and suffering long-term health risks.[1] Notably missing in discourses about and studies of smartphones are middle-aged people, who are the main focus of the ASSA project, and who comprise a significant proportion of smartphone users in Italy. The middle-aged are a dominant segment of the population in Italy, where the median age is 46.[2] Conducting in-depth interviews with middle-aged and older adults in NoLo, I found that most of the people I carried out research with and came to know who were between the ages of 45 and 80 used smartphones, and particularly WhatsApp, frequently. But what was the effect of this on their individual experiences of age, health, care and daily life? To begin the chapter, let us consider three examples of how the smartphone is embedded into people's daily lives, before teasing out some of the particular contradictions, affordances and problems it poses for people.

Introductory portraits

Each morning at 6.45, the alarm clock tone on Dario's smartphone rings, at which he wakes. Before Dario, aged 63, reaches for his glasses amid piles of reading materials, crosswords and a bedside lamp on his side cabinet, he has reached for his smartphone. With his smartphone already in his hand, he opens WhatsApp to check for any new messages that have come in overnight, holding the screen some millimetres from his face, squinting and contorting his face into a strained shape so that he can read the content of the screen without putting his glasses on. If there is a voice message from his family, he may play it: in a recent instance, with the volume accidentally turned up to maximum, the voice of his 88-year-old mother, who lives in another region of Italy, reminded him that it was a cousin's birthday that day. Rooting around in the dark for the volume button on the side, he turns his mother's voice down, listening to the rest of her message closer to his ear, so as not to wake his wife. From there, his thumbs slide over to 'open email' (briefly he thinks, with self-judgement, 'No, this isn't the proper place or time for email'), before gliding over to the weather app to see the temperature and decide what clothes he should wear that day, perhaps reflecting on how he feels about the weather today in relation to the seasonal norm. Finally, having put his glasses on, Dario pulls himself out of bed and heads over to the kitchen in his pyjamas to prepare coffee for himself and his wife. In winter, this is done in the dark (*il buio*); in summer, the humidity (*l'umidità*) is felt and present in this part of the city from sunrise. Dario's two children, in their early twenties, who live with their parents, make their own coffee an hour or two later as they head off to university and work. They themselves often stay in bed scrolling on their phones before they rise. Perhaps the ritual of checking the smartphone first thing has surpassed even putting the coffee on the stove as a widely practised first ritual of the morning.

People like Dario are among the many research participants who acknowledge the ubiquity and utility of the smartphone in their daily lives. However, this high level of use in everyday life leads people to feel that the smartphone 'robs them', as they would say, of their time, their attention or their offline presence with others. For example, sitting at the kitchen table or on the sofa in the evenings in her apartment, Anna will often browse Facebook or WhatsApp for sustained periods of time. She enjoys this, but simultaneously sees it as getting 'trapped' in the phone, feeling ashamed that she is wasting so much of her time doing so. Yet she clearly adores her phone and its endless possibilities for searching for information and connecting with her family. It is, in her word, a constant 'companion' (*compagno*).

She sits in the cold winters of Milan on many evenings, knitting in front of the TV. 'I like it [knitting] because it distracts the mind, which is very important.' Knitting takes Anna's mind off things and her daily worries. Her close-knit online circle of relatives and long-term friends is kept together via WhatsApp chats and calls, wherein she discusses family news, recipes, TV shows and daily life. Comparing the two activities, although it is the smartphone that digitally knits her family and friends together, it has not, at least as yet, accrued the positive moral connotations of knitting as a traditional motherly or grandmotherly craft which she undertakes to create clothing for her children and grandchildren, or for the church, meaning that it remains a somewhat ambiguous object that brings about mixed feelings as a 'companion'.

Karima, in her late forties, did not express particular guilt or concern about the amount of time she spends on her smartphone. This activity is regarded above all as an opportunity to be online with family and friends, both in Alexandria, Egypt, where she was born and grew up and in Milan where she lives. Karima, and a number of other research participants, did not express a moral distinction between on- and offline communication. Given the way it facilitated social communication, and offered practical help in daily life such as apps for translation, maps and searching for information, Karima's smartphone seemed a blessing.

Smartphone use is of course heavily situated in socio-economic context and includes those who have no Wi-Fi in the home. People in some low-income households would rely on mobile data packages to connect to the internet, as well as making use of public Wi-Fi hotspots such as cafés, bars and libraries, often accessing it by providing their *codice fiscale* (Italian tax code, akin to a National Insurance number in the UK or a Social Security number in the US). Members of a family that I came to know had been applying for a visa to visit their immediate family in the US, who they have not seen for years. The couple, in their mid-forties, apply every year for entry to the US. The family do not have Wi-Fi in their home and have limited mobile data on their individual phones. In one instance they recalled that they had received a letter saying that they needed to check the status of their visa application on a website within a specific time period. The couple had tried to do this in the hours when they were not working, which left them little time before the deadline as they could not stay in internet cafés for long periods. The site kept crashing and needed regularly refreshing, and entering the application details in English, a language neither of them speaks, is time-consuming. Family members took it in turn to repeat the process over and over again on their basic smartphones, in free public Wi-Fi zones in the city, or with their limited data. They repeated this ritual daily for some time, trying and failing to get through. Eventually, the couple learned that their application, as last year, had been refused, which they stoically accepted; they will try again next year. The example is a small but telling moment in this family's – and many others' – experiences; lacking easy-to-access digital infrastructure in the home can make important bureaucratic matters that are online or accessed via apps challenging and exclusionary.[3]

These portraits establish a sense of the widespread experience of living with (and sometimes without) smartphones, as well as introducing some of the practices and problems they produce and entail in a range of individuals' daily lives. Further examples of the role of smartphones in everyday life can be seen in a short film made with friends in NoLo (Fig. 5.3).

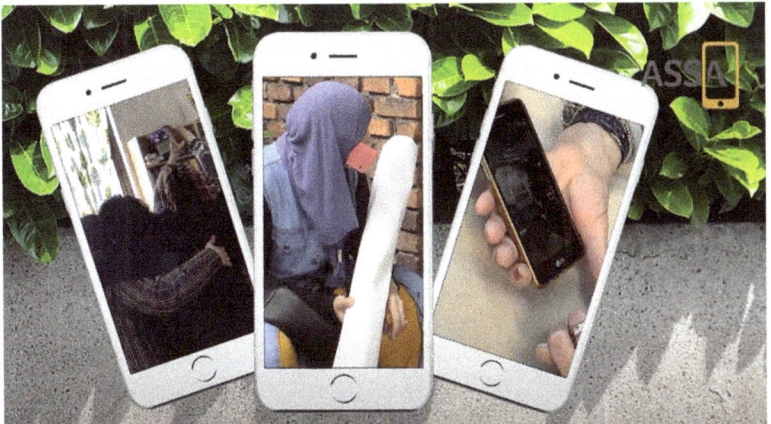

Figure 5.3 Film: *My smartphone*. Available at http://bit.ly/italymysmartphone.

An anthropological examination of the smartphone requires an appreciation of the kinds of infrastructure and discursive contexts within which smartphones in Milan and Italy exist, which I will turn to now.

Local infrastructure and information

Italy has a substantial telecoms market, with one of the highest mobile penetration rates in Europe. Among the top mobile network providers in Italy are TIM (Telecom Italia) (34.5 per cent), Vodafone Italia (30.5 per cent) and Wind Tre (29.8 per cent). Government investment aimed at developing the fibre broadband sector nationwide has played a significant role in developing this market, including 5G services.[4] In connection with its thriving telecoms market, smartphone penetration in Italy is growing rapidly. In 2018, the number of smartphone users was 34,394,000 in a population of 60 million, giving a penetration rate of 58 per cent.[5] The nationwide market is dominated by the Apple iPhone and Samsung Galaxy models, which were in the top six places in a list of the 12 most popular smartphones in Italy in 2019.[6]

As outlined in chapter 1, Milan has been recognised as a leader in technological innovation in Italy and urban 'smartness'. Across the city there are a number of free Wi-Fi spots, around the main stations, and in public parks and libraries, where people may charge their phones or access Wi-Fi. While the telecoms infrastructure in Italy supports the development of smartphones within the smart city of Milan, discourses about smartphones present a less optimistic picture. I will describe some of the dominant discourses about smartphones in Italy below, before considering how some of these themes play out in the lives and practices of research participants.

Smartphone discourses

Smartphones in Italy can be conceived of – in academic literature, governmental and NGO policy reports and media discourses – in negative terms. Children, adolescents and young adults, who are invariably described as 'digital natives' growing up in an age of ubiquitous digital technology and communications, have been subjects of research on smartphones in Italy. Reports and media commentaries tend to lump together the internet, social media, video games and smartphone usage, and the results frequently point to addiction and anti-social behaviour.[7]

Such reports have fuelled national debates about smartphone penetration in Italy, and politicians and the media have echoed them in raising smartphone addiction as a public concern. In 2019, politicians proposed a bill to tackle 'widespread smartphone addiction', particularly among younger people, based on reports that 'Half of Italians aged 15–20 consult their phone at least 75 times a day'.[8] Vittoria Casa, a politician in the Five Star Movement, who proposed the bill, stated that the problem is 'getting worse and worse and must be treated like an addiction … it's the same as gambling.'[9] The bill proposes courses in schools on the dangers of smartphone addiction, as well as campaigns to inform parents. There are also discussions of possible health centres, similar to rehabilitation centres, aimed at 're-educating' the young away from their phones towards a more 'conscientious use of the Internet and social networks'. The press in Italy reports on 'no-mobile-phone phobia' or 'nomophobia', which is anxiety caused by not having access to social networks or messaging apps. In September 2018, a headline in the Italian daily general-interest newspaper *La Repubblica* read 'Italians, more and more smartphone mania: 61% use them in bed, 34% at the table'.[10]

Despite the focus on the young, older adults also feature in discourses on smartphone use and are of increasing interest to the press and policymakers in Italy. A survey conducted by Ipsos of 6,000 people in Italy, Australia, France, Germany and the US found that over-55s constituted a significant demographic of smartphone users.[11] Seventy-six per cent of senior Italians were claimed to be 'inseparable' from their smartphone, primarily using it for social media, while the survey reported that 78 per cent of the participants said that the smartphone 'simplified' their life, with 83 per cent saying it allows them to do things that they could not do before and noting the ease of long-distance communication. Reporting on this study in September 2018, *La Repubblica* wrote: 'In Italy the smartphone has conquered the hearts of the "silver generation". … Set aside the bowls and the playing cards, the over-55s spend their time on Facebook, Twitter and Instagram.'[12]

Research participants in my own study of ageing and smartphones in Milan talked about the smartphone as being useful. 'I need it' or 'I find it useful' (*Mi serve*) was a phrase frequently heard during my research. However, my wider ethnographic research revealed that smartphone practices extended far beyond how it served individuals, but was often closely linked to being with and, indeed, connecting with or supporting others, through activities such as arranging grandparenting duties or running a community activity group. Moreover, the spectrum of uses, as we shall see, exceeded notions of functionality or utility altogether. In short, alongside the dominant discourses about smartphones, there is much variation in how smartphones are incorporated into everyday lives and practices.

Disinformation and misinformation

'Fake news'[13] has become a significant feature of media coverage and public and political conversation in Italy. In July 2018, an example emerged on social media, when a public Facebook post gained attention across Italy and the world. An individual had posted an image ostensibly depicting hundreds of people at a crowded port, with boats carrying people (Fig. 5.4). The caption read: 'Libyan port … They will never let you see these images … They are all ready to set sail to Italy.' The intention was to stoke anger about a supposed imminent 'invasion' of migrants, and the image was shared across the internet within the political context of anti-immigrant rhetoric espoused by the far-right politician and former

Figure 5.4 A widely shared social media post that falsely depicted Libyan migrants as being ready to 'set sail to Italy'. Source: Twitter. Screengrab by Shireen Walton.

Interior Minister of Italy Matteo Salvini. Within a few hours, however, the image was revealed as a photo of a Pink Floyd concert in Venice from 1989. Across NoLo, the image first appeared on individuals' social media in its subsequent, 'revealed form' as a fake news hoax. I observed that in the neighbourhood, where there is a strong liberal presence, the image was transformed into a resource for people to express their opposition to racism, xenophobia and disinformation. People shared the image of the hoax after the scandal for its significance as 'ridiculous' fake news, not for its claim to be a truthful depiction. Thus, a principal concern across social media in NoLo and beyond was to communicate both the ridiculousness of the scam, and the often malicious intention behind representations of and narratives about migrants.

In Italy, as elsewhere, there is concern about the ability of smartphones to enable the spread of fake news quickly and easily, but at the same time people recognise that the root issue – disinformation – has deeper historical roots. A number of the country's established media had been used, for instance during the Berlusconi period, to promote anxiety about a number of topics, particularly immigration;[14] some people, whose parents had lived through and witnessed the propaganda of the fascist era, expressed their concerns about the perils of disinformation.[15]

Apps

'For everything, there is an app' (*Per ogni cosa c'è un'app*), read a line from a *La Repubblica* article in 2018.[16] The report suggested that the 'young elderly' in Italy have an application for *every* need. In the study described in the article, chat was shown to be the most common reason for the use of apps, with 87 per cent of Italian participants using WhatsApp (a high rate within Europe, compared to 76 per cent in Germany and 27 per cent in France) and 40 per cent using Facebook Messenger.[17] The study is fairly congruent with my own results about the high prevalence of WhatsApp use among my research participants. However, there are some important points of departure, in methodology, approach and how results are understood, that require clarification here.

It has been an important part of the ASSA project to ask what constitutes an app, and app usage, and to explore this with research participants, for instance in semi-structured interviews and in the broader contexts of their daily lives. Given the person-centred and long-term ethnographic approach to studying apps and smartphones as practices of everyday life, an important distinction has been made in our project between an app as an 'application' and the broader socio-technological processes and constellations of procedures that the use of, say, a single app is embedded in. These processes and procedures may not even concern the app itself. For example, although people use YouTube or Wikipedia, they may do so via a search engine such as Safari or Chrome, and may not actually have or use the YouTube or Wikipedia app for the platform: some people may not even know that an app *for* YouTube or Wikipedia exists, although they engage with these platforms frequently. Hence there is a distinction to be made between the app and the wider process of engaging with the smartphone, with the internet and with searching for information. For these reasons, the suggestion of 'an app for every need' is something of a simplification of both apps and needs.

Moreover, the smartphone was not always the device for which an app (or a process for engaging with the internet) was configured. Here, the notion of ('Screen Ecology') discussed in detail in the ASSA project's group volume *The Global Smartphone* is important for describing people's movements between platforms and their use of different apps on different devices for various reasons. Sometimes, it might be because a tablet is easy to read from, since it has a bigger screen than a phone. Or a particular device might be easier to hold, or to place on one's lap, to play a game or scroll through photos. Apps are therefore routinely present digital objects, but they are also potentially obsolescent things that are vulnerable to their users' or company's abandonment or collapse. The meaning-making surrounding apps is wide-ranging and anthropologically diverse, from basic, routine searching for information to conscious or subconscious time spending, or time 'losing' as I often heard it described, to online communication, navigation and exploration.

During the course of my research, I undertook a study in NoLo of the use of smartphones of 30 people between the ages of 45 and 80. Most of the participants were in their sixties. I studied people's phones with them, often in their own homes, paying particular attention to the apps they had on their phones, and this interview context was supplemented by wider discussions and my broader relationships with these individuals throughout the research. As can be seen in the infographics in Figs. 5.5–5.7, most people with smartphones used Samsung devices (80 per cent). Apple phones were used very little (10 per cent), alongside other companies such as LG, or more affordable smartphones imported from abroad (see Fig. 5.5). All of these research participants had only one smartphone; some also had a landline and others not. Within this selective group, 97 per cent of people used smartphones, but 63 per cent also used tablets, 42 per cent used laptops and 30 per cent used personal or desktop computers at home (see Fig. 5.6).

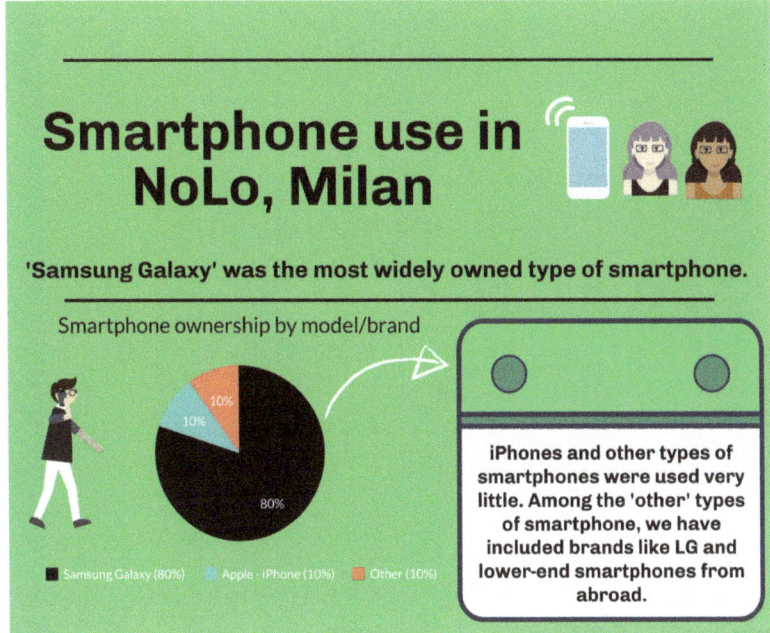

Figure 5.5 An infographic illustrating smartphone use in NoLo, based on data collected in the field. The sample was 30 participants. Created by Georgiana Murariu.

All the participants used WhatsApp, as well as search engines such as Chrome or Safari, for searching for information of all kinds. All the participants used the camera on their phone to take photos and the photo gallery to view them. Almost everyone used Facebook Messenger for messaging (96 per cent): Messenger even surpassed the use of Facebook more generally, though only slightly (94 per cent). Among the others, the most used apps (Fig. 5.7) were maps (90 per cent) for navigation and searching for places in NoLo or Milan and daily, habit-based uses that affect daily life, such as the weather app (85 per cent) for the forecast and the alarm clock to wake up each morning or the calendar to set reminders. Use of the smartphone to make calls was prominent (as opposed to using WhatsApp for one-way written or voice messages), as was checking email. Apps that relate to travel around Milan were fairly popular (Fig. 5.8), from ATM, the Milan city transport app, to bike-sharing apps and apps that tell an individual what parking spaces are available in certain smart car parks, though these are among the more bespoke apps that

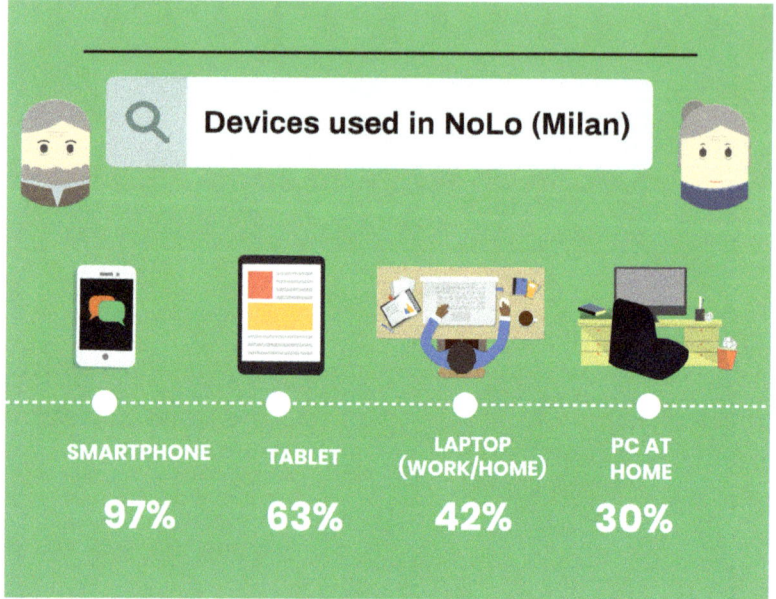

Figure 5.6 An infographic illustrating the use of different devices in NoLo, based on data collected in the field. The sample was 30 participants. Created by Georgiana Murariu.

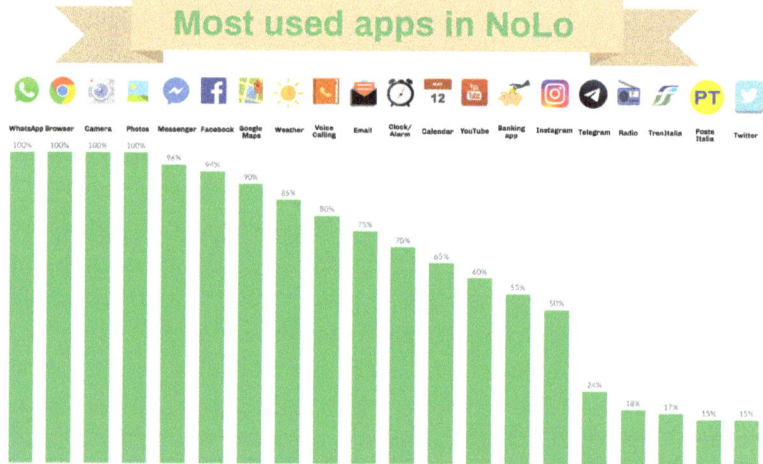

Figure 5.7 An infographic illustrating the most used apps on participants' phones in NoLo, based on data collected in the field. The sample was 30 participants. Created by Georgiana Murariu.

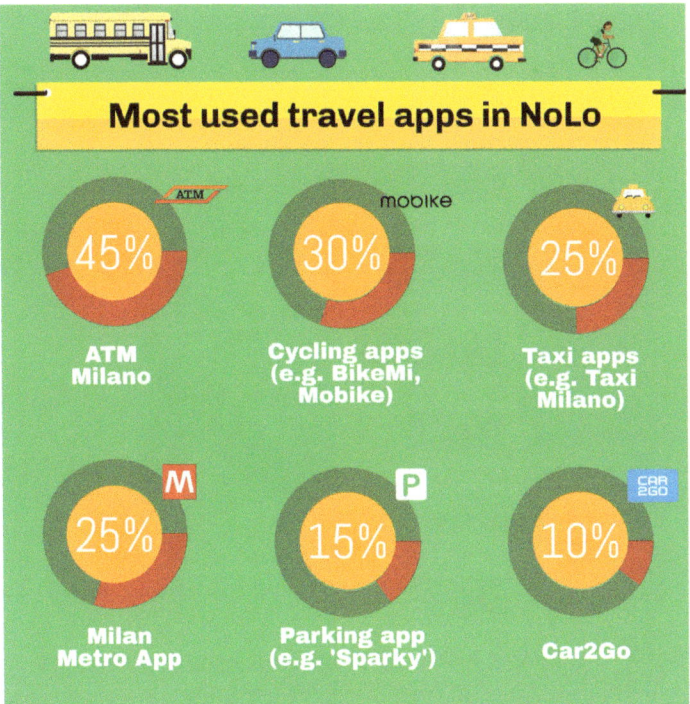

Figure 5.8 An infographic illustrating the most used travel apps in NoLo, based on data collected in the field. The sample was 30 participants. Created by Georgiana Murariu.

people have, and they tend to use them more rarely. Step-counting was also prominent (60 per cent) among health-related apps (Fig. 5.9).

In my ethnographic research, YouTube was seen as a source of information that was an alternative to the mainstream. It would be used for listening to music in the home and watching online tutorials or lessons related to things of personal interest. YouTube was a popular way for people to access music from their countries or regions of origin, which would be played aloud on smartphones or connected to speakers, at festivities, parties and gatherings, such as Eid al-Fitr celebrations to mark the end of Ramadan. Recipes were also popular sites of YouTube engagement (Fig. 5.10).

On the feast day of Santa Lucia (13 December), Maria had located online, via her smartphone, a particular recipe for *cuccìa*, a typical Sicilian dish eaten on this occasion, made with boiled wheatberries and sugar. She shared this recipe, and photos of the *cuccìa* she had made, on Facebook and WhatsApp with family and friends – and shared batches of the dish itself with her daughters in Milan and with close neighbours in her apartment block.

Figure 5.9 An infographic illustrating the most used health apps in NoLo, based on data collected in the field. The sample was 30 participants. Created by Georgiana Murariu.

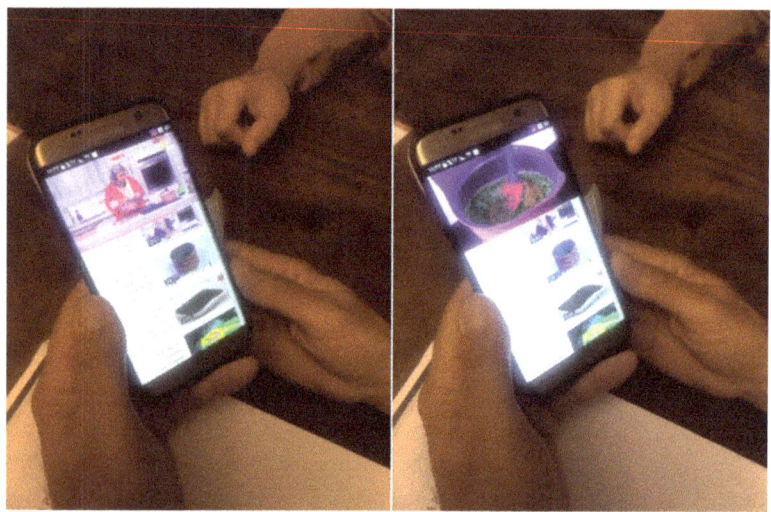

Figure 5.10 Watching an online cooking tutorial on the smartphone. Photo by Shireen Walton.

The smartphone can also be used to pursue a dominant hobby or interest, which, in the case of 60-year-old Domenico, originally from southeast Italy, but living in NoLo for the last 25 years, is politics. Teaching history in a local state school, and not seeing himself as particularly technologically savvy, he is nevertheless somewhat *attaccato* ('attached'), in his word, to his phone primarily because of his attachment to politics and current affairs. While mindful of his pupils' own use, particularly in the classroom, Domenico confesses to checking his own phone regularly during breaks at work. He is in touch throughout the day with his family in Milan, as well as with the community organisations he runs with friends. He spends his time contributing to Facebook pages and WhatsApp groups dedicated to education and awareness of local history, and to a number of causes he is committed to.

In some cases apps mark a clear reflection of individuals' personalities, hobbies and outlooks. Mario, aged 65, introduced in chapter 2, is actively involved in the community allotments. Alongside social media apps, he much enjoys using a plant-identifier app. Apps that were not well integrated into Mario's life – his daily routines, exercise activities, social networks and retirement activities – were generally abandoned.

Apps were placed by research participants on a spectrum between importance and almost total irrelevance. For some participants, apps were something of an indulgence, an attitude that might be summed up as 'I know it's not essential, but it's fun, or useful'. In this respect, the use of apps might be considered akin to owning certain kinds of material possessions that may be non-essential or superfluous, but are nice to have.[18] Apps can reflect and refract individual taste or consumption patterns in context. Taking this material culture anthropology[19] analogy further, in the smartphone as 'wardrobe' apps resembled clothing items that reflected the tastes, desires and practices of the individual, thereby enhancing the expression of the person.[20] At the same time, apps can be ephemeral digital objects. Once purchased, downloaded and engaged with, they could also be abandoned, forgotten about, ignored and outmoded by newer things, like old clothes moved to the back of a wardrobe or a tamagotchi gathering dust in the bottom desk drawer. The currency of apps was not mainly financial, since the ones my research participants used mostly cost nothing (beyond the costs of accessing the internet and owning and using a device) or very little. The material and social currency of apps enhanced the individual self, including in relation to others. Sometimes people would speak about a certain app to friends, neighbours and family members as a matter of pride or enthusiasm that reflected their own engagement with the digital world, but they can simultaneously feel conflicted about these possessions or lose interest in them.

While some people demonstrate more care for curation, or ordering of their apps on their phones, than others, for example by arranging them according to categorical types (such as news, communications, games, travel) or by colour, or even in alphabetical order, there was a clear impression that a number of people personalised their smartphones. Others demonstrated far less care for aesthetics or order, or the appearance of the object; they prioritised the basic use and function of the smartphone. Despite the variety of apps that research participants used, the heart of app usage was communication apps, specifically WhatsApp, and this requires a separate discussion.

WhatsApp

WhatsApp was the most-used app among the research participants, which reflects the fact that WhatsApp is the most-used communication app in Italy.[21] Its popularity does not exclude the use of other social media apps, such as Facebook Messenger, Telegram or Viber. A common use of WhatsApp among participants was for organising and administrating their social lives, work and activities. There were WhatsApp groups for almost every activity, on numerous scales, from gym classes, Italian language lessons or knitting groups, to culture- or identity-linked groups such as those for 'Sicilians … Egyptians … or Filipinos … in Milan', to community allotments, semi-private residential apartment building groups and the more intimate and widely used family and friends groups.

WhatsApp can facilitate a space of sociality tied to specific groups in transnational settings. Consider Jasmine, who is from the Philippines and is in her late forties. Jasmine's husband and two children live in the Philippines and the children are being raised by their maternal grandparents. Jasmine's experience of family separation is not uncommon among migrants from the Philippines, as a number of academic studies have shown. Deirdre McKay's research on the transnational lives and digital practices of Filipino migrants, for example, identifies 'archipelagos' of care networks among Filipino workers across the world.[22] This concept describes the webs that care is enmeshed in, and how belonging is negotiated, in lives that are lived transnationally. In public, Jasmine appears lively and energetic. She has consistently built her social life with other Filipinos in the three countries that she lived in for work before coming to Italy. These networks sustain her emotionally as she plays out her life across a spectrum of physical and digital places and spaces. In the offline context, her social life consists of eating at friends' restaurants around Via Padova, and taking short trips or days out in other cities across Italy for tourism with friends. Her smartphone was 'where my heart is', as she put it to me, placing her smartphone on her heart as she said so. As she is physically distant from her family, and the phone contains a significant part of her social universe, she explained, she carries them all with her everywhere through the device.

Furthermore, WhatsApp demonstrates how ageing with smartphones can have poignant implications for social life and wellbeing in retirement. Pietro, in his seventies, has severe walking difficulties and rarely leaves his apartment. He has his smartphone tied around his neck so that he is never without it. WhatsApp has become one of Pietro's main portals to the wider world. He checks it regularly for messages from family, friends and his family doctor, engages in a few chats, and then has another cigarette as he dives into the *Corriere della Sera* newspaper or continues with a novel until lunchtime, when his wife Maria, who is also retired and volunteers in the neighbourhood, will prepare the meal for the two of them. In the afternoon he will take a nap, return to his reading, browse the internet on the home PC in the study, and in the evening after dinner he will watch television. When he and his wife were added to a new WhatsApp group representing the apartment building they have lived in for 30 years, the two had different reactions. Maria welcomed the wider sociality and its usefulness for communicating on practical matters, such as the use of communal spaces and corridors, or issues to be shared and discussed. Pietro was more ambivalent about this unfamiliar mode of sociality, especially as it quickly morphed from the supposed function of information exchange to the wider postings of emojis, memes and even poems. At the same time the notifications he receives on his phone, including news alerts, bring him pleasure throughout the day, making him feel connected to a certain buzz of 'being-in-the-world', a place his physical condition had gradually removed him from.

While some feel comforted, accompanied and even empowered by being involved in WhatsApp groups that contain the 'voices' and posting activities of – often – dozens of persons, others find the scale of group dynamics intrusive, over the top and part of the 'noise' of technological modernity, of people taking things too far or being *troppo* (too much). Furthermore, though joining – or being invited to join – a WhatsApp group is one thing, it may not necessarily lead to increased social participation or inclusion, and in some cases can have the opposite effect, of making individuals feel annoyed or excluded by what they perceive as a lack of etiquette, decorum, rules and awareness of others, or a lack of regulation. On the whole, however, WhatsApp plays a fundamental and crucial role in everyday life. It is often the main reason people pick up their smartphones, and tends to shape an extraordinary amount of how daily life is organised, discussed, shared and experienced. In the next chapter, I will consider the role of WhatsApp in the field of health and care.

Talking without talking (*parlare senza parlare*)

Audio messages

Communication techniques on WhatsApp tended to vary according to individual personality and preference, or reflected more social forms of communication. A number of research participants from Sicily were fond of using WhatsApp to leave audio messages. These were mainly family communications, and were often laden with emotion and affectionate greetings and salutations. For example, a Sicilian mother greeted her daughter in her own voice, starting the message with 'My joy, how are you?', and following up with a detailed rundown of the day's events, specific goings-on in their lives, reminders about birthdays and what happened at a grandchild's nursery that day. This style reflected the person's offline communications, which were tactile as well as vocal, creating colourful and vibrant forms of expression.

Visual communication: memes and stickers

A significant development in smartphone-based communication in recent years has been the rise of visual messaging, in particular the sending of memes. Elena is visibly affectionate in her online social relations. She particularly enjoys communicating on WhatsApp via memes. 'I send up to seven or eight memes a day, mostly to friends but also to particular family members who would understand them – one of my sisters, a cousin who lives abroad….' The memes Elena finds and shares with friends and family express a mixture of humour, irony and satire, love and friendship, and spiritual content. Often it will be the same sets of individuals that she communicates with in this manner, as a kind of regular keeping in touch. Memes are significant in the sense that they reflect Elena's sociality and sense of humour, through which she expresses herself to friends in playful contemporary ways. Memes can be ways of talking without talking. Such emotion-laden messages and the way these platforms have developed and provide environments for people's communicative and emotional languages recall what Sara Ahmed calls 'affective economies' in describing how emotions, rather than being of the private self, are socially organised.[23]

Another research participant explained: 'I send them [memes] because they make me feel happy. It makes me happy knowing I'm reaching out to people.' Part of the appeal of sending memes is precisely for the kind of communication they afford. Though dialogical, memes do not necessarily incur reciprocal meme-based conversation, because they already fulfil the objective of holding other people within a certain 'force field' of contact and care, through which people – at the desk at work, on the metro, at home in the evenings – express care and humour, and connect with each other. Examples of expressions of affection, care, and friendship in meme-sharing across the neighbourhood (and beyond) can be seen in Figs. 5.11 and 5.13. The prevalence of meme-sharing may be playfully acknowledged in meme-sharing itself, as in Fig. 5.12.

Figure 5.11 A greetings meme in NoLo. The text reads: 'Hello/good morning full of hugs'. Screengrab by Shireen Walton.

Figure 5.12 A meme sent in NoLo. The text reads: 'Tell the truth, you were waiting for my good morning!!!'. Screengrab by Shireen Walton.

Figure 5.13 Meme sent among friends. The text reads: 'Good morning'. Screengrab by Shireen Walton.

While memes were a favoured mode of not necessarily reciprocal communication among some people, emojis were most commonly used as a kind of punctuation or added emphasis to a message aimed at affecting someone or a group of people. While, in other ASSA fieldsites, such as those in Japan and China, Line and WeChat stickers can comprise a significant majority of social media communications, emojis in the Milan fieldsite context played an important role, but not necessarily as primary forms of communication.

Talking and expressing care

Among middle-aged Italian research participants, 'frequent calling' was a fairly common use of WhatsApp.[24] Many research participants made phone calls via WhatsApp as they saw it as a helpful way of calling for 'free' in the sense that there was no financial cost other than being connected to the internet and using a device. Because of this it was particularly favoured for calling relatives and friends abroad.

Although the cases presented so far are mostly positive uses of WhatsApp, for care and communication, a number of middle-aged research participants highlighted a number of pressing concerns they had about smartphones and social media, such as the disinformation discussed earlier in the chapter and the safety and wellbeing of their children. The Rossi family consists of two parents, Cristina and Davide, who are in their late forties/early fifties, and their two children. Cristina Rossi was connected to both her children and her husband on social media: they all used WhatsApp as their main mode of intra-family communication and they all had Facebook and Instagram accounts. The children also used Snapchat. Although the smartphone accompanied the family members everywhere, the lack of control associated with it was something that Cristina, as a parent, had spent many hours thinking about, worrying about and dealing with mentally. In particular, a recent online bullying incident, in the form of a fake Instagram account prank, that had affected one of her children at school was at the forefront of her mind when we met. With just a cruel swipe, like or post, she explained, years of careful hard work as a parent could potentially be undone.[25] Public and policy discussion about online bullying, care and surveillance continues as the digital age unfolds, and as one generation after another ages with smartphones, social media continues to occupy a significant and complex place in contemporary family life.[26, 27]

Objects of everyday life

While a central theme in the study of smartphones concerns their use, how people use them in the compelling and commonplace ways they do forms another crucial area of anthropological interest in relation to the phone as object. A key finding across age groups is the personalisation of the phone. We have seen how this plays out with apps, but personality, character and an individual's social universe are also reflected in the 'objectness' of the phone itself.

As an illustration of this, consider Eleanora. Her smartphone is a visual homage to her grandchildren. The smartphone's wallpaper is a photograph of them on holiday. Other photographs of the grandchildren are sellotaped to the back of her smartphone. The collage that Eleanora has created resembles her fridge door, replete with photographs of her family and memories rendered as fridge magnets. The fridge from which she feeds her grandchildren and the smartphone from which she connects with her family have become sites where she can see them even when they are not physically present.

Dina has a habit of tucking her phone into her headscarf, and may feed her baby or use a sewing machine while speaking on the phone. Elisa playfully experimented with combining her smartphone with a receiver intended for a landline. The newly assembled device (Fig. 5.14) combined the ability to talk for an 'unlimited time' with the feel of a landline, illustrating the abundance of creativity by which people make the smartphone into what they want it to be, in this case, an object halfway between the familiarity of an old landline telephone and a hyperconnected and 'useful' smartphone.

Further to this kind of domestication of the phone as a household object or as an object for expressing love, Teresa, in her early fifties, who has a busy working life in the centre of the city, also uses the phone case in a functional fashion, as an on-the-go material hub for holding other key possessions such as credit cards and receipts, and adorns it with a photograph of her beloved dog. In short, there are instances of how the smartphone as object and container of social universes comes to reflect, and shape, the personality of the person.

But what about the experience of living and ageing without a smartphone? Beatrice is in her mid-seventies and lives with her husband. She has two adult children and four grandchildren and does not have a smartphone. She feels that 'the house phone gives us [herself and her husband] everything we need'. The family has orientated itself around

Figure 5.14 This device, halfway between a landline and an internet-enabled smartphone, was assembled by research participant Elisa. Photo by Shireen Walton.

Beatrice's preferences: her sons call home via the house phone up to three times a day to check in with their parents. Her house phone constitutes a familiar friend that she knows well, something that has served her for many years. Beatrice prefers to 'be in control of technology, rather than it being in control' of her. Despite the fact that her children have asked her if she would like or would use a smartphone, she insists that she does not *need* one. The only situation in which Beatrice acknowledged that such a phone would be 'useful' is when one is out and about and needs to look something up or briefly be in contact with someone outside the home. For the latter, she does have an old basic mobile phone, which she uses very rarely.

We should not put this rejection of smartphones down to a general 'technophobia' that is sometimes ascribed to older adults, however. A closer look at Beatrice's daily life reveals more about how the smartphone is perceived as both an excess, as she does not 'need' it, and an intrusion that she is not keen to invite into her life. Beatrice suffers from acute claustrophobia, which means that she regulates her life accordingly.

For example, she will not take the tram or the bus because of the enclosed space formed by the roofs, doors and windows, and she rarely rides in a car. For this reason, she still uses her bicycle to do the shopping. Beatrice feels that a smartphone would be an intrusive presence in her life, an object she 'must carry around everywhere all the time, charge it, use it so much, otherwise people may be offended …'. The house phone, by contrast, feels like a benign object, one that she knows very well and which has served her well for many years.

Beatrice is not alone in expressing these experiences of ageing *without* smartphones. Many of the middle-aged research participants described a similar situation with their parents, who refused, with varying degrees of emphasis, to use a smartphone. Clearly, then, while the smartphone adds value to life for some by making things easier, and making them feel more connected, comforted and informed, or protected in unfamiliar environments, like all technologies and objects they must be placed within the individual and social conditions, practices and infrastructures of people's lives, and it is through contextualising the smartphone in this multi-scalar manner that we can more concretely understand the value they present for people at different ages and stages of life.

Conclusion

Peeling back the layers of hyperbolic discourse about smartphones in Italy, we discover the range of activities, practices and rituals that smartphones are both implicated in and come to shape. These include connecting with family, friends and community, organising daily life, work and finances and, as I will show in subsequent chapters, navigating health, bureaucracy and citizenship. The chapter shows that there is significant diversity in how smartphones are incorporated into individuals' lives, because of differences in socio-economic circumstances, availability of data and storage, concerns about privacy and about bullying and harassment, and the digital, socio-economic and material infrastructures that shape people's experiences and practices. Wi-Fi, mobile data and connection speeds are all part of everyday social realities and part of how people experience any given day as they live with digital technologies, including in a smart city such as Milan.

The relationship between the smartphone in ethnographic context as it is and as it is often perceived to be, for instance as an object of addiction or social rudeness, has been an important theme that must be nuanced with respect to age, socio-economic and cultural context.

The value placed on the phone was shown to relate both to the content it contains (such as data, contacts and photos) and to the phone as physical object, as illustrated by the ways individuals adorn, personalise and make their phone meaningful by pouring and extracting meaning into and out of it as an object in connection with the various social worlds and networks contained within it.[28] If the phone is lost or stolen, this can be a matter of great distress, particularly if the data has not been backed up, as smartphones exist as a kind of intimate headquarters of people's private and public lives. Apps, I have suggested, are iterations of material culture in the digital age. Like clothing, which can be both functional and mundane, and performative, playful and expressive, apps have been shown to be part of people's repertoire of everyday expressions, based on their variegated engagements with digital-material worlds.

In short, how and to what extent people shape their lives around smartphones encapsulates multiple issues, including addiction, ill health, cyberbullying and forms of surveillance, issues that were not the specific focus of my research and lie outside the scope of this book.[29] For some of the research participants in this study, the smartphone formed a 'constant companion', both in daily life and, as we shall also see in chapter 8, for living amid life's many complexities and contradictions. Seen in this light, the smartphone can be understood within the constellations of practices in which people in midlife and older age engage to craft their lives in the current socio-technological moment, with or without smartphones.

Notes

1. De Pasquale et al. 2017.
2. Hall et al. 2019, 29.
3. During the Covid-19 pandemic in 2020, many documents, advertisements and images aimed to raise community awareness about health, safety and wellbeing, and digital accessibility. For example, in March 2020, an awareness initiative administered by a local NGO dedicated to the needs of families and children in the neighbourhood called on neighbours to share their wireless connections within apartment blocks, to assist children who did not have an internet connection at home to follow school lessons online. Often such campaigns are translated by NGO groups into languages spoken in the area, such as Arabic and Spanish, in order to reach more members of the community. As with many expressions of solidarity under lockdown, the tagline read 'Thank you! Together we'll do it!'
4. TIM launched 5G services in Turin, Rome and Naples in mid-2019 (TIM 2020).
5. From 2017 global statistical reports on smartphone usage: https://newzoo.com/insights/rankings/top-50-countries-by-smartphone-penetration-and-users/; Statista Research Department 2016; Poushter 2016.
6. Kielty 2019.
7. De Pasquale et al. 2017.
8. *The Local* 2019.

9. Scancarello 2020.
10. Merola 2018.
11. The survey, conducted by Ipsos and promoted by Amplifon, is titled 'Smart ageing: Technology has no age'. It found that smartphones surpassed all other technologies used by Italians: 76 per cent used smartphones, compared with laptops, used by 63 per cent, and tablets, used by 41 per cent of the sample. The main uses of the smartphone are documented as passing time (59 per cent), staying informed (48 per cent), and keeping up with family (46 per cent) and distant friends (43 per cent). Thirty-five per cent said they used smartphones for bettering their health. The results of the survey can be found in *La Repubblica* 2018. See also *Wired Italy* 2019.
12. *La Repubblica* 2018.
13. The *Oxford English Dictionary* (*OED*) defines 'fake news' as '[originally *U.S.*] news that conveys or incorporates false, fabricated, or deliberately misleading information, or that is characterized as or accused of doing so', and adds: 'The term was widely popularized during and after the 2016 U.S. presidential election campaign, and since then has been used in two main ways: to refer to inaccurate stories circulated on social media and the internet, esp. ones which serve a particular political or ideological purpose; or to seek to discredit media reports regarded as partisan or untrustworthy.' *OED Online* 2020, s.v. 'fake'. See Wardle and Derakhshan 2017.
14. For more on this see Foot 2001, chapter 8.
15. The spread of false information became a significant issue during the coronavirus pandemic in Italy in 2020, leading to government and medical authority interventions. See chapter 6 on health and care.
16. *La Repubblica* 2018.
17. The study also documented, among the most used apps, looking at weather forecasts (62 per cent), surfing Facebook (54 per cent), looking for directions on maps (53 per cent), and making online purchases (30 per cent), as well as general searching for information such as road and motorway information (*La Repubblica* 2018).
18. On the social worlds of possessions from the perspective of material culture anthropology, see Miller 2001.
19. For an overview and critical contemporary discussion of lineages and advancements in material culture anthropology see, for example, Carroll et al. 2020.
20. The idea that apps add something extra to the self is not a long way from what anthropologists of photography write about in connection with the everyday performative potential of photography for 'adding something to ourselves' which lets us 'review our varied appearances'. See MacDougall 1992, 104.
21. Research participants from different countries used other messaging services, alongside WhatsApp, that tied in better with social networks in their home countries; for example, Viber and Telegram are used widely in the Middle East.
22. McKay 2016. See also McKay 2012.
23. Ahmed 2004a, 2004b.
24. Ahlin 2020.
25. The theme of care and surveillance in relation to the smartphone and the digital age is critically discussed in detail in Miller et al. 2021.
26. For a critical discussion of the datafication of family life and the data traces of children see Barassi 2020.
27. Sonia Livingstone's work has extensively examined children's rights in the digital age, including the issue of cyber-bullying, parenting and digital futures. See Livingstone and Blum-Ross 2020.
28. See the theory of 'objectification' employed by Daniel Miller (drawing on Hegel), which argues that 'people create themselves through the medium of stuff' Miller 2010, 99.
29. For further critical discussion of these and wider issues concerning smartphones see Miller et al. 2021, particularly chapter 9.

6
Health and care in digital times

Introduction

The previous chapter examined the variety of ways in which the smartphone has embedded into and transformed people's lives in the neighbourhood and beyond. This chapter anchors the discussion of ageing with smartphones in the themes of health and care. It provides an overview of the national and regional healthcare systems in Italy, looking at the region of Lombardy (in which Milan is situated) and exploring how this region is particularly developed within the healthcare context of Italy. The chapter illustrates how the national and regional healthcare systems have been and are experimenting with digital health 'from above'. This forms the backdrop to understanding how individuals are practising their own forms of digital health and care in their daily lives 'from below', with a range of implications for health and care, social relationships and well-being across a range of socio-economic contexts. Concurrently a range of factors affect the equity and experiences of healthcare access and delivery across Italy, such as income, legal status and regional location; as will be discussed throughout the chapter, these factors and wider logics and practices of inclusion or exclusion affect the differentiated experience of health and care as a central part of ageing with smartphones in NoLo, Milan, Lombardy and beyond.

The national healthcare system in Italy and in Lombardy

The national healthcare system, the *Servizio sanitario nazionale* (SSN), was established in Italy in 1978, in recognition of the emphasis following the Second World War on the 'right to health' (*diritto alla salute*) as a basic human right. The SSN is free to all Italian citizens, as identified by a national health number,[1] and free or reduced-cost emergency healthcare is available for EU citizens, via a European Health Insurance Card (EHIC). As in many aspects of life in Italy, there are acute regional differences in the official healthcare system. The early 1990s saw the official regionalisation of the SSN, a policy that granted broad discretion in planning and organising healthcare services to individual regions, so that the national system effectively consists of 20 regional systems.[2] This policy has been claimed to have exacerbated the historical north–south divide,[3] deepening tensions between the more and the less economically developed regions, and posing challenges to the central government's guarantee of uniform levels of care across the country. Such distinctions in the system explain the prevalence of health mobilities, labelled within the EU context 'health tourism', which relate to the entitlement of EU citizens to access healthcare in different member states.[4] In Italy, such mobilities involve the movement of people from different regions to access particular healthcare services, and are another example of the many forms of movement and mobilities historically and contemporaneously taking place within the country (as outlined in chapter 1). Lombardy, particularly Milan, is a healthcare hub. The city hosts several leading medical establishments, including the Istituto Nazionale dei Tumori (National Cancer Institute) in Milan's zone 3 and zone 2's Ospedale Niguarda. The latter has its own ethno-psychiatry unit, which offers services for refugees and asylum seekers and deals particularly with trauma and post-traumatic stress disorder (PTSD). Milan and Lombardy also form a hub for social care and welfare programmes in Italy, with active volunteer, church, charity and NGO communities (see also chapters 3 and 4).[5]

Middle-class and middle-aged research participants said they received good-quality healthcare. Valeria, aged 55, who works full-time and leads a busy life in the city, acknowledges that the Italian healthcare system is 'generally good overall'. Along with others, she gladly acknowledges its value as a public system. At the same time people expressed everyday complaints about the functioning of and pressures experienced within the system. Issues identified by research participants included the limits on time and personal attention from medical staff: restricted time for consultations was a particular concern. 'They don't have much time for you, unfortunately, the doctors,' Valeria sighed, shaking her head in disappointment, not seemingly with the doctors themselves, but with the fact that the system more broadly was being put under pressure. Seeing a doctor was first and foremost about attending to a medical issue, but it was also considered a significant contact point of care and listening. 'Patients are brought in and out so quickly that the doctors can become quite automated in their response – you can even say they're going through the motions or following a routine in dealing with you.'[6]

Research participants from outside Lombardy conveyed other views. Antonietta, aged 48, had moved to Milan from another region in her twenties for work. She married in Milan, had two children and settled in NoLo. Members of Antonietta's family have since travelled to Milan for health treatments, and Antonietta has hosted family members in her home on a number of these occasions. An uncle underwent major heart surgery, while a cousin came to consult an orthopaedic surgeon following a leg injury, which she followed up with surgery in Milan. In return for such services, Antonietta felt, 'one does not really complain'. 'It's good, the system here – you pay tax for it, and it's very good.' Antonietta's and her family's exposure to differences in regional healthcare services across Italy had shaped her attitude towards the system in Lombardy, which she was keen to support in the hope that members of her family might receive what she had experienced as high-quality treatment. Personal experience, location, mobilities and socio-economic factors all play a role in the experience of and access to health services across Italy. A major area of cross-sector development within the field of health and care in Italy, which forms a significant part of the context of ageing with smartphones in urban Italy, is the development of digital health or mHealth (mobile health) in the country, which I now discuss.

The development of digital health in Italy

The uptake of digital or mobile health in Italy has been steady, but slower than in other European countries such as Estonia and Denmark.[7] Since 2016 a few regions of Italy – Lombardy, Emilia-Romagna, Tuscany and a few others – have been active in the area of digital health, and Lombardy's development of digital healthcare is above the national average.[8] The picture I gathered in Milan in 2018 and 2019 from interviews with patients and doctors, national and EU reports, and participation in hospital meetings was one of work in progress in the field.[9] The work in this area has since been significantly impacted by the coronavirus pandemic during 2020, in Italy, and in Lombardy in particular, which saw the highest number of cases in Italy in early 2020. Digital technologies played a significant role during the pandemic in a number of core areas, including regional and national healthcare access, communication and delivery, in governance and communications, in new public–private partnerships and in the everyday experience of lockdown. I will refer again to the impact of Covid-19 on the field of (digital) health and care, with a number of examples, at the end of this chapter.

An early beneficiary of investment in digital health facilities in Italy was the Electronic Clinical Record (CCE), implemented by the Italian government in 2012.[10] With electronic health records, individuals can access their medical history and make appointments with doctors. All citizens are given a *tessera sanitaria*, a national health card which contains a chip with their health ID number as well as their national insurance number.

The Digital Innovation in Healthcare Observatory in the School of Management at the Politecnico di Milano is a hub for the development of, and communication about, digital health in Italy.[11] In research carried out by the Observatory in 2016, in the early days of digital health in Italy, on the use of digital technologies in communications, based on a sample of 656 general practitioners, 83 per cent of doctors were reported to use email, 70 per cent text messages and 53 per cent WhatsApp (which is up 33 per cent compared to 2015).[12] WhatsApp, according to the report, is 'used to exchange data, images and information', and was therefore seen as having the potential to open up possibilities for avoiding physical visits. Paolo Locatelli, Scientific Officer at the Observatory, said in 2016 that Italy needed to build 'a multi-channel health system that allows us to improve and make the system more efficient by allowing citizens to access information and services both through websites and apps and through self-service counters in health facilities, pharmacies and supermarkets'.[13] The idea put forward imagines a larger 'ecosystem' of health practices in communities – a 'multi-channel health system' which goes hand in hand with the development of Milan as a leading smart city in Europe and which is part of a vision of a system that allows citizens to access information and services easily through their smartphones and apps. These kinds of visions of urban and digital health ecosystems were shown to be prevalent in ageing policy in Italy, and in Milan in particular, which, as outlined in the discussion of 'active welfare' in chapter 2, emphasises an 'integrated system of subjects and public and private interventions where, through informal networks, the State, the Third Sector and individual citizens all work to build the social welfare of people, thus strengthening the concept of community and of social cohesion'.[14] Key concerns in such developments are the use of citizens' data and surveillance, particularly when these are posited as requisites for public health and the safety of citizens, as widely seen and debated in 2020 during the coronavirus pandemic.

According to studies undertaken since 2015 at the Observatory, patients in the Italian regions who engage with mHealth have used digital technologies mostly for searching for information and for organisational purposes, including the online booking of appointments via apps and websites. According to a 2016 report, 26 per cent of Italian citizens have accessed the internet to look up information about health facilities such as specific health departments, timetables and specialist doctors. Online booking of medical tests and visits was carried out by 24 per cent of citizens, with an increase of 85 per cent since 2015. Facilities for accessing and consulting clinical documents and paying for health services are used by 15 per cent and 14 per cent of patients respectively (up 88 per cent and 180 per cent on 2015).[15] Physicians, citizens and general practitioners have been reported to be communicating more and more through digital channels, though this form of communication is by no means standardised or widespread throughout the SSN. The age group recorded as using digital technologies for health the most in Italy is 35–54-year-olds.[16] My own research revealed a high proportion of over-sixties using smartphones and WhatsApp, but not necessarily specifically or officially for health-related purposes.

The use of WhatsApp for health in Italy is currently undergoing development and experimentation within the Italian healthcare system. My research found WhatsApp to be strongly present in daily life (as was discussed in chapter 5), with only a small number of research participants engaging with medical authorities via WhatsApp. Understanding the role of new channels for health requires an evaluation of the role of traditional ones, as part of the picture of how health information and authority are perceived, valued and engaged with. The following examples illustrate how a number of research participants evaluated digital health or incorporated it into their lives.

Luca, aged 60, who is originally from a city in the Emiglia-Romagna region, lives with his wife Isabella. He has recently retired from his job in marketing and is settling into retirement with enthusiasm as 'a new period of life'. Regarding health issues, Luca is very clear: 'Me, I do what I've always done. We [himself and his wife] never go to the doctor!' Luca explained that his wider family (his parents and his wife's parents) were exactly the same in preferring to visit medical authorities only for very serious matters. Luca disliked constantly seeing doctors and treating common ailments (colds, temperatures) with medicines. This reflects an attitude seen in members of the older generation who would see unnecessary fussing or visits to doctors as evidence of being an *ipocondriaca* (hypochondriac). Although he avoids visits to the doctor, Luca frequents the local pharmacy: it is just three minutes' walk from his home, and he has become good friends with the people who run it. Pharmacies in Italy are mostly independently run, and can be expensive. Pharmacists often offer health advice alongside selling pharmaceuticals and can build a rapport with (regular) visitors.[17] It was not uncommon for people to speak to their local pharmacist and engage in mini-consultations and chats over minor issues or get to know them on a more personal basis.

At the other end of this spectrum of attitudes towards seeing a doctor is Alessia, aged 71, who came to Milan from Sardinia in her twenties to study and work. Alessia prefers to see a doctor whenever she becomes ill, for this, in her words, is a person she knows and can trust. Although this attitude towards seeing the doctor is different from Luca's, it is quite traditional in another respect. The idea of the family doctor who, traditionally, saw over the whole family's health plays an important part in community – and particularly village – life across Italy. Alessia had described aspects of village life in her home town as providing little opportunity to develop her educational and socio-economic aspirations, but the position of the village doctor is something she retained as valuable, and, clearly, this value is present in the way she perceives doctors and visits her doctor today in the 'urban village' of NoLo.

Enzo, aged 68, is somewhere in the middle of Luca and Alessia's attitudes to doctors: an admirer of medical authority, but not overly keen on visiting clinics or hospitals, Enzo makes use of his smartphone to bridge the two. A retired designer, Enzo is particularly attentive to his and others' daily health. In the words of his wife Chiara, he has 'always got something *not quite* right'. Although he has no major health concerns and leads an active retired life filled with walking, and trips to the mountains and the seaside in summer, Enzo is highly sensitive to changes in his body, to the temperature, to the seasons and to air pollution. He uses a pedometer app to count his steps, taking pleasure in this use as part of his repertoire of 'paying attention' to his health, which involves keeping track of his wellbeing, including his fitness. Enzo is in touch with his family doctor on WhatsApp. The ease of this communication comforts him, and he has been known to send photographs of various symptoms, from skin rashes to tongue discolouring, to his doctor as part of monitoring his health with a trusted professional. Chiara is more sceptical about these habitual health concerns and is less concerned on this topic. In a discussion between the three of us over coffee at their home, Chiara gently implies, with a pinch of humour, that her husband might be something of a hypochondriac, a charge that Enzo, hearing this not for the first time, shrugs off.

Enzo, Alessia and Luca convey a range of attitudes towards health that reflect their preferences, experiences, backgrounds and upbringings. Ideas discussed in interviews about, for example, using webcam or video for medical consultations met with mixed reactions from research participants. Some highlighted that this could be a positive affordance of the digital, a form of mHealth that could work and be useful if patients could not leave their own homes. Others saw it as something they would only consider as a last resort, emphasising the importance of *being physically seen* by a doctor (and ideally by *their* doctor, the doctor they *knew*), as opposed to the unfamiliarity of a virtual consultation that may lack 'proper' human connection, and could be outside their usual frame of reference for what constituted care in a medical setting. There was also the in-between arrangement, in which Enzo, along with others like him, had taken to WhatsApp to communicate with his family doctor from home, including by sending images of particular health conditions; in this way he experienced personalised care in a digital setting, based on contact and visual-digital communication.

Health apps

Apps relating to health were used by a small number of my research participants. Roberta, in her mid-fifties, leads a busy working life and is always on the go. She uses her smartphone for many aspects of her life, from diaries and reminders to maps and personal and professional communications.

Roberta downloaded, and sometimes uses, Salutile, a regional healthcare system app for those who live in Lombardy, approved by the official Lombardy regional council,[18] which can be accessed via a national health service number. Residents of cities and towns in Lombardy can use it for a number of medical activities, including booking appointments with their local clinic.[19] Roberta uses it to make medical appointments. The app's ease of access and use makes things easy for her when she is out and about. She quite likes having aspects of her life 'all in one place', that place being the smartphone (Fig. 6.1).

Roberta uses different apps, in line with her general smartphone literacy and her social life. For example, concerning mHealth, she uses an insurance company app, which is tied to her work insurance; it holds her health insurance documents, helps her find the nearest hospital, is integrated with Google Maps and offers a range of health-related tools, for example one that helps users to find local equivalents of brand-name

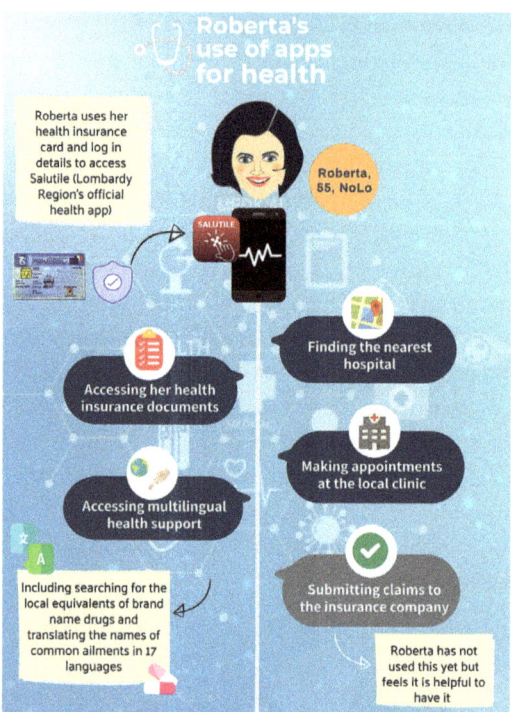

Figure 6.1 Infographic illustrating Roberta's use of health apps, based on ethnographic data collected during fieldwork. Created by Georgiana Murariu.

drugs, one that offers multilingual health-related support and another that allows them to submit medical claims to the insurance company. Roberta has not yet made a claim via the app, but says she likes having it on her phone 'just in case'. For Roberta, all of these apps contained within her smartphone serve as a kind of digital Filofax for arranging her life. Roberta's interaction with the healthcare system is more complex than her use of apps, and plays out via different avenues of engagement, but her digital engagements with the system via her smartphone are regarded as helpful, and appear to be appreciated in her day-to-day life.

In part because of the slow uptake of mHealth, and the host of considerations involved in its development, at the state level its most visible growth is in the private sector. Digital health start-ups and initiatives that have been, and are being, rolled out in Italy include remote monitoring of blood pressure. Some start-ups in Milan are focused on areas such as physical mobility issues in ageing, particularly rehabilitation and the restoration of motor function and control. Other companies have been developing mHealth solutions, and services delivering medicines to patients and *badanti* (carers) at home. Among my research participants, bespoke health apps were used very little, and their use often depended on whether an individual was accustomed to using other kinds of bespoke apps as part of their broader lifestyle and on their digital literacy. For Roberta, for example, apps formed part of how she organised and practised various aspects of her life.

In another example we see that technology is viewed in terms of care and social or family considerations. Bernardo, in his sixties, has recently retired. He is divorced and lives by himself. His son, Filippo, lives in another city, not far from Milan. Bernardo is a member of several retirement groups, such as walking meditation groups. He uses his smartphone 'a lot' as part of his daily life and to foster his sense of health and wellbeing, to provide a kind of self-care he has learned to give himself following the therapies he undertook after his divorce. Bernardo uses the step-tracking app on his smartphone and also has the Lombardy health app, mentioned above, through which he books appointments with his doctor. Bernardo, who, as a retired engineer, is keenly interested in technology, explained that he thought technology could make a positive difference in the experience of ageing in the future. He knew it was 'early days' with mHealth, but seemed excited to watch things develop globally, enthusiastically citing, for example, Japan as a 'place to watch' in this regard. Bernardo raised the issue of independence in older age. For now, in his sixties, he was mobile and had no major health concerns, but in 10, 15, 20 years' time he would be very keen to know what services might be available to assist in the experience of ageing and frailty. His interest in mHealth seems to coalesce around concerns for his son:

> I very much want to ease any duty of care or responsibility my son may feel towards me in the future – he doesn't need to worry about looking after his dad. I want him to be free, be with his girlfriend, and eventually maybe they will have their own family, maybe they will leave Milan, and that's all OK too. I want him to be free and to be happy. That's it.

Regardless of how his son Filippo may feel about caring for his father later in life, which may shift over time, depending on their relationship, this is how Bernardo feels at present, and evidently quite strongly. For Bernardo, remote digital services were envisioned as assisting in care practices in the future in one's own home. In particular, he expressed interest in being able to do a video consultation with the doctor from home, and in remote monitoring of, especially, heart rate and blood pressure:

> It would be useful if we could record and store these things through smartphones and send the data to our GPs, without having to always go into the clinic, without needing to be seen every time in person. I would use this, even now, but definitely later, in older age.

Bernardo's interest in technology-aided self-sufficiency (a notion introduced in chapter 2 on ageing and ideas about *autosufficienza*) is different from other ideas shared by, for instance, a number of women research participants in their fifties and sixties for whom care duties and responsibilities towards elderly parents who did not or could not use smartphones caused them some concern in daily life (see examples in chapter 2). These women, at least at the present time, had expressed less interest in imagining the potentials of digital technologies for future healthcare.

Among research participants who were interested in technology-facilitated healthcare practices for facilitating self-sufficiency, these ideas concerning independence formed a contemporary variant of their parents' traditional insistence, which many had seen in their childhoods, on self-sufficiency as part of personal dignity through autonomy. However, there was also a curiosity about digital models of care that might exist in years to come, models beyond those currently in existence. What might care via smartphones and digital technology offer in the future wondered people like Bernardo, who were adamant that they do not wish to burden their children and are not keen on the idea of live-in carers or traditional retirement homes. Ideas about self-sufficiency should be examined further to highlight how such discourses can come to shape how people think about their own ageing, now and in the future.

Self-sufficiency and digital technologies

Self-sufficiency is a framework within which active ageing has been considered in Europe and globally (as discussed in chapter 2). It is also an important concept and aim envisioned, described and rolled out in public and private mHealth initiatives in Italy. A report on digital health in Italy by a Milan-based initiative and platform dedicated to fostering education and knowledge about ageing, called Grey Panthers, stated that since 2011 (when mHealth emerged in Italy):

> A new definition of health has emerged. We have moved from a state of well-being to a capacity for adaption and self-management in the face of social, physical and emotional challenges. It is a change of no small importance, in which we begin to approach a culture of a digital kind, which places the Citizen in the centre, not just as a 'user' of technology, but as an active element in the process that concerns one's own health.[20]

The article reports on the contemporary push towards emphasising the citizen's responsibility to take care of their own health in the digital age and the potential of technology to be a tool of citizen empowerment. In some countries this push is and has been stronger than others. In Denmark, for example, the emphasis on individual responsibility for health, including the digital, comprises a core framework in the state's agenda on age and social care.[21] Older people in Denmark, for example, have been presented with top-down initiatives without necessarily taking into account how people feel about them. Accepting care workers into the home, for example, is presented as part of a person's duty to take care of themselves and take responsibility for their own ageing.[22]

A wealth of scholarship on active ageing has highlighted that such top-down policies and practices can reflect neoliberal emphases on and ideologies of individual responsibility. As seen in Bernardo's story above, discourses of self-sufficiency may place emphasis on individual responsibility and technology-assisted care in the home, but the rationale may not be wholly about the individual, or about promoting individualism. Bernardo's desire for self-sufficiency was mainly driven by not wanting to burden his son or his son's future family in years to come. His expressed desire to be self-sufficient thus reflects family or social concerns, issues and choices stemming from and feeding back into his life course and relationships, all of which were informing his attitudes towards, ideas about and foreseeable practices in ageing with technologies and the smartphone.

In any case, as this chapter seeks to highlight, there is an unfolding tension between what is presented from above, in macro-level discussion, within the EU, governments, businesses and start-ups, about tech and self-care, and the lived realities of individuals and their complex social and personal webs of health and care that play out in everyday life. The notion that the digital could 'help' in a number of capacities was widely acknowledged by a number of people who had witnessed how smartphones and the internet had been increasingly penetrating and transforming their everyday lives, in many ways and with positive implications. Yet this prospect was also met with mixed feelings, reflecting both preferences for traditional mechanisms and a more general ambivalence towards the new or towards things presented to people as 'solutions'. All of these factors affected how digital technologies were conceived of more broadly, as good and bad and as bringing negative implications along with positive affordances, ideas I will return to in the concluding chapter.

Care and communication

Beside developments within the healthcare system in Lombardy and Italy and the growth of digital health, caring in NoLo (broadly conceived) is rooted more locally and socially in the neighbourhood and the city, and is realised through a range of interactions between local institutions, non-governmental organisations and networks of volunteers. This complex network of social care makes up what has been termed the 'Milan model', which reflects the social history of the city of Milan as a centre of the civil and religious charity sectors and of a care industry comprised of public and private institutions.[23]

As was discussed in chapters 3 and 4, many institutions of social care and wellbeing are physically based in the neighbourhood, including Auser, the nationwide NGO dedicated to ageing, and local NGOs that focus on social participation and social support within the neighbourhood and more broadly. As seen in previous chapters, women play prominent roles in care and social work across the neighbourhood, and women's social and support groups play an important role in the local community.

A meeting at a multicultural centre's women's social group I participated in was dedicated to a particular event regarding women's and children's health. Representatives of an Italian health NGO that offers free healthcare (check-ups, consultations, advice, referrals, emergency services) to marginalised groups and communities in Italy (and across the world) spoke to the women who came to the centre. The meeting that day was attended by women from Egypt, Morocco, Cameroon, Tanzania and elsewhere, including local residents and asylum seekers, who had found out about the event from information posters put up around the neighbourhood, online via WhatsApp groups and through word of mouth. There were also volunteers and other participants present, including myself. The meeting was conducted in Italian, French and Arabic, and explanations of when and where to access different services were carefully relayed; a focus, given that this group included a number of mothers with young children, was on information relating to paediatric clinics and maternal and infant health.

At one point during the meeting, the conversation turned to the internet, smartphones and health, when those leading the session wished to ascertain how much smartphones and digital platforms were used to access health information or to engage in health services. Asking for a show of hands, they, along with one of the group's organisers, who followed up with clarifications, asked who used the internet or their phones for health purposes. No one raised their hand, and quite a few of the women seemed unsure what the question meant. When the question about digital practices was rejigged to 'Who uses Facebook …?', three-quarters of the participants raised their hands. Facebook was a familiar word, and smartphones were much present in the room. This example is not included as evidence for any claim about the uses of digital media for health, or about the participants at the meeting. However, it points to one of the core findings of the ASSA project – about the familiarity of platforms such as Google, Facebook, WhatsApp, and other apps like Telegram or Viber, and how they can be used for a range of purposes, by people in different contexts, including for health. Engagement with matters of daily life and health digitally, 'from below', via social media or googling, forms part of people's repertoires and reference points concerning digital and social practices, as I will illustrate in the rest of the chapter.

Initiatives and communication practices seen around the neighbourhood, aimed at spreading awareness about healthcare services in clear terms to different groups, reflect concerns with access and equality.[24] Studies have found that migrants in Italy are more likely to contact emergency services than to visit specialist doctors, because of the costs of specialist treatments.[25] Similar findings apply to the children of migrants, relating to whom records have suggested that there is a lower probability of their visiting specialist doctors, where specialist treatments are not subsidised and can involve several months of waiting.[26] A number of research participants, including Italian citizens originally from other countries, shared experiences along these lines, concerning costs, waiting times and issues such as discrimination. Hussein, aged 48, has worked and lived with his family in Milan for over ten years. He recalls an incident in which he had damaged his back at work. He went to the doctor and the doctor agreed that he needed an X-ray; he received an appointment for six months later. Hussein explained that he could not take the six-month time scale seriously in his mind: by then, he thought, any physical ailment would have either fixed itself, or caused severe damage. Hussein explained that, from the next day, he tried to forget about the back pain, took painkillers, sought advice on physiotherapy, and in time seemed to make a recovery: 'To this day, I've never taken up that X-ray appointment!' he said. Hussein felt that while the waiting time did not make sense, he was also not taken seriously or perhaps was not considered a priority as a perceived 'foreigner'. Money, he said, would have helped him to overcome some of these obstructions: 'If you have the money, of course you pay at a private clinic in the city and you will receive the X-ray within the next week – whoever you are!' Another research participant recalled an incident of hair loss, which they associated with acute stress. A doctor had prescribed an ointment that cost 50 euros on prescription. Recalling the story, they told me, 'The system is there, yes – but it costs!'

In sum, a range of factors help to contextualise the availability and access to healthcare services, including emergency services, which play a significant role in Milan. The NGO 'Emergency', for example, was founded in Milan in 1994 and plays a prominent role in healthcare in the city.[27] In addition, visual and digital media play an important role in disseminating health information across the neighbourhood. The posters shown in Fig. 6.2, for instance, are aimed at women's health, and include reminders to women to be vigilant for changes in their bodies, including checking for lumps, and to have regular check-ups. Information posters

Figure 6.2 Information posters in the area, directed at women's health. Photo by Shireen Walton.

for those for whom Italian is not their first language can be seen in the premises of NGOs, public parks and community centres.

Language remains a crucial aspect of communicating initiatives or interventions in the neighbourhood. During my long-term participation in a number of women's groups in the neighbourhood, and witnessing from time to time the confusion, lack of understanding, or misunderstanding, and disengagement that can result from language barriers, I noticed that visual illustrations made a difference by capturing people's attention, as well as by aiding understanding of the kinds of support available.[28] These information posters are also circulated digitally via WhatsApp to particular groups, NGOs, Italian classes and so on. The information can be kept close by and stored on smartphones, and is forwarded to others, sometimes translated and explained, for reference, forming an important practice in everyday and informal health communications.

While awareness campaigns around the neighbourhood aimed at providing support to certain groups, including minority and marginalised communities, I also learned more about health and communication practices and histories from female research participants in their seventies. Taboos surrounding the menopause, which have existed for a long time across Italian society, have long caused something of a gap in health communication. For Alessandra, aged 74, the menopause was 'quite a trauma'. At the time she had found it hard to access information about it in the community. Her first recourse was to head to the pharmacy and try out some remedies sold on the market at the time. After consulting her GP, she took up hormone replacement therapy (HRT) and was put on antidepressants for some time. Alessandra felt she became worse during this period, and 'extra-depressed'. Eventually, after incessant searching and tentative enquiring among herbalists and complementary medicine practitioners, people she liked and trusted, Alessandra found a local clinic specialising in holistic health. The clinic had an in-house doctor, a gynaecologist and a holistic health consultant working together. A female practitioner, whom she particularly liked, guided her through herbal and holistic remedies. A significant source of difficulty for Alessandra was that the menopause had never been talked about socially, as she recalled to me one afternoon as we took coffee together in her home:

> We never ever talked about periods or the menopause or anything like that, even among ourselves. It's utter madness that such a natural thing that happens to all of us women should never be

talked about. Why? What were we scared or ashamed of? Really, I don't know.

Alessandra links a lack of awareness and discourse in former decades to a generational point about women growing up, like her, in the 1950s and 1960s, whose mothers, aunts and sisters never dared speak about the menopause, just as they did not about their periods. The issue, Alessandra felt, was rooted deep in long-standing taboos and gender discriminations spanning decades. Recalling her youth, she said, 'Menstruation was also a very difficult time for me. It was something one just had to learn to cope with, and of course, I never talked about it – with anyone!'

Giuliana had a similar experience to Alessandra's, growing up in a small town in Lombardy where talking about women's health was off limits during her childhood and adolescence. She had suffered from endometriosis in her twenties and thirties, with extremely painful periods. Unlike for Alessandra, the menopause for Giuliana was less a trauma than a blessing. Given how severe her period pains had always been, and the symptoms she had experienced throughout her life, the menopause 'could not have come too soon', despite it being challenging to go through.

What both women acknowledge at the stage of life they are in now was the lack of communication about these issues at the time, within the intimate family context, among friends and in social and public-health settings. Notably, both women are keen smartphone users and engage heavily with digital forms of communication. They keenly seek out and circulate information within their social networks, and use Facebook every day to read and circulate news about events, current affairs and hobbies and to share memes. Though they had not joined Facebook or WhatsApp groups specifically relating to medical conditions, they both said they would be interested in such groups if they experienced health conditions in the future. Today both Alessandra and Giuliana derive much solidarity from digital forms of sociality, including by being members of all-women WhatsApp groups relating to hobbies and interests, from gardening to sewing to choirs. The sense of the collective gained by being a member of these WhatsApp groups seems to have provided a welcome accompaniment to their experience of ageing, as a more collectivised experience of 'togetherness', something that digital connections have helped to facilitate. The connections that had been lacking in earlier parts of their life, when they had struggled to contend with traditional knowledge regimes and sources, such as their mothers, and with social taboos (see also chapter 8) were being discovered and enjoyed.

The historical, generational and socio-technological shifts of recent decades, which have been instrumental in transforming information structures, have meant that many older adults are in the throes of a seemingly extraordinary present moment, in the potentially limitless 'information society'.[29] These experiences, and the currency of the present moment, are something I will specifically explore in chapter 8. It is within this broader context that practices like 'googling' (seeking information via Google) among older adults ought to be situated, as I will now consider.

Googling for health

'[Google] è la mia biblioteca – è la mia enciclopedia!'
Silvia, aged 60

Googling formed a significant part of the daily smartphone habits of many of the research participants. It was useful (*utile*) and convenient/handy (*comodo*) to 'google' things; the word could be a shorthand to describe more generally the act of searching for information on the internet. Googling was regarded as particularly helpful when one was on the move, outside the home, and wished to find out something quickly, but also inside the home, where one could get lost in browsing and surfing, jumping from topic to topic. For more serious searching about health matters, googling was perceived as potentially misleading and dangerous if unchecked by other facts, which recalls what was discussed at the start of this chapter concerning ideas about trust and where people located medical authority, namely among trusted healthcare professionals. Teresa, for example, who is retired, in her mid-sixties, felt it was 'dangerous to use Google for searching about health issues'. On this matter she was not alone. Her neighbour Giuseppe, retired, also in his mid-sixties and reasonably technologically active, exclaims that he would 'never google anything regarding health – never!', always opting to see his GP if there was something to enquire about. Giuseppe would often resort to Italian proverbs and older ideas regarding health issues – headaches and so on – including the idea that many major health matters are connected to the stomach and the gut, an idea he would not hesitate to share with people.

Despite their scepticism about using the internet for health matters, both Teresa and Giuseppe were avid smartphone users. Searching for information about the weather went hand in hand with communicating on WhatsApp, as well as with general conversation with friends and family and participation in searches on topics of interest as they come up in everyday life. Sometimes this would lead to trips down memory lane. Teresa had recently located a song she recalled from her childhood in the 1950s, from the Abruzzo region of Italy where her family are from, while Giuseppe's most recent online search was about a popular Italian water polo player he had forgotten the name of and had recently wanted to make reference to in a conversation with friends at a bar. Despite their frequent use of smartphones and searching for information, Teresa and Giuseppe are wary of the 'amount of information one gets on the internet' including 'all kinds of rubbish'. The examples highlight how much distrust there is about information on the internet, and although the smartphone was very helpful, it was potentially an instrument of mis- or disinformation. These criticisms did not deter the same people from using it avidly, though *not*, they insisted, for health.

Another frequent googler was Fatema, in her fifties. Fatema is, as she put it, '*attaccata*' (attached) to her smartphone, since it is how she communicates with – and knows the whereabouts of around the neighbourhood and the city – her teenage children, and how she co-ordinates her work commitments and timetables as an Arabic and Italian teacher and translator. She uses Google Translate throughout the day, such as at lunchtime, to assist with words and phrases if she needs to. Her children's paediatrician is a central authority in the constellation of health and care practices that relate to her family. She also enjoys preparing and exploring the natural remedies, foods and herbs associated with her socio-cultural background and her upbringing in Egypt: 'We have so many remedies for things in our culture – natural ones. I generally prefer natural options for keeping in good general health,' she explained.

Fatema's searching repertoires are restricted to the mobile data limit she pays for and accesses with her top-up SIM card. She and her family, like a number of other individuals and families, do not have Wi-Fi at home in their rented apartment. Unlike Teresa or Giuseppe, introduced above, who expressed an aversion to googling for health information, Fatema and some others did this within reason and with moderation, just as when she searched for language translations and other information on the internet – always with a degree of caution and contextualisation. As an educator, she was vigilant about misinformation and sought advice from wider sources and authorities, particularly when it came to the health and wellbeing of her children.

Research participants did not report any major issues of 'fake health information' they had experienced or got into trouble with personally, but they were very aware of the issue in general, as discussed in chapter 5. 'Fake news' has come to the fore again in Italy in 2020, during the writing up of this book amid the coronavirus pandemic. This period saw a significant pushback by Italian medical authorities against the 'fake health information' that was circulating via WhatsApp.[30] In March 2020, the Italian Ministry of Health published a warning list of ten particularly pertinent 'fake news' items about the coronavirus that were circulating within the Italian social web, urging the public to be vigilant.[31]

Official interventions concerning misinformation during the pandemic offered some comfort to a number of research participants in the anxious climate in which digital and daily updated information formed many people's lifeline to the outside world. Within this context interventions like these from the state had brought an assurance to some that the medical and administrative authorities were working together to keep people safe. The issues concerning official and unofficial digital health practices and infrastructures that I had been researching in 2018–19 in Milan remain salient today amid the Covid-19 pandemic, and against a backdrop, broadly mapped in this chapter, of the emergence of the digital as a major player in the healthcare and wellbeing infrastructure of the city of Milan, the region of Lombardy, Italy and Europe. These developments should remain a topic of ongoing critical discussion in the light of the currently unfolding relationship between (digital) care and surveillance, in Italy and beyond.

Conclusion

This chapter has examined health and care in the present digital moment in Italy, showing how formal and informal policies and practices exist within a nexus of an emerging digital health scene 'from above' and a variegated adoption of digital practices by people 'from below'. For smartphone users, googling for information about health and using WhatsApp to communicate with and care for others were activities not wholly distinct from broader uses of smartphones for care and communication, but the smartphone could also be a purveyor of mis- or disinformation. The use of digital sources of health information reflected socio-economic realities and inequalities, such as socio-economic status, language barriers and ideas about health and wellbeing from a range of sources, including traditional cultural and social contexts.

In addition, given the central role played by digital technologies during the coronavirus pandemic in 2020, when the country witnessed a dramatic increase in state intervention, as well as a range of public–private partnerships that offered 'digital solidarity' packages to citizens,[32] the chapter has offered a wider look at digital health and innovation. The experiences, detailed in this chapter and the rest of the book, of a number of research participants, who are practising their own improvised and creative forms of digital health and care 'from below' through existing channels such as social media, may call into question a view of mHealth apps and digital services that are aimed at specific sections of the population and that may foster greater digital inequality. Although Milan and Lombardy are leading sites within Italy for healthcare, charity and social work, a range of factors affect the equity of healthcare access and delivery, such as income, socio-economic status, regional location and language, and these factors all play a role in the differentiated experience of living and ageing with smartphones in NoLo, Milan and Italy. I will pick up the theme of inequality and exclusion in the following chapter, on 'coming of age' with smartphones, and examine, among other issues, the Italian citizenship framework and the role of smartphones and digital practices among younger people in Milan.

Notes

1. The Italian national healthcare system was designed in the post-war period. In 1948 the Italian constitution (article 32) stated, 'The Italian Republic safeguards health as a fundamental right of the individual and as a collective interest, and guarantees free medical care to the poor' (http://www.senato.it/1025?sezione=121&articolo_numero_articolo=32; accessed 12 December 2020). Ensuring equitable access to healthcare reflects a primary goal of the policy agenda outlined at the time by the EU, where 'universality, access to high-quality care, equity and solidarity are common values and principles underpinning the health systems in the EU Member States'. See Publications Office of the European Union 2011 on 'reducing health inequalities in the EU'.
2. Mapelli 2012.
3. Toth 2014.
4. Mainil et al. 2017.
5. For further insights on this theme see Muehlebach 2012, 2013 and Giordano 2014.
6. Roberta's comments here refer to patient consultation time. This is a main point of discussion between healthcare professionals, as I found at a meeting at the Istituto Nazionale dei Tumori in Milan in 2018 concerning patient experiences and satisfaction, the use of digital technologies in healthcare and patients' experiences of the impact of technology on healthcare services (see note 9 below).
7. See Kostera 2019.
8. See Postelnicu 2019.
9. In March 2018 I attended a meeting to discuss patient evaluation of medical services, with a focus on the use of digital technologies for patient evaluation, at the Istituto Nazionale dei Tumori in Milan, which is one of the leading healthcare institutions in Italy, some 20 minutes' walk from NoLo. This meeting was attended by the heads of different medical sections, university researchers and medical students. The digitisation of medical records (*la cartella clinica*) was discussed and concerns were raised about a 'digital divide' between different socio-economic, ethnic and age groups' ability to access (and sustain access to) digital health records and digital health services.
10. See Grey Panthers 2016.

11. See the Osservatori Digital innovation–Politecnico di Milano website: https://www.osservatori.net/it_it.
12. See Balabio 2016.
13. See Balabio 2016.
14. See the Associazione per l'invecchiamento attivo (Auser) website at http://www.auser.it.
15. See Balabio 2016.
16. See Balabio 2016.
17. During the Covid-19 pandemic in Italy, pharmacies remained open, alongside supermarkets, as essential services, building rapports on a community level.
18. For information about the Salutile app, see https://www.prenotasalute.regione.lombardia.it/sito/Menu-principale/Come-prenotare/App-Salutile-Prenotazioni. Accessed 18 November 2020.
19. The app offers a range of services, including access to medical electronic records (referral history, official appointments, access to medical history if requested), live emergency-service updates (it informs the user how many people are waiting in each medical site at any given moment), booking appointments for individuals and families, prescription pick-up services for electronic prescriptions, which can be sent to the smartphone and taken to pharmacies to be prepared, and vaccination records (lists of which vaccinations an individual and their children have had).
20. See Grey Panthers 2018. (Author's translation.)
21. Mikkelsen 2017.
22. As discussed also in chapter 2, critical discussion of active ageing discourses has highlighted that 'neoliberalisation' has extended ideals of productivity into old age and creates a binary framework in which 'activity' in phrases like 'active ageing' is seen as 'positive', and dependency, illness or loneliness is 'negative', without examining the complex relationship between dependency and independence. See for example Katz 2003, 2013 and Macnicol 2015.
23. On the specificity and history of 'the Milan model' in the field of social care in Italy, see Bini and Gambazza 2019.
24. Reports have highlighted acute healthcare inequalities in the light of the 2015 refugee crisis in Europe, and its implications for the health and care of migrants and refugees. One such report (CARE 2016) was produced by the EU-funded CARE project (Common Approach for REfugees and other migrants' health), which received funding from the European Union's Health Programme (2014–20). It aimed to promote a better understanding of refugees' and migrants' health conditions and health needs and to assess the general state of provision for refugees and other migrants in a number of EU countries in the wake of the 2015 refugee crisis. The project was launched in April 2016, with the participation of a consortium consisting of 15 partners from five EU member states (Italy, Greece, Croatia, Malta and Slovenia), along with local and regional authorities. Digital technologies are prominent in such reports, as is a concern with age. The report states that among the project's instruments are 'the use of a portable device containing the migrant's health data, the monitoring of infectious disease risk through an operational platform and the holistic model for age determination for unaccompanied minors'.
25. Devillanova 2012.
26. Devillanova 2012.
27. Emergency was established to provide free medical treatment to victims of war, poverty and landmines. Its headquarters are in Milan, but it operates around the world and particularly in conflict zones, including Afghanistan, Iraq, the Central African Republic, Sierra Leone and Uganda. Since 2005 it has operated in Italy to provide free healthcare to marginalised communities. Its slogan is 'Health is a human right'. Accessed 18 November 2020. See https://www.emergency.it
28. During the writing of this book in the spring of 2020, during the Covid-19 pandemic, I observe through remaining in contact with friends and research participants in Milan that health and care information, from government and regional levels through to community levels, has embraced digital-visual means of communication as never before. Digital platform services are currently being developed and launched at pace to provide many kinds of information, and infographics and visualisations feature prominently in information flows, community awareness and health and safety advice in NoLo, in Milan and across Italy. For example, the Ministry of Health had created a series of infographics about protocols to help prevent the spread of

the coronavirus, including what to do in the case of symptoms, many of which were circulated via WhatsApp. They can be found on the Italian Ministry of Health's website at http://www.salute.gov.it/nuovocoronavirus. Accessed 18 November 2020.
29. On the information society, see Castells 2010.
30. In the light of the false information being shared via WhatsApp, and in the context of the high anxiety and stress caused by the experience of lockdown, some people in NoLo (as seen in the previous chapter in relation to the 'fake news' about migrants coming to Italy) had asked others to stop sharing unverifiable information that was proving inflammatory and divisive and causing anxiety. Amid the coronavirus crisis, such information had spread very quickly across the community, the country and the world. The state stepped up its involvement in this issue with an attempt to communicate the facts about the virus. In March 2020, the Ministry of Health and individual health professionals took to the internet to communicate with the public about what and what not to believe. In early March, the Medical Director of Milan's Niguarda hospital pleaded with the people of Milan, and of the nation, to stop circulating unverified information about the coronavirus, including gossip and a stream of official-sounding voice messages that had been sent via WhatsApp to people across Italy about what doctors were or were not doing or who they were or were not treating. See Redazione Milano online 2020.
31. The examples that were cited as misinformation in this governmental online advice page included the notion that drinking tap water was dangerous to health, the rumour that wearing face masks in the home would help limit contagion, and the idea that taking a hot bath would kill off the virus. See Ministero della Salute 2020a.
32. In Italy in 2020 'digital solidarity' packages were offered to bridge some of the socio-economic and digital gaps highlighted and perpetuated by the virus, at a time when digital care and communications had taken on heightened significance. See Agenzia per l'Italia Digitale 2020.

7
Coming of age with smartphones

Introduction

Throughout the course of my research, I came to know a number of research participants' family members, and this complemented my research on the experience of people in midlife by enabling me to examine the related themes of age, digital technologies and identity at earlier ages. The voices and experiences of younger people add a multigenerational perspective on several core themes of the book, including care, community life and identities within and across borders. In this light, a focus in this chapter is on young adults, including those born in or growing up in Italy who have one or both parents from another country; they are invariably referred to in Italy and elsewhere in Europe as the 'second generation'. The chapter explores the role smartphones play in the experiences of growing up and coming of age for these young people, in the light of identity practices and claims to citizenship. The penultimate section explores questions of identity and belonging vis-à-vis smartphones and social media by drawing on insights from the Hazara community in Milan, who are originally from Afghanistan, and their practices of identity, activisms and awareness.

The theme of ageing with smartphones in Milan is expanded upon in this chapter by complementing the study of older people with these experiences of younger people. It charts younger people's experiences and pushes for various types of social, legal and political change in Italy and further afield, as seen in practices ranging from online activism and film-making to poetry, which play out against a backdrop of ongoing debates about Italian and European identity, including notions of 'new Italians'. To begin the discussion of young people in contemporary Milan, I consider the case, and the socio-political significance, of Mahmood's victory.

Mahmood's victory

In the cold evenings of January 2019 in Milan, I observed that many families huddled around the television after dinner, or turned on the television while still at the dinner table, watching a TV show with children as young as two and three. Sanremo is something of a national treasure in Italy, a singing competition dating back to the 1950s. It is a kind of Italian 'X-factor' contest that is screened by the state broadcaster Rai, and it enjoys popularity across the country.[1] In 2019, the top prize in the 69th annual competition went to a young Italian man, aged 27, with a Sardinian mother and an Egyptian father, named Alessandro Mahmoud, known professionally as Mahmood. The contest was voted on equally by the public and a professional jury of music journalists and industry professionals. Mahmood's debut single '*Soldi*' (money) is an autobiographical narrative that references his growing up in the 1990s with his mother in the Gratosoglio district in the working-class southernmost outskirts of the city, in Milan's zone 5. The lyrics directly address his father, referring to his abandoning of Mahmood and his mother when he was a child, and the family's socio-economic struggles. The lyrics are in Italian but also contain Arabic phrases and references to Ramadan, even though Mahmood is not a fluent Arabic speaker:

> *È difficile stare al mondo, quando perdi l'orgoglio, lasci casa in un giorno …*
> (It's difficult to be in this world if you lose your pride, you leave your home in one day only …)

The chorus line chimes repeatedly '*Come se avessi avuto soldi, soldi …*' (As if I had money, money …). The music video that accompanies the song features frames of Mahmood today, interspersed with flashback-type scenes that purport to show him as a young boy, depicting his innocence and naivety as he grew up in a difficult family situation and a socio-economic context that he and his mother figured out how to navigate together.

Mahmood's victory in the 2019 Sanremo contest coincided with a political moment in Italy of the prominence of the far right, epitomised by the then Interior Minister Matteo Salvini and his frequent public remarks about the importance of 'Italian identity' as based on a white, Christian, ethnonationalist model, ideas that are among the foundational tenets of his Northern League party. A high-profile event, Mahmood's victory was politicised very quickly in Italy. Salvini took to Twitter to question Mahmood's victory in the competition, questioning whether it was really 'the best Italian song', and subsequently criticising what he claimed were leftist agendas to support Mahmood as a figurehead of a progressive Italy.

Mahmood frequently acknowledges his background in his music, while stating that he feels Italian, his name being Alessandro Mahmood, and that he was born and grew up in Milan, which he considers home. Mahmood's emphasis on feeling comfortably Italian while also being in touch with his Egyptian heritage is not uncommon among young people growing up in Italy today, and is something I noticed often in Milan and NoLo. The young people with diverse backgrounds who are growing up in Milan by and large feel secure about these aspects of their identities and experiences, while acknowledging that the debate about identity and citizenship has been and remains a deeply politicised and polarised one that does not really reflect or represent their experiences. For example, consider 21-year-old Dina.

Dina

The eldest child in an Egyptian family, Dina came to Milan with her family at the age of six. She went to school in Milan and speaks both Arabic and Italian fluently. She was into both Egyptian and Italian pop music and could often be heard rapping in Arabic and Italian at street parties or festivals such as Eid. Dina felt comfortably Italian, showing bewilderment that anyone would think she was an outsider, since she was so culturally Italian and Milan was her home. At the same time, Dina comfortably connected to aspects of her 'Egyptianness'. From her early teens she had felt close to her Egyptian roots, speaking in Arabic with her mum, which also served as care and comfort to her mother. Rapping in Arabic was a way to 'get to know' the background culture that she embraced, which she felt lent her an edge of distinctiveness in her teenage years. To all intents and purposes, Dina felt Italian and Egyptian. She did not feel the need to quantify the percentage of her multiple attachments, which, incidentally, chimed with her Italian friends from other regions and places such as Sicily, Naples and Apulia who, like Dina, did not feel they were only 'Italian' but, in some cases, quite ardently Sicilian or Neapolitan.

Dina and Noor

Dina expressed a desire to leave Italy in the future. This was not uncommon among young people I knew in NoLo, as I learned about some of their aspirations for the future.[2] Dina and her boyfriend had often talked about getting married and moving to Australia to start a different life together. For her part, Dina's mother Noor (see chapter 2), envisioned her future as being with her children, wherever they were, and she hoped they would take care of her in her later years. The ideal model of ageing and care, in this urban and transnational family context, appears to be, for Noor at least, one of intergenerational reciprocity. Dina's aspirations to upward and transnational mobility, as they are currently expressed, call into question some of Noor's expectations or hopes that the family will remain physically close together.

Noor emphasised that, for her, her children were the future, revealing something of the sacrifice parents make, and something of the social pressure the subsequent generation is under to make a success of their lives for the sake of the wellbeing of the family as a whole. 'I work for my family to get ahead in their life – it is their future that matters. They are growing up here as Italians: they know the culture, the language, better than me. Their future is what matters,' Noor explains. It was through the health and happiness of her children that Noor primarily defined herself and, to some extent, her success. She spoke about her life as a kind of generational bridge, from the old world of life in Egypt to a new one in Italy, that she has been actively crafting and cultivating as a project centred on her children, to be with and enjoy now and in the long run. There was no sense of her speaking about her own future in individual terms, or about matters of 'retirement', the implication being that in-family care will be reciprocated by the rest of the family in later life, though when, where and how remains unknown.

Despite the nuanced experiences of the young people involved, this so-called 'second generation' has been carved up ideologically by people from across the political spectrum: they may be otherised along with their parents or viewed as a threat to 'Italianness', or, at the opposite end of the socio-political discourse, seen as the future solution to the country's identity crisis, as the 'involuntary pioneers' of social change in Italy.[3] In order to situate the place of younger people in contemporary Italian society more precisely, I will explore the notion and framing of the 'second generation' before returning to issues related to younger people's experiences of ageing with smartphones in NoLo.

Seconde generazioni and '2G' youth in Milan

Seconde generazioni is a term used to refer to the children, born or growing up in Italy, of whom one or both parents belong to the 'first generation' of migrants who settled in Italy from around the 1980s onwards, from a range of countries. The term is used by policymakers, governments, politicians, activists and NGOs in the country and elsewhere in Europe. It often provokes debate on a number of issues pertaining to 'Italian identity' and citizenship. 'Second generation' is explored here as an ethnographic category that stems from its use in the context of Milan and Italy which is being critically discussed. The term itself is ambiguous, and contains variously blended logics of inclusion and exclusion.[4] It is used to refer both to children born abroad, and to children born in Italy to parents of whom one or both are from another country, and does not take into account either the diverse experiences and subjectivities of young people or the variations in the socio-economic and class circumstances of first-generation migrants, in their countries of origin and after they settled in Italy.

Discussing the term 'second-generation migrants' in a book that unpacks the construction of 'European others', Fatima El-Tayeb writes: 'whoever is identified as racial or religious Other is necessarily conceptualized as a migrant, that is, as originating outside of Europe, even if the origin is two, three, or more generations removed. … [T]he children (and grandchildren) of migrants of color, rather than becoming first- or second-generation citizens, are considered second- or third-generation migrants.'[5] Bridget Anderson writes: 'Who sheds and who retains their migrancy is often bound up with nationally specific ways of encoding and remaking of race'.[6] The politics of exclusion that these kinds of differentiation reflect endure within the category of citizenship, where, as many critical migration studies scholars have written, citizenship does not guarantee social equality.[7] In sum, the concept is rife with problems, inconsistencies and exclusionary logics, and these form part of the ethnographic enquiry relayed here.

The shorter term 'second generation', and its abbreviation '2G', are used and taken up by young people themselves, in awareness campaigns and activism, to highlight racism and discrimination in society. Drawing upon terms such as '2G', young people across Italy develop generational bonds of solidarity, push for reforms to the citizenship laws and petition for better representation in Italian politics and society. The term is used accordingly when young people inform civil society organisations and policymakers about these issues[8] and in the titles of many NGO groups and associations in Italy and Europe.[9, 10]

An area that directly affects the 'second generation' is Italian citizenship law. Legally, citizenship in Italy is determined by *jus sanguinis*, which confers citizenship on the children of Italian nationals, by descent.[11] The *jus sanguinis* law encodes a more restrictive policy towards children born in Italy to parents from other countries: for instance, Italian citizenship can be granted to children living abroad without them having lived in Italy.[12] The current legal framework reflects legislation from 1992 (Law 91) passed in the wake of relatively new increased immigration to Italy, where emigration had been more significant ever since the late nineteenth century. This law established that children born in Italy whose parents were migrants were to assume their parents' nationality automatically, and if they remained continually resident in Italy, they could request Italian citizenship within one year of turning 18. Livia Turco, Minister for Social Solidarity in the 1990s, acknowledged that the system, systemically aimed at protecting descent, sends an exclusionary message towards these young people in Italy, who should be able to perceive Italy as their own country.[13]

The political context surrounding these issues involves longstanding and continuing debates about national identity and ideas about what was or is perceived to threaten particular ideologies of 'Italianness'.[14] Discriminatory discourse forms part of the context in which young people in Italy and Europe have developed their activism. A number of 'second-generation' organisations and groups are based in Milan.[15, 16]

Digital platforms and forms of communication via social media (Twitter, Facebook groups and YouTube channels) play significant roles in growing forms of second-generation collective awareness, as seen among those in their late teens and twenties who are communicating their experiences and voicing claims of belonging along these lines.[17] Much of the activism within these groups is directed at calling for a reform of the aforementioned citizenship law of *jus sanguinis* ('right of bloodline' through descent), which excludes the children of migrants from guaranteed citizenship even if they were born in Italy, and pushing instead for *jus soli* (birthright citizenship). Smartphones and digital media are also implicated in identity-making and negotiating in everyday life, from navigating state bureaucracy and healthcare to social media practices.

Not all of these young people engage with '2G' activism in public or visible ways, and nor do people necessarily identify with the concept. The young people of different backgrounds I came to know in NoLo reflected on identity and belonging in a number of different ways. Dina attempts to locate herself via a kind of upward social mobility through which she hopes she might one day be able to eschew a number of identity labels. She had long practised and claimed 'social citizenship'[18] as a social actor in NoLo through her participation and practices in the neighbourhood, and through the social capital she has accrued over the course of her life, from school and work and from hobbies, including participation in local support groups (including WhatsApp groups) and volunteering as an Arabic teaching assistant. Dina navigates her daily life and her greater subjectivity in the urban and digital context of Milan. Her smartphone practices are both reflective of and instrumental in shaping her overall 'citizenness', which is developed in line with her other social practices and aspirations regardless of the citizenship laws that had formally categorised her and others as non-citizens.

Digital connections and identities across borders

As outlined in chapter 1, my fieldwork in Milan involved getting to know a range of individuals and communities in NoLo and across the city, whose stories and experiences are reflected in this book. During my fieldwork, as a Persian speaker I came to know members of the Hazara community in Milan. The Hazara are a Hazāragi-speaking (a dialect of the Persian language closely related to Dari) ethnic group originating in the region of Hazarajat in central Afghanistan.[19] Afghan migration is situated in a longer history of population movements across the region.[20] Since the 1960s Hazara have been migrating to other areas such as Iran and the Gulf states to engage in different kinds of labour. Following the coup of 1978 and the Soviet invasion of Afghanistan in 1979, many people fled Afghanistan to neighbouring countries such as Iran and Pakistan, for a variety of political, religious and economic reasons.[21] Ongoing violent persecution of the Hazara and a lack of confidence in the political and economic systems are the main motivations for fleeing to countries such as Iran and Pakistan, Australia, the US, the UK and, more recently, other countries in Europe.[22] After the 2001 US invasion and war, and again after around 2010, a number of Hazara people moved to Europe to escape violence and persecution by the Taliban and to join family members who were already living there. The Hazara women and men in their twenties and thirties who live in Europe today therefore form part of a later generation of Hazara migrants who have left Afghanistan. At the same time, Hazara people around the world feel invested in the future of Afghanistan. In addition to sending remittances to family and friends, they are engaged heavily in online awareness campaigns, digital activism and entrepreneurialism to build support and raise money for communities, including the Hazara, in Afghanistan and to build businesses and economic links between Afghanistan and other countries.

Afghan-run businesses have developed in Italy in recent years, including restaurants, travel agencies and hotels.[23] My own experience of getting to know members of the Hazara community in Milan was through a newly established restaurant that doubled as a cultural centre promoting knowledge about culture and the arts from Afghanistan, Iran, Central Asia and the Middle East and around the world, which was run by a number of Hazara friends.

Among the Hazara people I came to know in Milan who had been in Italy for around ten years, a number have Italian citizenship, and speak fluent Italian. Matters of Hazara identity, belonging and social participation were tied in with entrepreneurialism in Italy, along with brotherhood, and forms of solidarity concerning social justice and human rights were seen in networks across the city and in online digital transnational networks, including a number related to Hazara people, accessed often via smartphones. The Hazara independent film-maker, poet and activist Amin Wahidi, a prominent figure in the Milan Hazara network, captures a number of themes pertaining to Hazara experiences in Italy in his 2017 short film *Behind Venice Luxury: A Hazara in Italy*.[24] The film tells the story of a young Hazara man, Ashraf Barati, who arrived in Italy ten years earlier as a refugee, seeking asylum and fleeing from the Taliban. Throughout the the film Ashraf, who is granted asylum, undertakes a range of jobs in Venice, from construction work to work in hostels. Developing his networks over time and working hard, Ashraf eventually opens his own fast food restaurant in the city and continues to build his life in Italy. The film, which won the 24th Venice City Award and was well received across Italy, is one of the first efforts to tell Hazara stories in Italy. These efforts tie into themes and questions about the lives of refugees and asylum seekers in Italy and the line between otherness and integration, as well as the significance of the place of Afghanistan and homeland among the Hazara people. Furthermore, in 2018, the film *Sembra mio figlio* (Just like my son), a research-informed story about two brothers who had escaped persecution by the Taliban in Afghanistan during the first years of the new millennium and come to Italy, marks another significant moment in the telling of Hazara stories in Italy. The film, written and directed by the Sicilian film-maker Costanza Quatriglio and featuring Hazara poet, journalist and human rights activist Basir Ahang, addresses the history, politics and violence of the wars in Afghanistan, and the experiences of the Hazara in Italy and elsewhere in Europe.

With Hazara friends I explored how aspects of belonging and place are accessed, negotiated and reconfigured through food and music, language and poetry; these take on acute significance as portals of connection in contemporary urban and digital contexts of daily life in present-day Milan. Hazara research participants in their thirties in Milan engaged socially and politically on different scales. Individuals lived and worked in Milan, and physically their social networks were dispersed across the world, including in Afghanistan. They participated in a number of transnational virtual communities via social media, namely WhatsApp, Viber, Telegram and Facebook, a number of which were tied together by their activism for the Hazara people, and by their raising of global awareness about the persecution of the Hazara by the Taliban in Afghanistan. Websites such as www.hazarapeople.com are key for connecting the Hazara across the world.[25] Activism concerning their identity is at the core of their ongoing quest for social and political justice, human rights and equality in their homeland. As they were for many other people featured in this book, smartphones were a key feature of daily life in Milan for Hazara, providing the main access points for engaging in global Hazara activism. A Hazara research participant reflected: 'The first thing I do in the morning is look at my smartphone. … When you leave the house, it's what you think of the most to remember to take with you.'

The digital connections enabled by social media as part of daily life bring individuals into proximity with violence and suffering, making them co-witnesses. This proximity has consequences for mental health and wellbeing that the smartphone, as a portal to the wider world, is implicated in. The smartphone assists in many areas of life, from apps that help users to navigate cities and other places to social media that allow them to connect with their families in other countries or on the move across Europe. Smartphones provide spaces for education, entertainment and connection. Telegram was a favoured app for sharing files and documents, as the storage space was viewed as sufficient. A research participant had used it for sharing articles, documents and books that had been translated from English into Persian; they described the app as 'my mobile library!' Others listened on YouTube to familiar songs and languages, and to classic works of Persian poetry such as those of Hafez. To others the smartphone 'notes' function offered a convenient way to pen one's own thoughts digitally, in Persian or Italian, in breaks at work, at restaurants or while riding on a bus or the metro. Poetry is a prominent art form among the Hazara: it is used for expressing political commentary, entering into socio-political dialogue and expressing personal and subjective experiences, thoughts and emotions. Many Hazara people are able to quote lines and lines of verse from well-known poets from Afghanistan and Iran, and poetry is deeply embedded in life, love and politics.[26]

Since poetry is a prestigious cultural form for the Hazara, particularly among refugees outside their homeland, it is a favoured form for conveying aspects of the experience of living in Milan, of being both Hazara and Italian and of living amid physical and symbolic experiences of uprootedness. In poems such as 'Wandering exile' in the volume *Sogni di tregua* (Dreams of truce), Basir Ahang, introduced on p. 137 in relation to the film *Sembra mio figlio*, writes that 'home' becomes a kind of rooting, which on the one hand is physically and symbolically rooted in Afghanistan, but on the other becomes something located in movement and in the act of moving, where 'my homeland is no more / than the soles of my shoes'.[27] This emphasis on movement as an existential condition is what anthropologist Alessandro Monsutti emphasises in his research, over many years, with Hazara communities, highlighting the salience of the term *âwâra*, a Dari/Persian word for 'wanderer(s)' that is reflected in the aforementioned poems.[28] Following on from experiences of movement, migration and generational responsibility, among younger people ageing is understood as a journey towards mental and physical maturity,[29] which may be conceived as a necessary stage of the life course, a rite of passage to adulthood.[30] This journey, combined with the more literal one of travelling from Afghanistan to Europe, becomes a stage in individual trajectories of development and growth. Social media and smartphone practices, information sharing and transnational forms of collective identification and solidarity constitute portals between worlds and places in motion.

Conclusion

The aim of this chapter has been to illustrate how growing up with smartphones in urban Italy can be observed in the examples of younger people with different backgrounds, journeys and upbringings, and their experience of growing up and 'coming of age', and how smartphones and digital technologies play a role in their processes of exploring identities and belonging, subjectivity and citizenship. We have seen in this chapter and others how people at different ages – in retirement or in their twenties – and from a range of backgrounds and experiences, individually or within families or other social groupings, are living with the questions not just of 'Where do I belong?', but also of 'Who should or could I be?' The smartphone presents no ready answers to these questions, but in many cases it is there all the same in this broader figuring out of life and love, politics and identities, in Milan, and beyond national borders through transnational social fields and digital environments.

We have seen how a number of younger people in NoLo and Milan express themselves and work through issues of identity politics and social change. Whether through digital activism, film-making and poetry, or through social media and community activisms, from citizenship rights and social equality for the '2G', to human rights, equality and social and political justice, the online is demonstrably connected to a wholly 'on*life*' engagement.[31]

As the examples in the chapter highlight, being young in Italy moves way beyond discourses of 'smartphone addiction' or the alleged egoism and social apathy of the young. A number of the generalised discourses highlighted in chapter 5 were shown to apply to youth in Italy. Being a younger person or citizen in NoLo, Milan and Italy brings encounters with legal obstacles and institutional and social exclusions, and with different degrees of visibility and invisibility within contemporary Italian society. It can also be about practising and figuring out social participation, social citizenship and solidarity, offline and online amid a range of practices and alignments, in which smartphones and social media play prominent roles.

The themes of identity and belonging discussed in this chapter are facets of the multigenerational story of ageing with smartphones explored in this volume. I examine these threads in more detail in the following, penultimate chapter, which is concerned with life purpose and examines the role of narrative in meaning-making, in the light of digital and social change.

Notes

1. For an anthropological discussion of the Sanremo competition in the context of Italian popular culture, society and politics see Favero 2017, chapter 3.
2. Jacqueline Andall's ethnographic research on second-generation African-Italians in Milan has highlighted young people's desire for social and transnational mobility in seeking opportunities beyond Italy and in shaping progressive social change within the country and across Europe. See Andall 2002, 401–2.
3. Andall 2002, 390.
4. In a conference paper stemming from a symposium on 'Italy's Second Generation' at the American University of Rome in November 2009, which formed part of a series of events on the theme of past and present racism in Italy organised by the university's Centre for Research on Racism, anthropologist Bjørn Thomassen (2010, 21) questioned the terminology with

which this youth demographic in Italy is described, asking whether they are 'second-generation immigrants' or 'Italians with immigrant parents'.
5. El-Tayeb 2011, 180.
6. Anderson 2019, 8. See also Goldberg 2002, 2006.
7. Anderson 2019.
8. See Clough Marinaro and Walston 2010.
9. The EU-funded research project entitled 'New Italians' (2016), led by Marco Antonsich, for example, sought to explore the question 'What kind of nation do migrants and their children envision?' The multimedia project website includes videos and interviews with second-generation Italians, along with a directory of resources that includes groups and communities of the second generation across Italy. See Antonsich et al. 2016.
10. For example, see the website of the Bologna-based organisation 'Next generation Italy' (Next Generation Italy 2020), which says 'We hope for the construction of a society of Italian citizens made up of a multiplicity of peoples, genders and generations, countering all types of discrimination'.
11. The *jus sanguinis* (citizenship by descent) law differs from *jus soli* (birthright citizenship), which confers citizenship on all children born in a country.
12. Reform of the current citizenship legislation has been proposed since the late 1990s by liberal groups, but such proposals are met with fierce opposition, particularly from the far right. Salvini has generally targeted his inflammatory remarks at first-generation migrants and refugees. However, the second generation has also been subjected to far-right attacks.
13. Turco, L. 1999. 'Perché riformare la legge sulla cittadinanza?'. In Commissione per le politiche di integrazione degli immigrati, *Riformare la legge sulla cittadinanza*, 22 February 1999, 4–11, cited in Andall 2002, 395.
14. O'Healy 2019, 11. See also Cole 1997 and Favero 2017.
15. Along with Milan, Rome is a core site of second-generation organisations and activity. See for example 'The National Co-ordination of the New Italian Generation', a group that aims to develop solidarity and increase inclusion within Italian society, and in particular to lobby against the citizenship law that recognises Italian citizenship only by blood. See Coordinamento Nazionale Nuove Generazioni Italiane 2020.
16. See for example the Twitter page of the Milan-based group 'Yalla Italia', a blog for the 'second generation', https://twitter.com/yallaitalia?lang=en, and a Facebook page for 'Giovani Musulmani d'Italia', https://www.facebook.com/GiovaniMusulmanidItaliaGMI/. Both accessed 19 November 2020.
17. Zinn 2010.
18. Classic discussions of citizenship have focused on civil, political and social citizenship. The distinction relates to those that include legal rights and those that may not. See Marshall 1950. For further discussion of the concept of social citizenship see Çağlar and Glick Schiller 2018, chapters 1 and 4.
19. Hazāragi is the language spoken by the Hazara people from Afghanistan and within the Hazara global diaspora. It is a dialect of the Persian language closely related to Dari, which is one of the main languages of Afghanistan, and the linguistic boundary between Hazāragi and Dari is not clear-cut. See Kieffer 2020.
20. See Monsutti 2004, 2005 and Olszewska 2015, 37–46.
21. Olszewska 2015, 38–41. See also Hanifi 2000 and Monsutti 2004, 2005.
22. Information relating to migrants from Afghanistan in Italy can be hard to come by and many individuals do not have official documentation. In 2017 an unofficial estimate found that there may be around 20,000 Afghans in Italy, including many unaccompanied minors (Foschini and Bjelica 2017).
23. See https://globalvoices.org/2017/10/26/ex-refugee-who-slept-rough-in-rome-now-runs-several-businesses-dreams-of-rebuilding-afghanistan/.
24. See the trailer for the film at https://vimeo.com/253161715.
25. Hazara International 2011.
26. Ethnographic research on Afghan refugee poetry has shown that prominent poetic themes are love, home and the pain of exile, and some works question or subvert social convention. For anthropological discussions of poetry and personhood among young Afghan refugees in Iran see Olszewska 2007, 2015.
27. Ahang 2015. See https://www.festivaldepoesiademedellin.org/en/Festival/25/News/Ahang.html. Accessed 20 November 2020.

28. Monsutti 2018. See also the book of poems *Quando la luna c'è* (2019) (When the moon is there) by the Hazara poet and film-maker Amin Wahidi.
29. Monsutti 2018.
30. Monsutti 2007, 169.
31. I adopt the term 'onlife' from a research paper on digital ethnography by Edgar Gómez Cruz (2014), in which the author uses the term 'onlife ethnography' to describe a number of methodological techniques for doing ethnography online in digital environments. My own use of 'onlife' here is analytical, intended to describe a high level of engagement with social and political life through activism online – or 'onlife'– that the examples of social media and smartphone use among various sets of young people seen throughout this chapter demonstrate. More broadly, the concept chimes with the various scales of 'life' explored in this book, from the minutiae of everyday life to the broader frame of the life course.

8
Life purpose: narratives of ageing

Introduction

This chapter zooms out of the book's focus on the practices of everyday life to consider a larger picture, viewed through the screens of smartphones, of how people talk about their lives, what they have been, what they are today, what they might be in the future. An overarching question explored throughout the chapter is how people live in the present moment, and why ideas about the present have such significance for my research participants. As ageing unfolds within and alongside the 'information age', individuals move along with, and narratively co-construct, the life course along the way, and the smartphone plays a notable role in this.

Chapter 2 examined ageing from the perspective of institutional and classificatory definitions, looking at how ageing has been defined in Italy, including how it has been constructed in policy terms. That and subsequent chapters explored how people are navigating these classifications and structures through their everyday practices, hobbies and healthcare, and through creative forms of self-expression. This chapter focuses on the *narratives* of ageing, with respect to *moving* selves and unfolding lives, as contexts of value shift over time and space. It highlights how the smartphone plays a central role in narrating the self through engaging with digital and visual forms of expression and communication, as well as the broader processes of *moving* the self through life and through learning, education and personal journeys of awareness.

Movement and mobility are two areas in which the meaning and value of life have been experienced and were articulated by a number of research participants. As stated in chapter 1, many people in the area had moved to work and live in Milan or elsewhere in Italy, or both, over time. My research illustrates and supports the idea that movements, physical and metaphorical, can be part of the pursuit of human dignity and agency;[1] many of the people I came to know in Milan had moved in order *to live*: to quote from the Portuguese poet Fernando Pessoa, 'what moves lives'.[2] The smartphone, as we shall see, serves as a mediating tool for navigating some of these movements, along with the accompanying uncertainties and ambivalences involved, while playing a prominent role in nurturing individual aspects of the moving self in the process.[3]

As I thought through life with friends and research participants over the course of 16 months, a prominent theme emerged as a feature of the life course, that of 'awareness', with which this chapter begins. A number of older adults had used the Italian verb *svegliare* ('to awaken') in conversation or in interviews as they searched for words to describe their experience of growing into their own and into more collective forms of education about life, and about themselves. The following examples will show a parochial concept of awareness, stemming from experiences such as the claustrophobia and constraints of being brought up under strict Catholicism and conservative family values. Ageing in these life stories became associated with a gradual cutting through a kind of 'darkness' to be in a position to acknowledge and take advantage of adult education and fields of knowledge and information that people felt brought them into a kind of 'light'. But why was awareness emerging as a dominant narrative about the life course? Why now? The present digital age has evidently played a significant role in nurturing individual curiosity and comparisons, with other people and contexts, with other ways of doing things, of being and living, that link to biographical journeys of development and change, desires and movements. The smartphone, as we have seen, can be a tool for exploring the possibilities of individuals' 'enlightenment' in older age, by learning new things, taking up hobbies, joining choirs, rediscovering old songs from childhood on marvelling at knowing the names of flowers or plants within seconds via an app. First, I describe the context in and motivations for which research participants in their sixties and seventies had begun to foster their curiosity and desire to learn and 'move', in one form or another, including in certain ways of being, thinking or doing, and then consider how the smartphone comes into play.

Awareness and awakenings

A number of research participants aged from their forties to their seventies described a process of 'waking up' from aspects of a conservative childhood, or from particular traditional or religious dogmas and societal pressures and taboos; others described escaping from abuse, violence or war. Though the processes by which people had come to different forms of awareness, through education, travel and work, long pre-dated digital technologies, their experiences of ageing with smartphones today present opportunities to reconfigure the self in relation to information, to themselves and to others. Ideas about awakening and awareness, whether of society or of the self, and about transformation and enlightenment, have multiple origins, histories and iterations in cultures and contexts across the world. Today, in global social justice movements and activisms across the world, awareness continues to be linked to attention to racial or social discrimination, injustice, and inequality. In Italy, social awareness took its own historical and social trajectory over the course of the twentieth century, and I came to learn more about this through the life stories and narratives of research participants.

Individuals in their sixties, seventies and eighties had lived through societal confrontations with a number of significant social and historical phenomena, for example the legacy of fascism, the post-war internal migration and urbanism that saw the social and economic development of Milan during the 'miracle' years of the 1950s and 1960s, the liberation theology that emerged within the Catholic Church in the 1960s (discussed later in this chapter), the activities and impact of Italian feminism in the 1970s and increasing international migration to the country from the 1980s. Since the 1990s, the convergence of capitalism and neoliberalism and the rapid development of the information society or 'information age'[4] have paved the way for a new digital era in twenty-first century Milan, witnessed by the city's burgeoning smart city development. Concurrently, environmentalist, anti-fascist and anti-racist movements are active in the city, and in the neighbourhood in particular.

These developments have inevitably affected people's lives, social experiences and attitudes to life and to themselves and others, as detailed in a number of case studies throughout the book. So what did people mean when they talked about coming into an or into their awareness? Let us begin with Ugo.

Ugo

A retired mechanical engineer, Ugo, aged 77, lives with his wife Isabella, aged 70, a retired teacher, in an old palazzo building. Ugo grew up in a large family in a working-class suburb on the outskirts of Milan during the economic boom of the post-war period. He feels that the best thing about those times was the underlying social foundation of living a 'simple life', based on his notions of morality, derived from a Christian education, which had become compromised by the speed and pressures of modern life.[5] The home and the family were at the centre of his and many others' lives then, a time he now views with a certain nostalgia.

> We were five children at home. There was no space for all of us really, but we managed it. Every evening we – my brothers and sisters and I and my parents – sat round the table to eat whatever we would be eating that day, and somehow it was complete. Or rather, we felt complete.

Ugo's experiences of family life and his nostalgia for the secure sanctity of it link to his present-day life in his seventies, as he experiences ambivalence about growing old in the city, away from his adult children who live in another city and another country, while he despairs about the sweeping spread of populism in Italy and Europe, which he feels is corroding society and politics.

Central to the vision of moral goodness espoused by Ugo and Isabella is a propensity for curiosity and education, on which they both place great value. Encyclopaedias of different types, nature magazines and stacks of books, particularly historical novels, fill their bookshelves. They mark a certain continuity with Ugo's childhood, in which curiosity and knowledge featured poignantly. Ugo recalled a practice, a kind of game, he used to undertake with his father Umberto when he was a child in the 1950s. After work each evening, his father, exhausted and hungry from working all day at a factory on the outskirts of the city would sit in his chair with Ugo hovering above him seeking attention, information, engagement. Umberto would routinely ask him, 'Tell me, son, what does this word mean?', referencing a passage from the newspaper he read daily. Ugo would spend the next few hours calling on neighbours and school friends, perhaps locating a dictionary or encyclopaedia, trying to find out what certain phrases, foreign words or complicated words meant. Upon discovering the word, Ugo would be exhilarated, as if he had come a notch closer to uncovering the 'fountain of the earth's knowledge' or 'secret treasure', a feeling quietly shared by Umberto. Ugo has kept up iterations of this practice throughout his life, which brings him into an affective orbit with his father. Ugo himself, during his working life, after work and dinner, while winding down in front of the TV, would take a pencil and notebook which he kept on a side table in the living room, jot down words or phrases he had heard on the TV or the radio that day and look them up in a dictionary or encyclopaedia or via an encyclopaedia program on a CD-ROM, on the PC that he and Isabella bought.

Contemporary iterations of this 'information game' can be seen in Ugo's smartphone practices, where he draws on the apparent plenitude of the Wi-Fi at home to spend hours surfing the web. For some people, the smartphone and the internet are viewed as a denigration of older skills (skills involving patience, effort and a sense of reward), in the same way that Google Maps might diminish old cartographical memory skills. Ugo, however, embraces digital technology, because he believes it has enhanced his practice of searching and learning in ways his father could never have imagined and, Ugo feels, would have been equally enthusiastic about. For this reason, the Wikipedia app has become one of Ugo's favourites and each time he opens it, he feels a warm jolt that brings him into proximity with his father.[6]

Ugo describes his appetite for information and learning as something that has developed over time, through work, reading and general life experience, and has since become part of his character: '*Sono molto curioso*' ('I am really curious'), he confessed. At the same time, there is a deeper-rooted explanation of this curiosity, which can be linked to what Ugo described as the 'sleepy blindness' of members of the older generation who were not curious, and did not embrace new information, knowledge or change. Ugo feels his father was somewhat exceptional in this way. Umberto was Catholic and, Ugo explains, 'curious' and 'critical'. Ugo's mother Maria was more socially conservative, and strict in her religious practices in the home and in daily life. Ugo explains that at quite an early age – in his early teens – he 'woke up' ('*Mi svegliai*'). He explained:

> I participated [in religious matters], of course, socially, but I just could not follow as my parents did – particularly my mother. It was a kind of blinded behaviour and I could never understand it. I wanted to be free of it. Many of us did.

Like a number of other research participants, Ugo emphasised a broad moral conception of 'goodness' that was linked to a wide-ranging notion of living an ethical life that was rooted in Christianity but was not tied to religious doctrine or practice.

Ugo describes a certain kind of awareness that he has developed throughout his life through books, reading and now the internet, one that has become valuable to him: 'We are here, life is a cycle, we die – just like all other animals,' he states with a certain pointed matter-of-factness. The information age has been a personal journey for Ugo, with historical roots in other forms of information 'technologies' such as books and encyclopaedias, the television and CD-ROMs. However, today, smartphones add a further dimension to his life and have shone more light on the meaning he derives from it in his late seventies. His experience of ageing with smartphones has drawn attention to how much he felt he missed before, as he put it, he 'woke up'. Embracing social and technological change has given him greater access to opportunities for learning and personal growth in older age. A similar process of finding alternative ways of learning and doing things was described by Augustina.

Augustina

Augustina is in her mid-seventies. She was an only child from a low-income household; her father had worked in a textile factory on the outskirts of the city and her mother took sporadic work as a seamstress. Augustina described growing up as a process of maturing that she had developed, like Ugo, through education and learning, mainly through reading.

> I was the only child, in those difficult times after the war. Everyone was trying to make things work, to tie things together and to make some kind of progress one way or another. Both my parents worked all day long and I had to fend for myself during the day. I didn't go to school until later. I stayed alone in the house all day as I wasn't a particularly sociable child, and children could be very cruel! Books were my saviour. I read everything I could see and get hold of. It helped me grow up – in a way, this saved me.

Ugo and Augustina are not alone in highlighting the memory of growing up in 1950s Italy in a religious and socially conservative family context coupled with a lack of communication and information about aspects of life from adolescence and periods to sexual relations (see also chapter 6). As she put it, quite pointedly, '*Tutto era tabù! Tutto tutto tabù!*' ('Everything was taboo! Everything, everything taboo!'). Reprimands were not uncommon in Augustina's childhood. She recalled that no mirrors were allowed in the house, since they would be seen as vanity. These early childhood experiences – specifically about lack of communication within the family – she brings up when talking about her experiences throughout the rest of her life.

Umberta

Umberta, in her seventies, who has adult children, has always been and continues to be fiercely independent, and devoted to her family, but in a way that she describes as 'practical', rather than in a 'romantic' or emotional way. This practicality was a feature of her own upbringing: her parents did not explicitly express much emotion or affection within the family. Umberta's digital communication practices are filled with affection and visual forms, including frequent use of emojis and memes to express emotion, friendship and affection. She does not align herself with normative gender constructions of femininity or emotional expressivity. Her WhatsApp chats and groups nevertheless appear to afford Umberta spaces in which she expresses tactility, affection and sociability, including through emojis and memes, in ways she seems to feel comfortable with. The digital and visual mediums appear to lend her a safe way of expressing her emotions, finding a balance between proximity and distance in which she finds her '*equilibrio*', between too much and too little. Through these practices, she partly transcends her own image of herself.

Ugo, Augustina and Umberta, like other research participants, demonstrate the importance that awareness and a type of coming into their own have had in their lives and, as they implied, on members of their generation. This is a post-war generation that grew up during an economic boom in the north of Italy and in other parts of the world, but which had also experienced close-knit families, village life and lives played out in contexts of intense sociability and religiosity, and then left these contexts and moved to cities, developed autonomy and experienced new lifestyles. The generational experiences seen in Ugo and Augustina's stories reveal something wider about the shifting role of Catholicism in Italy today and the centrality of Milan and Lombardy in the field of social welfare (see chapters 3 and 6), which requires further discussion.

Roman Catholicism in Italy, home to the Vatican and the papacy, is deeply ingrained in the social fabric. In his book *The Dark Heart of Italy*, the English journalist Tobias Jones describes a deep absorption of Catholicism into 'Italianness': 'Catholicism is Italy, and vice versa. Even for a non-believer, being Italian implies absorbing the mores and morality of Roman Catholicism.'[7] Writing in 2003, Jones highlighted a distinction between Catholic and Christian, with a far greater emphasis on the former in the Italian language and society: 'One hardly ever hears the words "Christian" or "Christianity" in Italian. The words have been almost entirely replaced by "Catholic" and "Catholicism". People talk not about the "Christian commandments" but of the "Catholic commandments".'[8]

Notwithstanding the deep embeddedness of Catholicism in Italian society and culture, my ethnographic research revealed shifting attitudes and positionings that in a number of cases reflected a moral outlook located in Christianity. Some research participants who were religious and practising Catholics had made a point of describing themselves as 'Christian'. Giuliana, for example, in her late sixties, who is married and has three adult children, is retired and attends church on Sundays. She was keen to describe how she positions herself vis-à-vis her faith: 'I am Christian, I believe in Christian principles and I try to uphold them throughout my life.' Similarly, for Gianluca, aged 62, 'being Christian' was about a certain conception of expressing good social values, while the Church was a social space he had enjoyed since childhood.[9] What these research participants had in common was either a move away from a more direct association with the institution of the Church as a whole, including its conservatism, doctrines and dogmas, and scandals and abuses, or a move away from more traditional forms of faith. Faith could be expressed on grounds they felt comfortable with and aspired to live their lives by, based on the Church's moral and ethical teachings All of this figuring out formed part of broader life courses and journeys.

In this short film portrait (Fig. 8.1), made with a friend in NoLo, we see another significant theme in life trajectories: the city of Milan, and how the social and economic opportunities of the city had become important to people throughout their lives.

Figure 8.1 Film: *Short film portrait 2*. Available at http://bit.ly/filmportrait2.

So far, the chapter has explored how research participants have 'moved' over time, perhaps to the city of Milan, or to Italy, or more metaphorically through education and awareness. In the next section, I examine these kinds of mobilities as journeys in life that have involved transnational movements. Here again, the affordances and moral assemblages contained within and shaped by the smartphone can be observed as the experience of life in middle age plays out.

Transnational mobilities and well-being

Kemala's story reveals how aspects of upbringing and background interact with personal journeys and aspirations as life is made meaningful across time and place.[10] Kemala was born and grew up in Southeast Asia. She has been in Italy for ten years, and is married with young children. Kemala is from a small island and grew up in humble circumstances in a large family. She went to university in her home country before getting a job in marketing and working for five years in other countries in the region. I learned about Kemala's life story over time, and how the journey of her life course is narrated, as part of how she speaks about herself and her children today.

Kemala feels deeply connected with her upbringing and cultural background, and is particularly close to her mother, who in her seventies still runs a small business she established in the village 40 years ago. Reflecting upon her life in middle age and the values she has accrued over time and place, Kemala said, 'My mother and what she taught me about life and working hard, my children and my hope of helping them grow to have a good life, and one's thoughts – these should be fluid, like a river, always refreshing itself and never stagnant.'

Kemala's care and attention are multidirectional, spread over offline and online contexts,[11] physically and digitally across Milan but also in the virtual spaces of her family and friends across the globe.[12] She leads a busy life, between taking care of her children's daily and weekly routines and carrying out different jobs, some paid, some voluntary within community groups. Kemala has visited her country of birth with her family but is unable to do so often. She engages in social contact and transnational care 'at a distance',[13] and in a way that enables her to maintain her sense of balancing her time and her life between countries and socio-cultural groups.[14] She is sensitive to when and how she participates in family WhatsApp groups, responding on the transnational family group (consisting of over 30 people) only on important occasions, such as birthdays or religious occasions. Knowing that this group exists, however, and that 'everyone is there', Kemala confesses, provides comfort to her, physically distant as she is. The frequency of calling is modulated by her wish to maintain a certain social distance by not engaging too much in sociality online, but enough contact enables her to bridge the physical and social distance.[15] The smartphone's socio-technological capacity for facilitating 'distant-closeness'[16] allows her to practise care at a distance,[17] and at the same time navigate her own *equilibrio*.

Kemala is happy with the life she has carefully carved out as a site for her children to grow up in. At the same time, as with other research participants who were physically far from ageing close family members, the emotions she carries in relation to this distance show in her everyday life. As Kemala continues to craft her life in her forties, this is done at the intersection of her emotional proximity to but physical distance from her kin and her natal village, and her determination to provide the best life she can for her children, who were born in Milan and are growing up in the neighbourhood. The smartphone is central to mediating these different attachments to place and people, and assisting in the maintenance of forms of 'Care Transcending Distance'.[18]

The theme of education, awareness and learning through life's literal and metaphorical journeys is further illustrated by Azad, who is a Hazara from Afghanistan. He has been in Italy for over ten years, having travelled to Europe via other countries, fleeing persecution by the Taliban. He has Italian citizenship. His wife and children are currently in another country in Europe and the family see each other whenever possible. Azad studied Italian rigorously, becoming fluent. Over the years he has undertaken a variety of jobs and has developed social and economic networks.

The smartphone constitutes a companion to daily life in Italy and is a particular kind of portal of connection with food and language, with family, with aspects of Hazara culture and with his personal biography. Through social media, Azad participates in a number of different groups that reflect his various 'lifeworlds',[19] which are linked to different-sized transnational family- and Hazara-linked groups on Viber, Telegram and WhatsApp. The family social media group, consisting of over 35 people, is used for sending greetings, good wishes for occasions such as Eid and memes that relate to, among other things, humour, health, morality and the changing seasons. As Azad's close family members live in different countries, he feels both with them and apart from them, and so, like those of many of the people I came to know, his life is dispersed economically, socially and linguistically. Food, poetry and music accessed via YouTube, and the occasional sound of the Persian language, rarely heard in Italy, bring him much comfort as markers of connection. Azad also enjoys passing spare time on YouTube, watching science documentaries and videos related to nature, videos about the Hazara people, and historical and anthropological documentaries relating to human lives and experiences across the world.

Azad highlighted education as a core aspect of and aspiration in life, linking his sense of its importance to a discourse about the need to support education for Hazara youth in Afghanistan. Azad emphasised how persevering and hard-working Hazara youth were in Afghanistan and abroad.[20] Many Hazara around the world are committed to raising awareness and supporting the Hazara people in Afghanistan and other countries through activism, transnational social media campaigns,[21] fundraising and remittances.[22] Moreover, as it did for Ugo, Augustina and Kemala, education for Azad entailed a journey of personal enlightenment, of being awake, alert or, as he put it, having your eyes open to life. Explaining this idea further, Azad said, 'A dead life is not to open your eyes'. Azad's description links literally having one's eyes closed or open to the difference between being 'alive' or 'dead' in a socio-ethical sense. Azad's experiences of life (*zendegi*) and wellbeing (*khoshbakhti*) were deeply intertwined with his own life story, with his growing up in Afghanistan and his journeying across countries to Europe.[23]

This emphasis on the life course brings us back to the chapter's theme of the experience of ageing, and of age as narrative. Age, among the Hazara, is socially constructed in various ways. Elders are greatly respected and honoured, particularly by younger people, and a significant feature of elders' status is their role as keepers of stories, poetry and wisdom, particularly in the past when books and written records were scarce. Age is defined in social terms through notions of maturity (mental and physical) and capability in adulthood (*bâlâ-ye sin*). The social construction of age also relates to the fact that in Afghanistan, within the context of a precarious and shifting political and bureaucratic state, official birth certificates are rarely issued and birth registration can be challenging.[24, 25] Azad rarely thought of his age as such:

> It's not like I think 'When I'm 50, I want to do this or that'. Instead, I observe – often by looking in the mirror! – that I have arrived at a certain age. And however long I live, I will do the same. Life is a path on which you reach different moments, but you should always try to be useful, for your family, for your people, for others. If I was born to this world, so I must grow, and so I must become old, if it

is God's will. I should be happy if I were an older person, because I would be alive! I don't think so much about what will happen tomorrow. It's best not to!

According to Azad, expressing himself in Italian and in Persian, age is a mark of a lived life, measured in a social and ethical sense by being useful to family and kin, to the Hazara people, and to people generally. Azad connected ageing with ideas about maturity and responsibility that link to mobility and masculinity. Young men, he explained, needed to leave home in order to undertake mature pursuits such as searching for work and an income to support one's family.

In their research on notions of wellbeing, adulthood and futures among young Afghans in Europe, Khadija Abbasi and Alessandro Monsutti have suggested that 'migration to Europe is conceived as a school of life where … young adults who move to Europe are invested in the double mission to prove their individual value and prepare a better future for their community'.[26] These young people's experiences of strict border regimes and immigration policies, and of discrimination, can be a long way from the images of Europe they might share with families via social media as a sign of 'successful migration'.[27]

There was another side to the always-on-ness of the smartphone and its capacity to bring places and events to people in real time. Hazara research participants in Milan were in touch with family and friends in Afghanistan and at times witnessed violence there on smartphones and social media. Frequent digital connection to such events and to multiple instances of violence and suffering can have a number of psychological consequences for mental health and wellbeing, including PTSD, which form part of people's experiences of living with smartphones in the context of ongoing violence and persecution. Such cases reflect the sociopolitical systems and blended spatial and temporal frameworks that the smartphone is enmeshed with and in.

Within the complex nexus of attachments, detachments and movements described in the chapter, the smartphone can form a kind of 'Transportal Home', as we call it in the ASSA collective volume *The Global Smartphone*. It is at once a 'home' site and a moveable portal for experiencing multiple worlds in motion, which at the individual level can provide comfort and a sense of continuity and connection amid the ruptures and uprootings of life. The smartphone as Transportal Home can also be a collective space for developing awareness online through transnational solidarity campaigns, as seen in global Hazara online activism aimed at the reconstructing of home in Afghanistan. Many Hazara social media groups are viewed as collective spaces for developing the political project of establishing social and political justice and equality for the Hazara people in their homeland.

Crises and contradiction

A key feature of the role of smartphones in people's lives is how, via their socio-technological affordances concerning relationships, information and connectivity, individuals experience, acknowledge and work through the contradictions of their lives. Anthropologist Jarrett Zigon employs the term 'moral assemblages' to describe many of the contradictory conditions in which human beings live their lives.[28] Normative notions of what a good life should be, he argues, are often in conflict with one another, as well as with the practices of people's lives. Across NoLo, moral frameworks, ethical notions and belief systems, from a range of sources, overlap with and shape everyday life and experiences – and how life is made meaningful – through narrative and practice. Case studies earlier in the chapter discussed, for example, the role of religion and morality in individuals' lives, but what about the theme of contradiction and crisis as part of the life course and of experiences of ageing?[29]

Amid the various contradictions and crises of life, the smartphone becomes some*thing* and some*where* that people may go to and be in, particularly in midlife, when life's complexities are contained and perhaps confronted, if not altogether resolved.

In the case of one couple we see a poignant example of contradiction being played out in midlife in a family context. Gloria works full-time and is married. She is a devout, practising Catholic and attends Mass every Sunday. Gloria grew up loving books, and her parents nurtured the value of education and informing oneself about politics, society and the world. Gloria and her husband have experienced socio-economic pressures over the years, as well as some family tensions concerning their faiths, which are different, and these matters, together with some work and care responsibilities, have posed challenges. During particularly difficult periods a person Gloria felt she could talk to was her priest. She has known this priest for many years, and she considers him a family friend who her husband also came to know. Gloria draws much strength from her religious faith, as well as from her faith in people. From time to time she suffers from anxiety. As she explained, aspects of her life do not match up to the ideas she had had about her life and its path when she was younger.

When her husband took up a job in another country, he gave Gloria her first smartphone. The smartphone is a constant companion to Gloria in her daily life, present with her at the dinner table in her apartment, beside her at night, and on her desk at work. The smartphone, while being the container of a broader social universe, represents her husband's presence in his physical absence, not only because it enables the couple to communicate, but also as a gift he had bought and given to her to signify their remaining connected. Among the photos she likes to take and share are pictures of her husband at tourist spots around Italy or on a weekend break the couple had taken together. The images reflect both presence and absence, feelings that the smartphone itself captures and is a kind of repository of. As life plays out for this couple and others, the smartphone as a container of social universes, including loved ones, family and friends, forms a 'constant companion' in daily life.

The smartphone occupies a prominent place in the navigation of the moral and ethical entanglements of people's lives. Though it brings no simple solutions or moral resolution to life's cruel complexities and conundrums, such as how to live together and earn incomes as a couple physically apart, or how to negotiate aspects of religious faith, love and marital or other family relationships, it is centre stage in many of life's quandaries. The smartphone and social media play prominent roles in how transnational couples and families keep connected, and express care and love, by allowing them to hold a certain intimacy in place in the face of challenges such as physical separation. In such a role, amid the more general theme of living with contradiction and searching for balance, the smartphone can be a kind of life companion, providing both a way to pass the time and a place and space to inhabit.

Conclusion: the moving self and the smartphone

> Mobility must, therefore, be understood existentially …. It is a metaphor for freedom as much as a means for accessing life-giving resources.[30]

The stories, ages and life experiences covered in this chapter have illustrated how life is conceived of and narrated in terms of mobilities of various kinds, and as a journey of awareness, education, maturity and agency. The chapter has illustrated how research participants 'moved' themselves in and through life, to learn new things and to undertake physical, emotional and educational journeys, which at times involved unlearning and relinquishing things like taboos, judgements and other socialised practices. Many research participants were shifting constantly between off- and online environments in order to be with people and to explore things, including aspects of themselves, for example by learning to do things or express care in different ways, which had brought about some positive effects on social lives and relationships. By the same token, acquiring new things or moving to new environments had undoubtedly led to losses, of older values, attitudes or faith. As part of this, some relationships were jeopardised, particularly if transgressions from norms were significant, or if an individual had moved 'too far' away from something, somewhere or someone. The smartphone may bring these discrete lines together in a space of convergence that reflects these complexities, without altogether resolving or simplifying the contradictions in people's lives.

In Ugo and Augustina, we saw how people in their seventies are constructing lives in contradistinction to their parents' patterns and practices and linking this to a sense of self-agency that stems from their desire and ability to 'choose', 'awaken' or simply 'move on' from the grip of traditional or conservative social practices that had marked their childhood. This is, after all, a post-war generation in Italy, who left their villages and moved to cities to work and so had to make adaptations of personhood from village collectives towards more individually crafted lifestyles. The value they put on this new-found freedom, which afforded them an *equilibrio* (equilibrium or life balance), has come to define how they attribute meaning or purpose to life today, as a state of recognition that is collective in its moral outlook but also respects and celebrates individual self-awareness. Many call this an 'awakening', when they 'grew up', escaped ignorance or, to link back to Azad's metaphor, did *not* close their eyes and, in deciding to live in these new ways, ceased to be 'dead', a notion that invokes the sociological concept termed 'social death' by Erving Goffman, which for many research participants was the opposite of wellbeing.[31] The awareness of and ability to decide what was good or bad for one's own wellbeing, and act upon it, were ideas that for some people represented a great leap from those they had grown up with in more conservative and traditional family and social contexts, but which formed part of their explorations of the smartphone and of the moving self.

Education formed part of an (ongoing) process of encountering contradictory experiences, attitudes and practices, and ultimately living with and and working through 'ethical entanglements' through various logics, narratives and practices of reason.[32] Ageing, for many research participants, threw up more and more complexity and contradictions about their own lives and the world around them. However, as people got older and engaged with various struggles, life itself became partly defined by an attempt to keep things in balance, to find *equilibrio*, in the aforementioned sense, within daily life. This response, of searching for *equilibrio*, constituted a general aim of life for many of the research participants, and captures how being older was about their individual and collective processes of *becoming*.

The existential object

If, as I have suggested, the smartphone is centre stage in many of these ethical entanglements (because it is an object *and* a space and place[33] for the self), then the smartphone can be seen as a contemporary 'existential object',[34] by virtue of the fact that it forms an intimate link with the self and with narrative, that, as many research participants would say, 'accompanies' them throughout their daily life. This aspect of daily accompanying highlights the significance and scale of data tracking in the era of the smartphone, in which the other side of constant connectivity is constant surveillance.[35]

The existential object describes a socially alive repository of the self, which shapes the possibilities of *what* people become with and through it, and *where* and *who* they feel they are and are in the process of becoming. At the same time, even though it caters for people's needs by providing these connections, the smartphone has no answers to life's big questions and challenges. It is neither a Magic 8-Ball to reveal fortunes or futures nor a *sang-e sabour* magic stone from Persian mythology, which, when placed in front of a person, will shield them from unhappiness or suffering. What the smartphone as existential object may do, however, as we have seen throughout this volume, is *exist* for people, as a companion or a distraction, a mirror or a canvas. It may even flourish amid contradiction, accompanying people in the uprootedness and ambiguities of life as they experience shifting experiences of place, time and the self that make many feel younger (see chapter 2), physical frailties that make them feel older or rapid socio-technological change that can prove both dislocating *and* locational.

The smartphone is a device for meaning-making through the production of narratives. Through the socio-technological affordances and affective pulls of the device, including individual apps, social media practices and algorithms, and haptic and kinaesthetic engagements with alerts, messages and triggered responses, individuals engage in a range of active, reactive and passive forms of meaning-making all the time, about daily life, social relationships, themselves and others.[36] These shape the formulation of meta-narratives about what they are doing with their daily life, how they receive, qualify and share information, how they spend time with others and themselves, and how these activities reflect onto and shape people's sense of themselves as they age with smartphones.

For some research participants, the purpose of life was to live and act in the present, which means figuring out how to integrate a kaleidoscope of reference points, normative claims and practical demands from the past and the present into the formation of an everyday or 'ordinary ethics',[37] which the smartphone, as a repository and co-constructor of narratives, can become an active tool for. From this perspective, ageing with smartphones is perhaps best described through an image of a constantly swinging pendulum, an idea that also invokes the image of a ticking clock, marking the moral, social and geographical points that make up people's lives, including contradictory ideas people had about their own use of smartphones as, for example, an object of love and of guilt, or stealer of time, as was discussed in chapter 5. Living with smartphones mediated – and modulated – the experience of ageing, and, concurrently, life went on, one's literal age, in many cases, going unnoticed or even unknown, unless, as Azad put it, one caught oneself in the mirror and *saw* something of age.

Notes

1. See Jackson 2013b.
2. Pessoa 2001, 30.
3. The emphasis on individuals' life stories and journeys in this chapter is inspired by anthropological approaches to writing ethnography that acknowledge that '[t]here is wisdom to be had … in approaching the social through the biographical' (Jackson 2013b, 24). In *The Wherewithal of Life*, anthropologist Michael Jackson highlights common existential questions and ethical dilemmas faced by individuals in different contexts, such as the balance people seek between personal fulfilment and the moral claims of kinship, along with the struggle to differentiate between 'concrete' and 'abstract' utopian visions.
4. The 'information age' is a phrase employed by the sociologist Manuel Castells in the late 1990s to describe the rise of the network society and a new age as part of globalisation. According to Castells, it is an era beginning in the late twentieth century that has seen a significant shift in social evolution and a move away from traditional industry to one centred on information storage, transmission and access, and computerisation, or 'informationalism'. See Castells 2010.
5. The emphasis on and negative evaluation of the speed of modern life in Ugo's narrative recalls the notion of 'dromology' in which Paul Virilio (1986) describes the speed of modern mass communication as destructive of human presence and experience.
6. For a discussion of the role of photography and digital technologies in the experience of absent presences and as a way of 'opening up time' and acknowledging the present see Favero 2018, particularly chapter 5, 'Images of living and dying'.
7. Jones 2003, 166.

8. Jones 2003, 166.
9. As part of the liberation theology of the 1960s, the Second Vatican Council (1962–5), attempting to involve bishops and the laity in the decisions of the Church, had talked about a social rather than an authoritarian religion, which represented the 'true church'. This social-facing conception of the Church plays a significant role in explaining the history of social work in the Church and in the charity and care sectors in Italy, in areas from homelessness and addiction to working with refugees and asylum seekers. For more on the role of the Church, and on the practices and politics of social care in contemporary Italy, see Giordano 2014.
10. For an anthropological work on the role of narrative and meaning-making throughout life in contemporary Japan, see Kavedžija 2020.
11. Sarah Lamb's extensive work on ageing details these intergenerational care practices across time and space (Lamb 2009).
12. Deidre McKay's work (2012, 2016) highlights the complexities of care practices in transnational and migrant contexts. Within the global networks of Filipino migrant care workers resident in the UK that McKay studied over a number of years, she discovered what she terms an 'archipelago' (2016) of care practices taking place on- and offline. The concept helps explain how people create a sense of stability for themselves and close kin through practices of care exchange and co-operation within the acute circumstances of uncertainty that accompany migration.
13. Pols 2012.
14. Kemala's use of smartphones recalls, in part, Tanja Ahlin's notion of 'frequent calling' in the ethnographic context of transnational Indian families for whom keeping in touch constitutes 'good care at a distance'. See Ahlin 2020.
15. See also Miller and Madianou's work (2012) on transnational care practices.
16. See Van House 2007.
17. Tanja Ahlin's (2018) notion of 'transnational care collectives', for example, describes how information and communications technologies (ICTs) allow family members to enact care for one another, while individuals care for themselves too. Ahlin's idea of the transnational care collective builds on the concept of a 'care collective', which describes how people and things, such as medical technologies, may 'tinker' together with the aim of enacting care. See Mol et al. 2010.
18. For more discussion on Care Transcending Distance see Miller et al. 2021.
19. Existential anthropologist Michael Jackson (2013a) adopts the term 'lifeworld' from Husserl, whose original concept described how humans live in a world of inter-subjective relationships.
20. See also Monsutti 2018 and Abbasi and Monsutti 2017.
21. For example, in 2011 a significant protest against the killing of Hazara populations in Afghanistan took place outside Milan's Centrale station. See Hazara International 2011.
22. On remittance practices among the Hazaras see Monsutti 2004.
23. On the theme of movement more generally, seasonal and historical migrations are a prominent part of Hazara history. For further discussion on this theme see for example Monsutti 2005.
24. Donini et al. 2016, 11.
25. See Donini et al. 2016, 8.
26. Abbasi and Monsutti 2017, 8.
27. Monsutti 2018, 451.
28. See Zigon 2010.
29. 'Moral responsibility, Max Weber wrote, was … cyclical in Catholicism … (Weber 1992, 36–7). … "[M]an was not an absolutely clearly defined unity to be judged one way or the other, but … his moral life was normally subject to conflicting motives and his action contradictory" (Weber 1992, 116.). Such contradictions could be temporarily resolved through the giving of alms …, the doing of charitable works, the saying of prayers and the participation in the miracle of the Eucharist' (Muehlebach 2013, 461). See also Schneider 1991, 198.
30. Jackson 2013b, 119.
31. In the social sciences 'social death' is the loss of social identity that accompanies the removal of a person from one particular or many social worlds. In Goffman's seminal 1961 essay he describes how a person becomes a 'non- person' through the process of institutionalisation in asylums that leads to a 'mortification of the self'. For a broad discussion of the concept across the social sciences, see Králová 2015.
32. 'Entanglement' is a term I employ here to describe theoretically the complexity and heterogeneity of the experiences, practices, values and ethics that people live with in daily life, which

include contradiction and can lead to crises. The term is used in line with the work of the anthropologist Tim Ingold, who describes entanglement as 'a meshwork of interwoven lines of growth and movement' (2010, 3). Ingold's conception of entanglement as the 'entwining of ... ever-extending trajectories' (2010, 11) describes processes rooted in flow and flux, and resists conclusive directionality or reduction to an individual point of origin. Entanglement, for Ingold, is concerned with processes or lines of becoming and conditions of possibility. The phrase 'ethical entanglements' brings these ideas together with Michael Lambek's (2010) notion of 'ordinary ethics', which highlights the centrality of ethical practice, judgement, reasoning, responsibility, cultivation and questioning in social life and locates ethics in the actions (performance and practices) of social life.
33. For more on the social affordances of understanding digital objects as places and vice versa, see Walton 2020.
34. My use of the term 'existential' is a theoretical articulation, chiming with the field of existential philosophy derived from Jean-Paul Sartre and others who link narration with selfhood. In this chapter the term describes the intimate link between the smartphone and narrative – the smartphone as connected with multimedia/multimodal practices and algorithmic creations (textual, visual, audio) that play central roles in how people define and perform aspects of themselves in the present. These multimedia creations exist alongside other meaning-making forms such as memories, reflections and dreams.
35. On surveillance capitalism see Zuboff 2019. For further discussion of surveillance and constant tracking, see Miller et al. 2021, chapter 9.
36. For further discussion of technology and intersubjectivity, see Jackson 2013a, chapter 9.
37. Lambek 2010.

9
Conclusion: threading together

Introduction

The stories, words and experiences contained in this volume have presented an anthropological account of the ways in which people live and incorporate digital technologies into their lives at a global moment of rapid digital change and innovation. The book has illustrated how people live within, and form domains of, shared experiences and urban digital sociabilities, in and beyond the neighbourhood of NoLo in Milan. These have been shown to be significant at various stages in people's lives, in the experience of ageing and in the ongoing social development of the area and the city.

'Threading together' in the title of this chapter is a metaphor inspired by my participation in a women's sewing group at a Centro Multiculturale (Fig. 9.1). It highlights the theme of close-knit togetherness that is a feature of life and social activity in the neighbourhood and, accordingly, of my experience of living and spending time with people in the area. The value of sociality is seen in a number of cross-generational groups in NoLo, and the book has aimed to show how this is reflected in and refracted by the smartphone and what it has become for people. WhatsApp groups and chats have become valuable spaces to be together, to let off steam, to pass the time *in compagnia* (in company) and send messages and memes to demonstrate and reciprocate care. The book has sought to demonstrate that the smartphone is at the centre of many of the contradictions and ethical entanglements of lives and relationships because it is so deeply embedded within them.

'Threading together' also refers to the way the research on ageing with smartphones that informs this book was undertaken, and how the volume was written. The book examines how individuals of various ages and backgrounds are living and figuring out their lives in the present digital moment, and how they create narratives such as those pertaining to and re-imagining 'active ageing', citizenship or belonging.

Figure 9.1 Objects and materials at the sewing group at the Centro Multiculturale. *Fascia per capelli* ('headband'). Photo by Shireen Walton.

Ageing with smartphones has been a multigenerational and cross-cultural story in this book, and this methodological openness has been the main approach to learning about ageing with different people in their everyday lives in this contemporary urban and digital ethnographic context. I was interested in exploring the urban digital environment – both as a site of sociability and as a site that people live and grow older in. While I carried out research among a range of people within and beyond the neighbourhood, I also critically examined logics of distinction and exclusion that I routinely encountered in the field. The volume has examined gender, race, ethnicity and citizenship in seeking an intersectional understanding of ageing in contemporary Milan. In analytically threading together the lives of a number of individuals in the book, I have endeavoured to highlight both the distinctive elements in people's backgrounds, lives and experiences, and the threads that connect them.

The emphasis on biography and narrative throughout the book reflects a method of how the research was carried out, through long-term participant observation and in-depth interviews about the life course over 16 months, which has been a principal tool for sharing these stories about ageing with smartphones. The emphasis on narrative was particularly salient in the penultimate chapter, 'Narratives of ageing', which brought together the main strands of the book by illustrating how people narrate and shape their life experience in the multiple contexts they inhabit, off- and online. We saw that life may have been something someone had dreamed of or planned in their youth, but that people had come to realise that life was also about living with unexpected events, compromise and contradiction. Gloria, for instance, working full-time in Milan and currently living physically far from her husband but connected to him through her smartphone, wonders 'what comes next' in life. Noor, introduced in chapters 2 and 7, had left her previous life in Egypt to bring her family to Milan, just as her eldest daughter imagines leaving Italy with her boyfriend. Kemala (chapter 8) is proud of the life she has created in Milan, and enjoys the weekly transnational WhatsApp video call she makes to mother and sister, but she still misses them deeply. Life becomes a kaleidoscopic experience of threading together aspects of the individual self – of idylls, responsibilities, socio-economic realities, the past, and the affordances of the present – while accommodating work, care duties, financial pressures, illness and loss. The result of this human-technological balancing act forms an everyday or 'ordinary ethics'[1] which the smartphone, as a repository and co-constructor of narratives, is a tool for. Attempting to keep things in balance and finding what some people called their *equilibrio* within daily life were important to a number of research participants and this attitude was likely to constitute one of their moral aims in life, which included monitoring one's smartphone usage so as not to use it too much ('*troppo*').

Being and becoming together

One of the main findings from studying ageing and digital technologies in Milan is the importance attributed to social life and communities, and that the character of NoLo emerges as an important feature of living and ageing in this place. The people I came to know in the neighbourhood generally enjoyed the experience of living '*in zona*' ('in the neighbourhood') and in Milan, which they viewed as a historically significant and vibrant city undergoing noticeable change, development and investment. NoLo was viewed by many as an up-and-coming 'social district' that offered a variety of opportunities for social participation across age groups.[2] Digital practices have opened up parts of the city to people in different but not equal ways.

As discussed in chapter 2, a number of research participants described the neighbourhood as a place in which they could envisage growing older. While in the past it was common to leave the city to retire to the seaside or the countryside, today a number of people felt that continuing to live '*in zona*' was appealing, specifically for the social opportunities it offered. Some people had discussed with friends ideas about growing old together in the neighbourhood ('*invecchiare nel quartiere*'), which seemed an attractive social proposition.

For example, a number of research participants in their fifties and sixties described possible future co-living arrangements for ageing in place, such as independent living with friends or others in multigenerational housing blocks. These plans reflect a global revival of interest in intentional co-living, seen in concepts like the contemporary cohousing movement, developed in Scandinavia in the 1970s.[3] One reason research participants in NoLo had envisioned future living in such collective but autonomous ways was the kinds of sociability they were used to and enjoyed in the neighbourhood. As chapter 4 set forth in relation to the characteristic *case di ringhiera* apartments, co-operation and care, particularly between people who lived alone, were valued, and regarded as a positive aspect of living together, yet apart. This was seen in the case of neighbours Clara and Claudia, who had established a kind of mother–daughter relationship through living next door to each other, which they both found emotionally sustaining and practically helpful, from watering the plants to receiving parcels to having someone to mull over the day with. In another example (chapter 5), residents of a building formed a WhatsApp group to take care of the building and communal spaces collectively, which became an affective space for fostering friendships between neighbours who had lived near each other for years. On the other hand, chapter 4 highlighted that apartment blocks were sites of socio-economic inequality. For a family who had recently had to give up their apartment in NoLo because of economic hardship and move to the outskirts of the city, life was a continuing cycle of renewal, in which strong bonds within the family structure proved a sustaining force that kept them together through conditions of precarity.

Notwithstanding the diverse experiences of sociality in the neighbourhood, how public and private lives play out in the urban environment and via smartphones depends on the individual as well as on socio-economic and cultural factors. As shown throughout the book, research participants in NoLo were engaged in navigating their own attitudes towards 'too much' or 'too little' sociality, a concept I described as 'social availability' in chapter 4. The issue here is individuals' sense of autonomy and privacy in the digital era, and how time for oneself may be carved out amid broader social and care responsibilities, and varying desires and capacities for sociality.

Moreover, while some people saw NoLo as an optimal site in which to *stare insieme* (stay together) in retirement, experiences of life in the neighbourhood and across the city are very varied, and ideas and perceptions about the neighbourhood are not all positive. Forms of discrimination that a number of research participants in NoLo had experienced continue to otherise citizens and minority communities within the national framework,[4] while, as shown in chapter 7, the urban digital context of NoLo can be an environment for challenging these constructions. This was illustrated in how, for example, so-called 'second-generation' youth solidarity is articulated alongside a push for changes to Italian citizenship law by advocating *jus soli* (birthright citizenship) and social justice and equality.

Smartphones play a prominent part in maintaining communication with friends and family members, regularly and conveniently, through the use of messaging or WhatsApp voice messages. Social relationships are forged and maintained through digital practices played out among families, neighbours, the community and the city, and transnationally online, and new kinds of 'second families' are formed (chapter 4) within the urban digital environment. The book has shown how individuals, from different generations and with varying backgrounds, demonstrated feelings of belonging and attachment in NoLo that the smartphone is an important instrument for accessing and modulating.

Age(ing) and beyond

One of the findings among older adults in NoLo is how traditional ideas about age have been shifting in the light of people's changing life experiences, expectations and expectancies, as a significant body of scholarship on ageing around the globe has demonstrated by charting a move from seeing ageing as frailty to regarding as signalling new leases of life and new opportunities.[5] As discussed in chapter 2, in Italy, in the rest of Europe and elsewhere, a host of initiatives have been developed since the 1990s to promote activity and productivity in older age in line with the EU's 'active ageing' vision ('successful aging' in the US) and its emphasis on individual responsibility for being autonomous and productive in later life. A similar emphasis has been seen in the development of mHealth in Italy (chapter 6), which is also steeped in narratives about empowering citizens through self-sufficiency.

The book has queried some of the dominant policy assumptions and narratives about how people (should) age with technology and who this typically concerns. It has examined how the lived experience of ageing and of individuals' own and others' health, care and autonomy play out at different ages and across society, and where care responsibilities play out in transnational family contexts online through smartphones and digital communications. Chapter 2 reiterated that the question of who gets to retire in future, on a state pension or otherwise, remains closely linked to social, economic and individual factors. While some people had enjoyed the new-found freedoms of retirement in NoLo, having planned for it over decades of investment, others felt that they could never afford to be old or retire but had to carry on working to make ends meet. The discussion of ageing in chapter 6 specifically explored the role of digital health services, smartphones and apps in the ageing, health and care landscape in Italy, highlighting the differences between top-down digital health initiatives, and the digital and non-digital health and care practices enacted by people 'from below'.

A principal finding presented in the book is how, for some research participants in their sixties and seventies, ageing was less about a sense of decline than about developing capacities, including the ability to explore the boundaries of social possibilities with and beyond smartphones. Giovanna (chapter 5), for example, had found a new lease of life in retirement through joining a women's choir that was socially and politically active in the community and on WhatsApp, while Luca (chapter 3) deeply enjoyed his part-time volunteering role as an Italian-language teacher, in which he felt socially engaged and useful. Being useful (*utile*) was a concept raised by almost all research participants in NoLo in describing their lives in retirement or as a general moral outlook. Utility was also the term most often used in connection with the smartphone: people described it as '*una cosa utile*' (something useful). '*Mi serve*' ('I need it'), they would tell me. At the same time, engaging with the smartphone was not always about its utility or doing things through it. Sometimes it was a case of 'old wine in new bottles', where older interests and hobbies were repurposed in new forms.

The sum of these experiences meant that many people felt younger, in a social sense, than their actual age, which was also a finding in the fieldsites in Ireland in the ASSA project. This is not to suggest that people altogether transcended their age, or age classifications such as retirement age, receipt of pensions, social benefits and care entitlements, as well as physical health and frailty. Age can also have symbolic connotations. Nonna Lina, who was actively involved in volunteering in the local community, prized her role as a grandmother: *'Nonna è sempre Nonna'*, she told me.

Despite normative ideas about, representations of or perceptions about ageing, ageing itself was marked by an acknowledgement that life was something to be crafted, through education, movement, and continued learning and social participation, as opposed to something that reflected being 'old' or that people had been socialised into or grew up with. A number of research participants used the verb *svegliare* ('to wake up') in conversation or in an interview, as they searched for words to describe their experience of growing into their own or more collective forms of awareness about their life and about themselves, throughout their lives as well as in the digital information age.

Crucially, the time for developing these aspects or capacities of the self in older age was now (chapter 8). But why now? As I have aimed to illustrate throughout the book, the emphasis on the present moment among older adults was not just to do with the limits of the human life span. The information age has played a significant role in nurturing individual curiosity, creativity, and comparison with other contexts, ways of doing things, and ways of being and living, which for many had formed a kind of renewable energy source for living life today. Examples of this energy or spirit have shown how people learn new things, take up hobbies or marvel at knowing the names of flowers or plants within seconds via an app. For these reasons life for many people involved a constant redesigning into midlife and later adult years, which called not for rest, reclusive behaviour or inactivity, but for creativity, and sometimes entrepreneurialism and pragmatism, to keep moving and to reconcile one's ideas about life with its challenges.

Despite a number of people in their sixties and seventies not feeling their age, there were cases when people did say they felt 'old'. This term tended to be employed negatively when people were describing an embodied feeling or a self-perception, such as changes in the body or to their health, or experiencing illness or fatigue from care responsibilities or depression. Some women research participants in this age group used the term 'old' to account for these feelings, which is indicative of the gendered distinctions in the experience of ageing, in contrast to ideals and norms promoted in areas like the beauty industry. In other cases, people had internalised narratives about ageing into their self-perception, like Bernadetta (chapter 2), who, in her early seventies, felt less active and that she was 'not designing anything new any more', despite her relative health and participation in the neighbourhood, cycling during the week to engage in volunteering activities. Through these examples the book joins a wealth of scholarship in highlighting the importance of combating stigmas and stereotypes about older adults, which, along with socio-economic inequalities, remain significant in the experience of age and ageing across the world.[6]

Ageing with smartphones: a 'constant companion' for the contemporary world

The stories featured in this volume on ageing with smartphones have shown that the smartphone forms a 'constant companion', as a physical object in everyday life, adorned with stickers or kept in a knitted bag around one's neck, but also in a social sense through its role in keeping relationships close across time and space. More broadly, it was a companion and a guidebook for living within the rapidly unfolding 'information age', defined by Manuel Castells as an era beginning in the late twentieth century that has seen a significant shift away from traditional industries to ones centred on information storage, transmission and access, and on computerisation.[7] We saw, for example, that for Rosalba the smartphone was a kind of presence, informing her about the weather or recipes found online. She drew comfort from the multiple presences contained within it, mostly those of her children and family whom she connected with through the smartphone or, if it was out of charge, via her tablet.[8] Nevertheless, the smartphone was an ambiguous object which some people felt guilty about using so much, while others expressed concerns about privacy, surveillance, fake news and online bullying.

Constant companion(ship) is a useful concept to employ in relation to the study of ageing with smartphones and the experiences of uprootedness that can accompany people as they undergo change within themselves, while moving through different stages of life, technological eras, geographical contexts or shifting socio-economic circumstances. However, life with smartphones taps into some of the anxieties of the present moment about ageing in Italy and globally, concerning lines between autonomy and surveillance in digital forms and contexts: another element of constant companionship is constant tracking.[9]

Given how intimately the smartphone is bound up with the self in all its complexity and contradiction, in chapter 8 I discuss the smartphone as 'existential object'. This term describes the particular type of human-technological hybrid object and narrative device that people incorporate into their lives, relationships and subjectivities. The existential object is a socially alive repository of the self, which shapes the possibilities of what people become with and through it, including how and 'where' they live.

Following on from this, a finding highlighted in this book and explained in further detail in the ASSA project group volume *The Global Smartphone*, is the theory of the smartphone as a 'Transportal Home', a digital-material home space that can provide, among other things, comfort and transnational connection amid movements, displacement and uncertainties.[10] The Transportal Home does not necessarily weaken the physical and symbolic significance of place. Nor does the smartphone as 'home' replace the physical home even if the home (*casa*) space is evolving amid socio-technological change. The smartphone is another kind of home, just as it is another kind of companion, wherein individuals exercise some, but not total, control over who or what is present or welcome.

Conclusion: ageing together, differently

Virginia Woolf described ageing as 'forever altering one's aspect to the sun'. This is a metaphorical description that Woolf employs, with an allusion to Shakespeare, to describe repositioning oneself vis-à-vis death, as the setting of the sun.[11] The story of ageing with smartphones presented in this volume has been about how people are altering their position to ageing, to themselves and to each other, through various forms of social participation. The longer-standing wisdom seen across Italy and the world, that social life is an important factor in ageing happily and healthily, partly explains the appeal of NoLo and Milan as a place in which to grow older – an urban-digital environment that is itself rejuvenating and growing. The smartphone is a key instrument for fostering forms of social participation, but also features in the modulating of it by allowing one to adjust one's 'social availability'. Through it, different people had gained exposure to new ways of accessing and sharing information about hobbies and activities, health and care, generational experiences and belief structures and moral systems.

The convergence of all the core themes of the book leads to the conclusion that ageing with smartphones in this contemporary urban and digital context in Italy is about living not only with ambiguity and contradiction, but also with hope and possibility, as people develop capacities in and curiosities about a changing world, changing selves and changing relationships with others.

If ageing is about living, then, as stories and conversations throughout this book illustrate, it is also about living together differently.

Notes

1. Lambek 2010.
2. On the creation and development of the concept of the social district in Italy, see chapter 1.
3. For contemporary examples of ideas about cohousing see the discussion by architect Grace Kim and others at Kim 2020.
4. See Anderson 2019.
5. For further discussion and historical overviews of scholarship on ageing, and a wealth of research in this field, see Sokolovsky 2020b.
6. Nussbaum and Levmore (2017) present a series of critical discussions about the stigmas of ageing in the US context and a number of recommendations for moving critical thinking about ageing forward.
7. Castells 2010.
8. On the relationship between how the smartphone is conceived of (in this book and among research participants) in relation to other devices such as tablets, see the notion of 'Screen Ecology' discussed in chapter 5, which is outlined in further detail in Miller et al. 2021.
9. The relationship between smartphones and surveillance capitalism is a significant topic of ongoing critical and public discussion, which is beyond the scope of this book. This theme is discussed in Miller et al. 2021 (especially chapter 9).
10. For more on the theory of the 'Transportal Home' see Miller et al. 2021.
11. Virginia Woolf often alludes to Shakespeare in her theoretical descriptions of ageing, quoting, for example, from *Cymbeline*, Act IV, sc. ii: 'Fear no more the heat o' the sun / Nor the furious winter's rages'. Cited in Sedon 2010, 167, 168.

Bibliography

Abbasi, Khadija and Alessandro Monsutti. 2017. '"To everyone, homeland is Kashmir": Cultural conceptions of migration, wellbeing, adulthood and future among young Afghans in Europe'. Becoming Adult Working Papers, Graduate Institute of International and Development Studies, Geneva. https://repository.graduateinstitute.ch/record/296938?ln=en. Accessed 21 November 2020.

Agenzia per l'Italia Digitale. 2020. 'Solidarietà Digitale al servizio di studenti e commercianti'. Solidarietà Digitale. https://solidarietadigitale.agid.gov.it/#/. Accessed 21 November 2020.

Agustoni, Alfredo and Alfredi Alietti. 2014. 'It doesn't seem like Christmas here anymore. Local representations of migrants and conflicts in a neighbourhood of Milan: A note from an ethnographic research'. *International Journal of Humanities and Social Science* 4 (12): 53–63.

Ahang, Basir. 2015. *Sogni di tregua*. Asola: Gilgamesh Edizioni.

Ahlin, Tanja. 2018. 'Only near is dear? Doing elderly care with everyday ICTs in Indian transnational families'. *Medical Anthropology Quarterly* 32 (1): 85–102. https://doi.org/10.1111/maq.12404.

Ahlin, Tanja. 2020. 'Frequent callers: "Good care" with ICTs in Indian transnational families'. *Medical Anthropology Quarterly* 39 (1): 69–82. https://doi.org/10.1080/01459740.2018.1532424.

Ahmed, Sara. 2004a. 'Affective economies'. *Social Text* 22 (2): 117–39. https://doi.org/10.1215/01642472-22-2_79-117.

Ahmed, Sara. 2004b. *The Cultural Politics of Emotion*. Edinburgh: Edinburgh University Press.

Al Jazeera. 2020. 'Italian grandma's coronavirus advice'. *Al Jazeera*, 23 March 2020. https://www.aljazeera.com/programmes/newsfeed/2020/03/italian-grandma-coronavirus-advice-200323105353496.html. Accessed 21 November 2020.

Amazon Web Services. 2020. 'Healthcare & life sciences: From benchtop to bedside, innovate faster to improve patient outcomes and lower costs'. Amazon Web Services website. 2020. https://aws.amazon.com/health/. Accessed 21 November 2020.

Amelina, Anna, Devrimsel D. Nergiz, Thomas Faist and Nina Glick Schiller (eds). 2012. *Beyond Methodological Nationalism: Research methodologies for cross-border studies*. New York: Routledge.

Amirkhanyan, Anna A. and Douglas A. Wolf. 2006. 'Parent care and the stress process: Findings from panel data'. *Journals of Gerontology Series B* 61 (5): S248–S255.

Andall, Jacqueline. 2002. 'Second-generation attitude? African-Italians in Milan'. *Journal of Ethnic and Migration Studies* 28 (3): 389–407. https://doi.org/10.1080/13691830220146518.

Anderson, Bridget. 2019. 'New directions in migration studies: Towards methodological de-nationalism'. *Comparative Migration Studies* 7 (36). https://doi.org/10.1186/s40878-019-0140-8.

Anthropology of Smartphones and Smart Ageing. 2020. 'Anthropology of Smartphones and Smart Ageing – UCL'. https://www.ucl.ac.uk/anthropology/assa/. Accessed 21 November 2020.

Antonsich, Marco, Silvia Camilotti, Lorenzo Mari, Stefano Pasta, Valeria Pecorelli, Roberta Petrillo and Sonia Pozzi. 2016. 'New Italians: The re-making of the nation in the age of migration'. New Italians research website. http://newitalians.eu/en/. Accessed 21 November 2020.

Auser / Associazione per l'invecchiamento attivo. 2020. https://www.auser.it/. Accessed 21 November 2020.

Balabio, Barbara. 2016. 'Sanità Digitale: Non più miraggio, non ancora realtà'. Osservatori.Net Digital Innovation. https://www.osservatori.net/it/ricerche/infografiche/sanita-digitale-non-piu-miraggio-non-ancora-realta. Accessed 20 May 2020.

Baldassar, Loretta. 2007. 'Transnational families and aged care: The mobility of care and the migrancy of ageing'. *Journal of Ethnic and Migration Studies* 33 (2): 275–97. https://doi.org/10.1080/13691830601154252.

Balibar, Etienne. 2002. 'The nation form: History and ideology'. In *Race, Nation, Class: Ambiguous Identities*, edited by Etienne Balibar and Immanuel Wallerstein, translated by Chris Turner, 86–106. London and New York: Verso.

Balibar, Etienne. 2004. Translated by James Swenson. *We, the People of Europe? Reflections on transnational citizenship* (Translation/Transnation). Princeton, NJ: Princeton University Press.

Barassi, Veronica. 2020. *Child Data Citizen: How tech companies are profiling us from before birth.* Cambridge, MA: MIT Press.

Barberis, Eduardo, Alba Angelucci, Ryan Jepson and Yuri Kazepov. 2017. *DIVERCITIES: Dealing with urban diversity – The case of Milan*. Utrecht: Utrecht University, Faculty of Geosciences. https://www.urbandivercities.eu/wp-content/uploads/2017/02/Divercities-City-Book-Milan.pdf. Accessed 22 November 2020.

Barnett, Rosalind C., Nancy L. Marshall and Judith D. Singer. 1992. 'Job experiences over time, multiple roles, and women's mental health: A longitudinal study'. *Journal of Personality and Social Psychology* 62 (4): 634–44. https://doi.org/10.1037/0022-3514.62.4.634.

Ben-Yehoyada, Naor, Heath Cabot and Paul A. Silverstein. 2020. 'Introduction: Remapping Mediterranean anthropology'. *History and Anthropology* 31 (1): 1–21. https://doi.org/10.1080/02757206.2019.1684274.

Bereketeab, R. 2007. 'The Eritrean diaspora: Myth and reality'. In *The Role of Diasporas in Peace, Democracy and Development in the Horn of Africa*, edited by Ulf Johansson Dahre. Lund: Dept of Sociology, Lund University.

Bergmann, Sigurd. 2008. 'The beauty of speed or the discovery of slowness – Why do we need to rethink mobility?' In *The Ethics of Mobilities: Rethinking place, exclusion, freedom and environment*, edited by Sigurd Bergmann and Tore Sager, 13–24. Aldershot: Ashgate.

Bernal, Victoria. 2006. 'Diaspora, cyberspace and political imagination: The Eritrean diaspora online'. *Global Networks* 6 (2): 161–79. https://doi.org/10.1111/j.1471-0374.2006.00139.x.

Bettio, Francesca, Annamaria Simonazzi and Paola Villa. 2006. 'Change in care regimes and female migration: The "care drain" in the Mediterranean'. *Journal of European Social Policy* 16 (3): 271–85. https://doi.org/10.1177/0958928706065598.

Bini, Valerio and Giuseppe Gambazza. 2019. 'The reception of asylum seekers in urban areas: The case of the city of Milan'. *Belgeo* (online) 1. https://doi.org/10.4000/belgeo.35559.

Birot, Megan. 2018. 'What does a plummeting birth rate mean for Italy's future?' *The Local*, 27 June. https://www.thelocal.it/20180627/italy-declining-birthrate-population. Accessed 24 November 2020.

Bonduel, Ludovic. 2018. 'Smart city development: The Milan model'. *Labgov.City* (blog), 6 November 2018. https://labgov.city/theurbanmedialab/smart-city-development-the-milan-mode/. Accessed 22 November 2020.

Bourdieu, P. 1989. 'Social space and symbolic power'. *Sociological Theory* 7 (1): 14–25.

Brenna, Elenka and Cinzia Di Novi. 2015. 'Is caring for elderly parents detrimental to women's mental health? The influence of the European North–South gradient'. Healthy Ageing and the Labour Market (HALM) Working Paper no. 1, Università Cattolica del Sacro Cuore, Dipartimento di Economia e Finanza.

Bryceson, Deborah Fahy. 2019. 'Transnational families negotiating migration and care life cycles across nation-state borders'. *Journal of Ethnic and Migration Studies* 45 (16): 3042–64. https://doi.org/10.1080/1369183X.2018.1547017.

Bullaro, Grace Russo, ed. 2010. *From Terrone to Extracomunitario: New manifestations of racism in contemporary Italian cinema: Shifting demographics and changing images in a multi-cultural globalized society*. Leicester: Troubador.

Çağlar, Ayşe and Nina Glick Schiller. 2015. 'A multiscalar perspective on cities and migration: A comment on the symposium' (*Rescaling immigration paths: Emerging settlement patterns beyond gateway cities*, edited by Eduardo Barberis and Emmanuele Pavolini). *Sociologica, Italian Journal of Sociology Online* 9 (2). https://doi.org/10.2383/81432.

Çağlar, Ayşe and Nina Glick Schiller. 2018. *Migrants and City-Making: Dispossession, displacement, and urban regeneration*. Durham, NC: Duke University Press.

Caglioni, Lorenzo. 2020. *Hipster: Subcultura della crisi*. Aprilia: Novalogos.

Camarda, Maria Teresa. 2019. 'Le nonne di Campoli con i bambini migranti in braccio. I messaggi sui social: "Questa è l'Italia che voglio"'. *Tpi.It*, 26 July. https://www.tpi.it/cronaca/foto-nonne-campoli-bambini-migranti-20190726380145/. Accessed 22 November 2020.

CARE. 2016. 'CARE: Common Approach for REfugees and Other Migrants' Health (press release)'. Care for Migrants. http://careformigrants.eu/wp-content/uploads/2016/07/CARE-Project_Press-Release_FINAL_rev.pdf. Accessed 22 November 2020.

Carroll, Timothy, Antonia Walford and Shireen Walton, eds. 2020. *Lineages and Advancements in Material Culture Studies: Perspectives from UCL anthropology*. London: Bloomsbury Academic.

Castells, M. 1996. *The Rise of the Network Society*. Oxford: Blackwell.

Castells, M. 2010. *The Information Age: Economy, society and culture. Volume 1: The Rise of the Network Society*. 2nd edn. Chichester: Wiley-Blackwell.

Centro Risorse LGBTI (2017) *#Contiamoci! Una fotografia delle famiglie LGBTQI in Italia*. http://www.risorselgbti.eu/contiamoci-famiglie-lgbtqi/. Accessed 24 November 2020.

Chisholm, June F. 1999. 'The sandwich generation'. *Journal of Social Distress and Homelessness* 8 (3): 177–91. https://doi.org/10.1023/A:1021368826791.

Civenti, Graziella. 2015. *Una casa tutta per sé: Indagine sulle donne che vivono da sole* (Transizioni e Politiche Pubbliche 18). Milan: Franco Angeli.

Clough Marinaro, Isabella and James Walston. 2010. 'Italy's "second generations": The sons and daughters of migrants'. *Bulletin of Italian Politics* 2 (1): 5–19.

Coe, Norma B. and Courtney Harold Van Houtven. 2009. 'Caring for mom and neglecting yourself? The health effects of caring for an elderly parent'. *Health Economics* 18 (9): 991–1010. https://doi.org/10.1002/hec.1512.

Cohen, Elizabeth F. 2009. *Semi-Citizenship in Democratic Politics*. Cambridge: Cambridge University Press.

Cohen, Elizabeth F. 2018. *The Political Value of Time: Citizenship, duration, and democratic justice*. Cambridge and New York: Cambridge University Press.

Cole, Jeffrey. 1997. *The New Racism in Europe: A Sicilian ethnography* (Cambridge Studies in Social and Cultural Anthropology 107). Cambridge: Cambridge University Press.

Collins English Dictionary. 2020. Definition of 'fake news'. https://www.collinsdictionary.com/dictionary/english/fake-news. Accessed 22 November 2020.

Comaroff, John L. and Jean Comaroff. 1997. *Of Revelation and Revolution. Volume 2: The dialectics of modernity on a south african frontier*. Chicago, IL: University of Chicago Press.

Comune di Milano. 2018. 'Popolazione residente nel Comune di Milano al 31/12/2018'. http://mediagallery.comune.milano.it/cdm/objects/changeme:111656/datastreams/dataStream5445508674048928/content?pgpath=/SA_SiteContent/SEGUI_AMMINISTRAZIONE/DATI_STATISTICI/Popolazione_residente_a_Milano. Accessed 22 November 2020.

Coordinamento Nazionale Nuove Generazioni Italiane. 2020. Home page. http://conngi.it/. Accessed 22 November 2020.

Coupaye, Ludovic. 2020. '"Things ain't the same anymore": Towards an anthropology of technical objects (or "When Leroi-Gourhan and Simondon meet MCS")'. In *Lineages and Advancements in Material Culture Studies: Perspectives from UCL anthropology*, edited by Timothy Carroll, Antonia Walford and Shireen Walton, 46–60. London: Bloomsbury Academic.

Cruz, Edgar. 2014. 'Onlife ethnography: Researching technologically mediated worlds'. Talk delivered at the Oxford Internet Institute on Thursday 13 March as part of the OxDEG seminar series. https://www.oii.ox.ac.uk/events/onlife-ethnography-researching-technologically-mediated-worlds/. Accessed 16 January 2021.

Daly, Faïçal. 1999. 'Tunisian migrants and their experience of racism in Modena'. *Modern Italy* 4 (2): 173–89. https://doi.org/10.1080/13532949908454828.

Das, Veena. 2007. *Life and Words: Violence and the descent into the ordinary*. Berkeley and Los Angeles: University of California Press.

Datta, Ayona. 2019. 'Postcolonial urban futures: Imagining and governing India's smart urban age'. *Environment and Planning D: Society and Space* 37 (3): 393–410. https://doi.org/10.1177/0263775818800721.

De Pasquale, Concetta, Federica Sciacca and Zira Hichy. 2017. 'Italian validation of smartphone addiction scale short version for adolescents and young adults (SAS-SV)'. *Psychology* 8 (10): 1513–18. https://doi.org/10.4236/psych.2017.810100.

Del Boca, Daniela, Marilena Locatelli and Daniela Vuri. 2005. 'Child-care choices by working mothers: The case of Italy'. *Review of Economics of the Household* 3 (4): 453–77. https://doi.org/10.1007/s11150-005-4944-y.

Del Giudice, Luisa. 1988. '*Ninna-nanna*-nonsense? Fears, dreams, and falling in the Italian lullaby'. *Oral Tradition* 3 (3): 270–93.

Deleuze, Gilles and Félix Guattari. 1987. Translated by Brian Massumi. *A Thousand Plateaus: Capitalism and schizophrenia*. London: Continuum.

DeviceAtlas. 2019. 'The most popular smartphones in 2019 [Italy]'. DeviceAtlas, 17 September. https://deviceatlas.com/blog/most-popular-smartphones#italy. Accessed 31 January 2021.

Devillanova, Carlo. 2012. 'Immigrants' access to health care services in Italy: New evidence from survey data'. MS. Università Bocconi, Milan. https://www.siecon.org/sites/siecon.org/files/oldfiles/uploads/2012/08/Devillanova.pdf. Accessed 22 November 2020.

Devillanova, Carlo and Tommaso Frattini. 2016. 'Inequities in immigrants' access to health care services: Disentangling potential barriers'. *International Journal of Manpower* 37 (7): 1191–1208. https://doi.org/10.1108/IJM-08-2015-0114.

Di Gessa, Giorgio, Karen Glaser and Anthea Tinker. 2016. 'The impact of caring for grandchildren on the health of grandparents in Europe: A lifecourse approach'. *Social Science & Medicine* 152 (March): 166–75. https://doi.org/10.1016/j.socscimed.2016.01.041.

Di Iorio, Martina. 2020. 'Daniele Dodaro: ovvero il sindaco di NoLo, creatore della NoLo Social District'. *Zero* Milano, 3/7 July. https://zero.eu/en/persone/daniele-dodaro/. Accessed 18 January 2021.

Di Minco, Lidia. 2017. 'Electronic Health Record (EHR): Implementation in Italy'. https://www.consorzioarsenal.it/c/document_library/get_file?uuid=ac838533-9ec4-4546-95f3-2356170acc43&groupId=10157. Accessed 23 November 2020.

Donini, Antonio, Alessandro Monsutti and Giulia Scalettaris. 2016. 'Afghans on the move: Seeking protection and refuge in Europe'. Global Migration Research Paper no. 17. Global Migration Centre, Graduate Institute Geneva.

El-Tayeb, Fatima. 2011. *European Others: Queering ethnicity in postnational Europe* (Difference Incorporated). Minneapolis: University of Minnesota Press.

European Commission. 2020. 'Italy – old-age benefits'. Employment, Social Affairs & Inclusion. https://ec.europa.eu/social/main.jsp?catId=1116&langId=en&intPageId=4625. Accessed 22 November 2020.

Eurostat. 2017a. 'Archive: People in the EU – statistics on household and family structures'. Accessed 31 January 2021. https://ec.europa.eu/eurostat/statistics-explained/index.php?title=Archive:People_in_the_EU_-_statistics_on_household_and_family_structures.

Eurostat. 2017b. 'When are they ready to leave the nest?' Eurostat News. 3 May. https://ec.europa.eu/eurostat/web/products-eurostat-news/-/EDN-20170503-1?inheritRedirect=true&redirect=%20per%20cent2Feurostat%20per%20cent2F. Accessed 22 November 2020.

Eurostat. 2019. 'Euro area unemployment at 7.5%, EU28 at 6.3%'. Eurostat newsrelease euroindicators. 29 November. https://ec.europa.eu/eurostat/documents/2995521/10075437/3-29112019-BP-EN.PDF/749d647b-6961-5d3d-a8c6-8eaca44a539d. Accessed 22 November 2020.

Eurostat. 2020. 'Marriage and divorce statistics: Statistics explained'. https://ec.europa.eu/eurostat/statistics-explained/pdfscache/6790.pdf. Accessed 29 May 2020.

Facchini, Carla. 2016. 'Invecchiare curando i genitori'. Osservatorio Senior. https://osservatoriosenior.it/2016/10/invecchiare-curando-i-genitori/. Accessed 2 June 2020.

Favell, Adrian and Andrew Geddes, eds. 1999. *The Politics of Belonging: Migrants and minorities in contemporary Europe*. Aldershot: Ashgate.

Favero, Paolo S. H. 2017. *Dentro e oltre l'immagine: Saggi sulla cultura visiva e politica nell'Italia conteporanea*. Milan: Meltemi.

Favero, Paolo S. H. 2018. *The Present Image: Visible stories in a digital habitat*. Basingstoke: Palgrave Macmillan.

Foot, John. 1995. 'The family and the "economic miracle": Social transformation, work, leisure and development at Bovisa and Comasina (Milan), 1950–70'. *Contemporary European History* 4 (3): 315–38. https://doi.org/10.1017/S0960777300003507.

Foot, John. 1997. 'Migration and the "miracle" at Milan: The neighbourhoods of Baggio, Barona, Bovisa and Comasina in the 1950s and 1960s'. *Journal of Historical Sociology* 10 (2): 184–213. https://doi.org/10.1111/1467-6443.00036.

Foot, John M. 1999. 'Cinema and the city: Milan and Luchino Visconti's *Rocco and his Brothers* (1960)'. *Journal of Modern Italian Studies* 4 (2): 209–35. https://doi.org/10.1080/13545719908455007.

Foot, John. 2001. *Milan since the Miracle: City, culture and identity*. Oxford: Berg.

Foot, John. 1995. 'The family and the "economic miracle": Social transformation, work, leisure and development at Bovisa and Comasina (Milan), 1950–1970'. *Contemporary European History* 4 (3): 315–38.
Foschini, Fabrizio and Jelena Bjelica. 2017. 'Afghan asylum seekers in Italy: A place of temporary respite'. Afghanistan Analysts Network. 13 September 2017. https://www.afghanistan-analysts.org/en/reports/migration/afghan-asylum-seekers-in-italy-a-place-of-temporary-respite/. Accessed 22 November 2020.
Galeazzo, P. 1994. 'La nuova immigrazione a Milano: Il caso dell'Eritrea'. In *Tra due rive: La nuova immigrazione a Milano*, edited by Giuseppe Barile, A. Dal Lago, A. Marchetti and P. Galeazzo, 367–441. Milan: Franco Angeli.
Georgiou, Myria. 2013. *Media and the City: Cosmopolitanism and difference*. Cambridge: Polity.
Giordano, Cristiana. 2014. *Migrants in Translation: Caring and the logics of difference in contemporary Italy*. Oakland: University of California Press.
Giuffrida, Angela. 2018. 'In Italy's "hospitality town", migrants fight to save mayor who gave them a new home'. *The Guardian*, 7 October. https://www.theguardian.com/world/2018/oct/07/migrants-fight-save-riace-mayor-who-gave-them-home. Accessed 22 November 2020.
Glick Schiller, Nina. 2014. 'Transnationality'. In *A Companion to Urban Anthropology*, edited by Donald M. Nonini, 291–305. Chichester: John Wiley & Sons.
Glick Schiller, Nina, Linda Basch and Cristina Blanc-Szanton. 1992. 'Transnationalism: A new analytic framework for understanding migration'. *Annals of the New York Academy of Sciences* 645 (1): 1–24. https://doi.org/10.1111/j.1749-6632.1992.tb33484.
Goffman, Erving. 1961. *Asylums: Essays on the social situation of mental patients and other inmates*. Garden City, NY: Anchor Books.
Goldberg, David Theo. 2002. *The Racial State*. Malden, MA: Blackwell Publishers.
Goldberg, David Theo. 2006. 'Racial Europeanization'. *Ethnic and Racial Studies* 29 (2): 331–64. https://doi.org/10.1080/01419870500465611.
Greiner, Clemens and Patrick Sakdapolrak. 2013. 'Translocality: Concepts, applications and emerging research perspectives'. *Geography Compass* 7 (5): 373–84. https://doi.org/10.1111/gec3.12048.
Grey Panthers. 2016. 'SANITÀ DIGITALE: Il miraggio diventa realtà'. 4 June. https://www.grey-panthers.it/speciale/speciali/digitale/. Accessed 12 December 2020.
Grey Panthers. 2018. 'Sanità Digitale, oggi: Facciamo insieme il punto, e monitoriamo anche le APP'. 23 September. https://www.grey-panthers.it/speciale/speciali/sanita-digitale/. Accessed 22 November 2020.
The Guardian. 2020. 'Coronavirus: Quarantined Italians sing from balconies to lift spirits – video'. *The Guardian*, 13 March. https://www.theguardian.com/world/video/2020/mar/13/coronavirus-quarantined-italians-sing-from-balconies-to-lift-spirits-video. Accessed 24 November 2020.
Hall, Suzanne, Kimberley Rennick and Rachel Williams. 2019. *The Perennials: The future of ageing*. Ipsos MORI. https://www.ipsos.com/sites/default/files/ct/news/documents/2019-02/thinks_theperennials.pdf. Accessed 22 November 2020.
Hanifi, M. Jamil. 2000. 'Anthropology and the representation of recent migrations from Afghanistan'. In *Rethinking Refuge and Displacement: Selected papers on refugees and immigrants*, vol. 8, edited by Elzbieta M. Gozdziak and Dianna J. Shandy, 291–321. Arlington, VA: American Anthropological Association.
Hazara International. 2011. 'Italian Hazaras' protest in Milan Italy'. 9 July. http://www.hazarapeople.com/2011/07/12/italian-hazaras'-protest-in-milan-italy/. Accessed 22 November 2020.
Iezzi, Vincent M. 2005. *More Coffee with Nonna: Stories of my Italian grandmother*. Cincinnati, OH: Servant Books.
Ingold, T. 2010. 'Bringing things to life: Creative entanglements in a world of materials'. In NCRM Working Paper no. 15. ESRC National Centre for Research Methods, University of Manchester.
Istituto di Ricerche Educative e Formative (IREF). 2007. 'Il welfare "fatto in casa": Indagine nazionale sui collaboratori domestici stranieri che lavorano a sostegno delle famiglie Italiane'. Rome. http://qualificare.info/upload/Il%20welfare%20fatto%20in%20casa.pdf. Accessed 23 November 2020.
Jackson, Michael. 2013a. *Lifeworlds: Essays in existential anthropology*. Chicago, IL: University of Chicago Press.
Jackson, Michael. 2013b. *The Wherewithal of Life: Ethics, migration, and the question of well-being*. Berkeley and Los Angeles: University of California Press.

Johnson, Miles. 2020. 'Italy's collapsing birth rate rings demographic alarm bells'. *Financial Times*, 17 January. https://www.ft.com/content/a9d1fe0c-2306-11ea-92da-f0c92e957a96. Accessed 9 January 2021.

Jones, Tobias. 2003. *The Dark Heart of Italy*. London: Faber and Faber.

Katz, Steven. 2003. 'Critical gerontological theory: Intellectual fieldwork and the nomadic life of ideas'. In *The Need for Theory: Critical approaches to social gerontology*, edited by Simon Biggs, Ariela Lowenstein and Jon Hendricks, 15–31. Amityville, NY: Baywood Publishing Company.

Katz, Steven. 2013. 'Active and successful aging. Lifestyle as gerontological idea'. *Recherches Sociologiques et Anthropologiques* 44 (1): 33–49. https://doi.org/10.4000/rsa.910.

Kavedžija, Iza. 2019. *Making Meaningful Lives: Tales from an aging Japan*. Contemporary Ethnography. Philadelphia: University of Pennsylvania Press.

Kertzer, David I. and Richard P. Saller, eds. 1991. *The Family in Italy: From antiquity to the present*. New Haven, CT; London: Yale University Press.

Kieffer, Charles M. 2020. 'Hazāra: iv. Hazāragi dialect'. *Encyclopædia Iranica*, online edition. http://www.iranicaonline.org/articles/hazara-4#. Accessed 22 November 2020.

Kim, Grace. 2020. 'Cohousing'. Schemata Workshop. https://www.schemataworkshop.com/passions-cohousing. Accessed 23 November 2020.

Kostera, Thomas. 2019. 'Digital health – Europe is moving at different speeds'. *The Digital Patient* (blog), 25 April. https://blog.der-digitale-patient.de/en/digital-health-europe/. Accessed 23 November 2020.

Králová, Jana. 2015. 'What is social death?' *Contemporary Social Science* 10 (3): 235–48. https://doi.org/10.1080/21582041.2015.1114407.

Kuruvilla, Gabriella. 2012. *Milano, fin qui tutto bene* (Contromano). Rome: Laterza.

La Bella, Cristina. 2019. 'Campoli, nonne italiane coi bimbi migranti in braccio: La foto stupenda diventa virale'. *UrbanPost* (blog), 26 July. https://urbanpost.it/campoli-nonne-italiane-bimbi-migranti-foto-virale/. Accessed 23 November 2020.

La Repubblica. 2018. 'Sorpresa, gli over 55 a tutto social: sono inseparabili dallo smartphone'. *La Repubblica*, 29 September. https://www.repubblica.it/tecnologia/mobile/2018/09/29/news/sorpresa_8_anziani_su_10_sono_inseparabili_dallo_smartphone-207710584/?ref=RHPPRB-BH-I0-C4-P1-S1.4-T1. Accessed 23 November 2020.

Lamb, Sarah. 2009. *Aging and the Indian Diaspora: Cosmopolitan families in India and abroad*. Bloomington: Indiana University Press.

Lamb, Sarah, ed. 2017. *Successful Aging as a Contemporary Obsession: Global perspectives*. New Brunswick, NJ: Rutgers University Press.

Lamb, Sarah. 2020. '"You don't have to act or feel old": Successful aging as a U.S. cultural project'. In *The Cultural Context of Aging: Worldwide perspectives*, 4th edn, edited by Jay Sokolovsky, 49–64. Santa Barbara, CA: Praeger.

Lambek, Michael, ed. 2010. *Ordinary Ethics: Anthropology, language, and action*. New York: Fordham University Press.

Lane, Jeffrey. 2019. *The Digital Street*. Oxford: Oxford University Press.

Leopold, Thomas and Jan Skopek. 2015. 'The demography of grandparenthood: An international profile'. *Social Force* 94 (2): 801–32. https://doi.org/10.1093/sf/sov066.

Levitt, Peggy and Nina Glick Schiller. 2004. 'Conceptualizing simultaneity: A transnational social field perspective on society'. *International Migration Review* 38 (3): 1002–39. https://doi.org/10.1111/j.1747-7379.2004.tb00227.x.

Livingstone, Sonia and Alicia Blum-Ross. 2020. *Parenting for a Digital Future: How hopes and fears about technology shape children's lives*. Oxford: Oxford University Press.

Luque-Ayala, Andrés and Simon Marvin. 2015. 'Developing a critical understanding of Smart Urbanism?' *Urban Studies* 52 (12): 2105–16.

MacDougall, David. 1992. 'Photo hierarchicus: Signs and mirrors in Indian photography'. *Visual Anthropology* 5 (2): 103–29. https://doi.org/10.1080/08949468.1992.9966581.

Macnicol, John. 2015. *Neoliberalising Old Age*. Cambridge: Cambridge University Press.

Madianou, Mirca and Daniel Miller. 2012. *Migration and New Media: Transnational families and polymedia*. Abingdon; New York: Routledge.

Mainil, T., E. Eijgelaar, J. Klijs, J. Nawijn and P. Peeters. 2017. 'Research for TRAN Committee – Health tourism in the EU: A general investigation'. European Parliament, Policy Department for structural and Cohesion Policies, Brussels. https://www.europarl.europa.eu/RegData/etudes/STUD/2017/601985/IPOL_STU%282017%29601985_EN.pdf. Accessed 12 December 2020.

Maly, Ico and Piia Varis. 2016. 'The 21st-century hipster: On micro-populations in times of super-diversity'. *European Journal of Cultural Studies* 19 (6): 637–53. https://doi.org/10.1177/1367549415597920.

Mapelli, Vittorio. 2012. *Il sistema sanitario italiano*. Bologna: Il mulino.

Marshall, T. H. 1950. 'Citizenship and social class'. In *Citizenship and Social Class and Other Essays*, 1–85. Cambridge: Cambridge University Press.

McKay, Deirdre. 2010. 'On the face of Facebook: Historical images and personhood in Filipino social networking'. *History and Anthropology* 21 (4): 479–98. https://doi.org/10.1080/02757206.2010.522311.

McKay, Deirdre. 2012. *Global Filipinos: Migrants' lives in the global village*. Bloomington: Indiana University Press.

McKay, Deidre. 2016. *An Archipelago of Care: Filipino migrants and global networks*. Bloomington: Indiana University Press.

Merola, Francesco. 2018. 'Italiani, sempre più smartphone-mania: Il 61% li usa a letto, il 34% a tavola'. *La Repubblica*, 26 June. https://www.repubblica.it/tecnologia/2018/06/26/news/dipendenza_degli_italiani_ad_internet-200069807/. Accessed 23 November 2020.

Michael, Janna. 2015. 'It's really not hip to be a hipster: Negotiating trends and authenticity in the cultural field'. *Journal of Consumer Culture* 15 (2): 163–82. https://doi.org/10.1177/1469540513493206.

Mikkelsen, Henrik Hvenegaard. 2017. 'Never too late for pleasure: Aging, neoliberalism, and the politics of potentiality in Denmark'. *American Ethnologist* 44 (4): 646–56. https://doi.org/10.1111/amet.12563.

Milano Digital Week. 2020. 'Città trasformata'. https://www.milanodigitalweek.com. Accessed 23 November 2020.

Miller, Daniel, ed. 2001. *Home Possessions: Material culture behind closed doors*. Oxford: Berg.

Miller, Daniel. 2008. *The Comfort of Things*. Cambridge: Polity.

Miller, Daniel. 2010. *Stuff*. Cambridge: Polity.

Miller, Daniel, Laila Abed Rabho, Patrick Awondo, Maya de Vries, Marília Duque, Pauline Garvey, Laura Haapio-Kirk, Charlotte Hawkins, Alfonso Otaegui, Shireen Walton and Xinyuan Wang. 2021. *The Global Smartphone: Beyond a youth technology*. London: UCL Press.

Miller, Daniel, Elisabetta Costa, Nell Haynes, Tom McDonald, Razvan Nicolescu, Jolynna Sinanan, Juliano Spyer, Shriram Venkatraman and Xinyuan Wang. 2016. *How the World Changed Social Media*. London: UCL Press.

Miller, Daniel and Shireen Walton. 2018. 'What's the opposite of Facebook? Err … it's (still) Facebook'. *UCL: Anthropology of Smartphones and Smart Ageing blog*, 28 June. https://blogs.ucl.ac.uk/assa/2018/06/28/whats-the-opposite-of-facebook-err-its-still-facebook-by-daniel-miller-and-shireen-walton. Accessed 23 November 2020.

Ministero della Salute (Ministry of Health). 2020a. 'Covid-19, occhio alle bufale'. http://www.salute.gov.it/portale/news/p3_2_1_1_1.jsp?lingua=italiano&menu=notizie&p=dalministero&id=4380. Accessed 23 November 2020.

Ministero della Salute (Ministry of Health). 2020b. 'Nuovo coronavirus'. http://www.salute.gov.it/nuovocoronavirus. Accessed 23 November 2020.

Mol, Annemarie, Ingunn Moser and Jeannette Pols, eds. 2010. *Care in Practice: On tinkering in clinics, homes and farms*. Bielefeld: transcript.

Monsutti, Alessandro. 2004. 'Cooperation, remittances, and kinship among the Hazaras'. *Iranian Studies* 37 (2): 219–40. https://doi.org/10.1080/0021086042000268183.

Monsutti, Alessandro. 2005. Translated by Patrick Camiller. *War and Migration: Social networks and economic strategies of the Hazaras of Afghanistan*. Abingdon: Routledge.

Monsutti, Alessandro. 2007. 'Migration as a rite of passage: Young Afghans building masculinity and adulthood in Iran'. *Iranian Studies* 40 (2): 167–85.

Monsutti, Alessandro. 2018. 'Mobility as a political act'. *Ethnic and Racial Studies* 41 (3): 448–55. https://doi.org/10.1080/01419870.2018.1388421.

Morning Future. 2019. 'Smart City? Milan is leading the game: Here are its 4 secrets'. *Morning Future*, 17 April. https://www.morningfuture.com/en/article/2019/04/17/smart-city-milano-roberta-cocco/596/. Accessed 23 November 2020.

Muehlebach, Andrea Karin. 2012. *The Moral Neoliberal: Welfare and citizenship in Italy*. Chicago, IL, and London: University of Chicago Press.

Muehlebach, Andrea. 2013. 'The Catholicization of neoliberalism: On love and welfare in Lombardy, Italy'. *American Anthropologist* 115 (3): 452–65. https://doi.org/10.1111/aman.12028.

Newzoo. 2017. 'Top countries by smartphone users'. https://newzoo.com/insights/rankings/top-countries-by-smartphone-penetration-and-users/. Accessed 4 June 2020.

Next Generation Italy. 2020. 'Next Generation Italy Intercultura Digitale'. https://nextgenerationitaly.com. Accessed 23 November 2020.

Nicolescu, Gabriela. 2020. 'Keeping the elderly alive: Global entanglements and embodied practices in long-term care in southeast Italy'. In *The Cultural Context of Aging: Worldwide perspectives*, 4th edn, edited by Jay Sokolovsky, 632. Santa Barbara, CA: Praeger.

Nonna's Handmade Pasta with Grandma (Chiara Nicolanti). 2020. 'Nonna's – homemade pasta with grandma'. http://www.Nonnas.it. Accessed 23 November 2020.

Nussbaum, Martha C. and Saul Levmore. 2017. *Aging Thoughtfully: Conversations about retirement, romance, wrinkles, and regret*. New York: Oxford University Press.

OED Online. 2020. Oxford University Press. December. https://www.oed.com/view/Entry/67776. Accessed 29 January 2021.

O'Healy, Áine. 2019. *Migrant Anxieties: Italian cinema in a transnational frame*. Bloomington: Indiana University Press.

Olszewska, Zuzanna. 2007. '"A desolate voice": Poetry and identity among young Afghan refugees in Iran'. *Iranian Studies* 40 (2): 203–24. https://doi.org/10.1080/00210860701269550.

Olszewska, Zuzanna. 2015. *The Pearl of Dari: Poetry and personhood among young Afghans in Iran*. Bloomington: Indiana University Press.

Osservatori.net. 2020. Osservatori Digital Innovation–Politecnico di Milan. https://www.osservatori.net/it_it. Accessed 23 November 2020.

Parco Trotter. 2020. AmicitrotterNews. http://www.parcotrotter.org/news/. Accessed 23 November 2020.

Pessoa, Fernando. 2001. *The Book of Disquiet*. Translated by Richard Zenith. London: Allen Lane.

Pieta, Barbara. 2020. 'Web Book Photo Essay: "Differently young" and "non autosufficienti": Managing old-age stigma in an Italian senior center, northeast Italy'. In *The Cultural Context of Aging: Worldwide perspectives*, edited by Jay Sokolovsky, 4th edn, 668. Santa Barbara, CA: Praeger.

Pink, Sarah. 2012. *Situating Everyday Life: Practices and places*. London: SAGE.

Pols, Jeanette. 2012. *Care at a Distance: On the closeness of technology*. Amsterdam: Amsterdam University Press.

Postelnicu, Leontina. 2019. 'Q&A: How Italy is working to digitise healthcare'. *Healthcare IT News*, 23 October. https://www.healthcareitnews.com/news/europe/qa-how-italy-working-digitise-healthcare. Accessed 23 November 2020.

Poushter, Jacob. 2016. 'Smartphone ownership and internet usage continues to climb in emerging economies'. 22 February. PEW Research Center. https://www.pewresearch.org/global/2016/02/22/smartphone-ownership-and-internet-usage-continues-to-climb-in-emerging-economies/. Accessed 23 November 2020.

Prieto-Blanco, Patricia. 2016. '(Digital) photography, experience and space in transnational families: A case study of Spanish-Irish families living in Ireland'. In *Digital Photography and Everyday Life: Empirical studies on material visual practices*, edited by E. Gómez-Cruz and A. Lehmuskallio, 122–40. Abingdon: Routledge.

Publications Office of the European Union. 2011. 'Reducing health inequalities European Parliament Resolution of 8 March 2011 on reducing health inequalities in the EU (2010/2089(INI))'. https://op.europa.eu/en/publication-detail/-/publication/264cecc9-c767-11e1-b84a-01aa75ed71a1/language-en. Accessed 23 November 2020.

Redazione Milano Online. 2020. 'Coronavirus Milano, video-appello e denuncia dell'ospedale Niguarda contro le fake news'. *Corriere della Sera*, 11 March. https://milano.corriere.it/notizie/cronaca/20_marzo_11/coronavirus-milano-video-appello-denuncia-dell-ospedale-niguarda-contro-fake-news-1c2c96b4-639a-11ea-9cf4-1c175ff3bb7c.shtml. Accessed 23 November 2020.

Regina, Sara. 2018. 'Milano, Giorgia Meloni contestata in via Padova: Lei si scatta un selfie'. *Corriere della Sera*, 24 February. https://milano.corriere.it/notizie/cronaca/18_febbraio_24/milano-giorgia-meloni-contestata-via-padova-de-corato-selfie-bella-ciao-9f144206-196a-11e8-9cdc-0f9bea8569f6.shtml?refresh_ce-cp. Accessed 24 November 2020.

Regione Lombardia council. 2020. 'Le app della sanità lombarda'. https://www.fascicolosanitario.regione.lombardia.it/app. Accessed 19 May 2020.

Riley, Lesley D. and Christopher "Pokey" Bowen. 2005. 'The sandwich generation: Challenges and coping strategies of multigenerational families'. *Family Journal* 13 (1): 52–8. https://doi.org/10.1177/1066480704270099.

Romei, Valentina. 2017. 'Italian emigration continues despite strong economic recovery'. *Financial Times*, 13 November.
Rosello, M. 2001. *Postcolonial Hospitality: The immigrant as guest*. Stanford, CA: Stanford University Press.
Rubin, Rose M. and Shelley I. White-Means. 2009. 'Informal caregiving: Dilemmas of sandwiched caregivers'. *Journal of Family and Economic Issues* 30 (3): 252–67. https://doi.org/10.1007/s10834-009-9155-x.
Rugolotto, Silvana, Alice Larotonda and Sjaak van der Geest. 2017. 'How migrants keep Italian families Italian: *Badanti* and the private care of older people'. *International Journal of Migration, Health and Social Care* 13 (2): 185–97. https://doi.org/10.1108/IJMHSC-08-2015-0027.
Salazar, Noel B. and Nelson H. H. Graburn, eds. 2016. *Tourism Imaginaries: Anthropological approaches*. Oxford and New York: Berghahn.
Salvioli, G. 2007. 'Gli anziani e le badanti: Old people and the minders'. *Giornale di Gerontologia* 55 (2): 59–61.
Saraceno, Chiara. 1991. 'The Italian family: Paradoxes of privacy'. Translated by Raymond Rosenthal. In *A History of Private Life: Riddles of identity in modern times*, edited by Antoine Prost and Gérard Vincent, 451–502. Cambridge, MA: Harvard University Press.
Sarti, Raffaella. 2010. 'Who cares for me? Grandparents, nannies and babysitters caring for children in contemporary Italy'. *Paedagogica Historica* 46 (6): 789–802. https://doi.org/10.1080/00309230.2010.526347.
Scancarello, Gea. 2020. *#Addicted: Viaggio dentro le manipolazioni della tecnologia*. Milan: Hoepli.
Schneider, Jane. 1991. 'Spirits and the spirit of capitalism'. In *Religious Regimes and State-Formation: Perspectives from European ethnology*, edited by Eric R. Wolf, 181–220. Albany: State University of New York Press.
Scrinzi, Francesca. 2007. 'Migrations and the restructuring of the welfare state in Italy: Change and continuity in the domestic work sector'. In *Migration and Domestic Work: A European perspective on a global theme*, edited by Helma Lutz, 29–42. Aldershot: Ashgate.
Sedon, Katherine. 2011. 'Moments of aging: Revising mother nature in Virginia Woolf's *Mrs. Dalloway*'. In *Virginia Woolf and the Natural World: Selected papers from the Twentieth Annual International Conference on Virginia Woolf*, edited by Kristin Czarnecki and Carrie Rohman, 163–8. Clemson, SC: Clemson University Digital Press.
Selmi, Giulia, Chiara Sità and Federica de Cordova. 2019. 'When Italian schools meet LGBT parents: Inclusive strategies, ambivalence, silence'. *Scuola Democratica* 4: 225–44. https://doi.org/10.12828/96372.
Simmel, Georg. 1949. 'The sociology of sociability'. *American Journal of Sociology* 55 (3): 254–61. https://doi.org/10.1086/220534.
Smart Building Italia. 2019. 'Milano Smart City Conference'. https://www.smartbuildingitalia.it/en/smart-city-conference/. Accessed 24 November 2020.
Smart Cities Information System (SCIS). 2020. 'Sharing cities site Milan'. https://smartcities-infosystem.eu/scis-projects/demo-sites/sharing-cities-site-milan. Accessed 24 November 2020.
Social Street. 2020. 'Dal virtuale al reale al virtuoso.' http://www.socialstreet.it/. Accessed 24 November 2020.
Sokolovsky, Jay, ed. 2020a. *The Cultural Context of Aging: Worldwide perspectives*. 4th edn. Santa Barbara, CA: Praeger.
Sokolovsky, Jay. 2020b. 'Introduction: A 21st-century global perspective on aging and human maturity in cultural context'. In *The Cultural Context of Aging: Worldwide perspectives*, 4th edn, edited by Jay Sokolovsky, xvii–liii. Santa Barbara, CA: Praeger.
Soysal, Yasemin Nuhoglu. 2000. 'Citizenship and identity: Living in diasporas in post-war Europe?' *Ethnic and Racial Studies* 23 (1): 1–15. https://doi.org/10.1080/014198700329105.
Statista Research Department. 2016. 'Forecast of the smartphone user penetration rate in Italy from 2014 to 2021'. Statista, 24 May. https://www.statista.com/statistics/568187/predicted-smartphone-user-penetration-rate-in-italy/. Accessed 29 May 2020.
Statista Research Department. 2020. 'Total contribution of travel and tourism to GDP in Italy from 2014 to 2029'. Statista, 6 February. https://www.statista.com/statistics/627988/tourism-total-contribution-to-gdp-italy/. Accessed 24 November 2020.
Strathern, Marilyn. 1996. '1989 debate: The concept of society is theoretically obsolete. For the motion (1)'. In *Key Debates in Anthropology*, edited by Tim Ingold, 60–6. London: Routledge.

Taladrid, Stephania. 2020. 'Meet the Italians making music together under coronavirus quarantine'. *The New Yorker*, 19 March. Accessed 24 November 2020. https://www.newyorker.com/culture/video-dept/the-italians-making-music-on-balconies-under-coronavirus-quarantine.

The Local. 2019. 'Italian government unveils plan to tackle smartphone addiction'. 22 July.

Thomassen, Bjørn. 2010. '"Second generation immigrants" or "Italians with immigrant parents"? Italian and European perspectives on immigrants and their children'. *Bulletin of Italian Politics* 2 (1): 21–44.

Tilley, Christopher. 1994. *A Phenomenology of Landscape: Places, paths and monuments*. Oxford: Berg.

TIM. 2020. 'Il Futuro. Insieme'. TIM company website. 2019. https://www.tim.it/reti-veloci-5g. Accessed 24 November 2020.

Today.it reporters. 2019. 'Le nonne italiane coi bimbi migranti in braccio: La foto (bellissima) diventa virale'. *Today.It*, 26 July. http://www.today.it/attualita/nonne-italiane-campoli-foto-bambini-migranti.html. Accessed 24 November 2020.

Toth, Federico. 2014. 'How health care regionalisation in Italy is widening the North–South Gap'. *Health Economics, Policy and Law* 9 (3): 231–49. https://doi.org/10.1017/S1744133114000012.

Tuttitalia. 2020a. 'Cittadini stranieri Milano 2017'. https://www.tuttitalia.it/lombardia/18-milano/statistiche/cittadini-stranieri-2017/. Accessed 24 November 2020.

Tuttitalia. 2020b. 'Italia'. https://www.tuttitalia.it/italia/. Accessed 24 November 2020.

Tuttitalia. 2020c. 'Popolazione per età, sesso e stato civile 2020'. https://www.tuttitalia.it/statistiche/popolazione-eta-sesso-stato-civile-2020/. Accessed 31 January 2021.

United Nations. 2015. 'World population ageing 2015'. ST/ESA/SER.A/390. https://www.un.org/en/development/desa/population/publications/pdf/ageing/WPA2015_Report.pdf. Accessed 24 November 2020.

United Nations. 2017. Department of Economic and Social Affairs, Population Division. *World Population Ageing 2017* (ST/ESA/SER.A/408). Accessed 9 January 2021.

Van Hooren, Franca. 2010. 'When families need immigrants: The exceptional position of migrant domestic workers and care assistants in Italian immigration policy'. *Bulletin of Italian Politics* 2 (2): 21–38.

Van House, Nancy A. 2007. 'Flickr and public image-sharing: Distant closeness and photo exhibition'. *CHI Extended Abstracts*. http://people.ischool.berkeley.edu/~vanhouse/VanHouseFlickrDistantCHI07.pdf. Accessed 24 November 2020.

Verga, Pietro L. 2016. 'Rhetoric in the representation of a multi-ethnic neighbourhood: The case of Via Padova, Milan'. *Antipode* 48 (4): 1080–1101. https://doi.org/10.1111/anti.12229.

Vertovec, Steven. 2007. 'Super-diversity and its implications'. *Ethnic and Racial Studies* 30 (6): 1024–54. https://doi.org/10.1080/01419870701599465.

Vertovec, Steven. 2009. *Transnationalism* (Key Ideas). Abingdon; New York: Routledge.

Vertovec, Steven. 2016. 'Super-diversity as concept and approach: Whence it came, where it's at, and whither it's going'. Keynote address for the conference on 'Super-diversity: A transatlantic conversation' (video), Graduate Center, City University of New York, 4–5 April. https://www.mmg.mpg.de/243448/online-lecture-2016-04-04-vertovec. Accessed 17 January 2021.

Virilio, Paul. 1986. *Speed and Politics*, trans. M. Polizzatti. New York: Semiotext(e).

Walsh, Katie and Lena Näre, eds. 2016. *Transnational Migration and Home in Older Age*. Abingdon: Routledge.

Walton, Shireen. 2016. 'Photographic truth in motion: The case of Iranian photoblogs'. *Anthropology & Photography* 4. http://www.therai.org.uk/images/stories/photography/AnthandPhotoVol4.pdf. Accessed 24 November 2020.

Walton, Shireen. 2020. 'Place-objects: Anthropology of digital photography/s'. In *Lineages and Advancements in Material Culture Studies: Perspectives from UCL anthropology*, edited by Timothy Carroll, Antonia Walford and Shireen Walton, 218–34. London: Routledge.

Wardle, Claire and Hossein Derakshan. 2017. 'One year on, we're still not recognizing the complexity of information disorder online'. *First Draft*, 31 October. https://firstdraftnews.org/latest/coe_infodisorder/. Accessed 24 November 2020.

Weber, Max. 1992. *The Protestant Ethic and the Spirit of Capitalism*. Translated by Talcott Parsons. London: Routledge.

Weibel-Orlando, Joan. 2009. 'La cura degli nostri cari anziani: Family and community elder care roles in contemporary Italy'. In *The Cultural Context of Aging: Worldwide perspectives*, 3rd edn, edited by Jay Sokolovsky, 536–49. Westport, CT: Praeger.

Wimmer, Andreas and Nina Glick Schiller. 2002. 'Methodological nationalism and beyond: Nation-state building, migration and the social sciences'. *Global Networks* 2 (4): 301–34. https://doi.org/10.1111/1471-0374.00043.

Wired Italy. 2019. 'Oggi la tecnologia non ha età'. https://www.wired.it/attualita/tech/2019/01/18/tecnologia-amplifon-eta/?refresh_ce=. Accessed 14 January 2021.

World Health Organization. 2015. 'World report on ageing and health'. https://www.who.int/ageing/events/world-report-2015-launch/en. Accessed 24 November 2020.

World Health Organization. 2020. 'Ageing: Healthy ageing and functional ability'. 26 October. https://www.who.int/ageing/active_ageing/en/. Accessed 24 November 2020.

Zamberletti, Jessica, Giulia Cavrini and Cecilia Tomassini. 2018. 'Grandparents providing childcare in Italy'. *European Journal of Ageing* 15 (3): 265–75. https://doi.org/10.1007/s10433-018-0479-y.

Zigon, Jarrett. 2010. 'Moral and ethical assemblages'. *Anthropological Theory* 10 (1–2): 3–15. https://doi.org/10.1177/1463499610370520.

Zinn, Dorothy Louise. 2010. 'Italy's second generations and the expression of identity through electronic media'. *Bulletin of Italian Politics* 2 (1): 91–113.

Zontini, Elisabetta. 2007. 'Continuity and change in transnational Italian families: The caring practices of second-generation women'. *Journal of Ethnic and Migration Studies* 33 (7): 1103–19. https://doi.org/10.1080/13691830701541622.

Zontini, Elisabetta. 2010. *Transnational Families, Migration and Gender: Moroccan and Filipino women in Bologna and Barcelona*. Oxford: Berghahn Books.

Zontini, Elisabetta. 2015. 'Growing old in a transnational social field: Belonging, mobility and identity among Italian migrants'. *Ethnic and Racial Studies* 38 (2): 326–41. https://doi.org/10.1080/01419870.2014.885543.

Zuboff, Shoshana. 2019. *The Age of Surveillance Capitalism: The fight for a human future at the new frontier of power*. London: Profile Books

Index

Abbasi, Khadija, and Alessandro Monsutti 153
Abruzzo 124
active ageing viii, 21–2, 25–6, 165
  policies 22–6
active welfare 24, 110
activism x, 56
  '2G' 134
  online 129, 136, 137, 139
addiction, to smartphones ix, x, 81–2, 86–7, 104, 139
adolescence 147
affective economies 15
Afghanistan x, 17, 129, 135–7, 138, 151–4
  elders in 152–3
  Soviet invasion 135
ageing
  and care 26–7
    see also care, caregivers
  classifications of vii, 21–2
  crafting of 167
  and existential questions 43
  experiences of vi, 21–2, 39–41, 122
  and life experience 38
  narratives of 16, 17, 39, 142–58, 161–3, 167
  perceptions of vii, 21–2, 35, 152–3, 165, 166, 167–8
  physical mobility issues 114–15
  and search for *equilibrio* ix, 61, 148, 151, 156, 157, 163
  with smartphones 22
  stigmas around 25
  tunnel metaphor 21, 41
ageism, in workplace 35
Ahang, Basir 137
  Sogni di tregua 138
Airbnb 36
alarm clock, app 91
Alexandria, Egypt 84
allotments viii, 13, 24, 34, 49–50, 96, Fig. 3.2
  apps for 95
  events held by sites 49–50
ambiguity xi, 84, 133, 157, 168, 169
Anderson, Bridget 133
anno scolastico (school year) 44
anthropology, material culture 95
anti-Fascism 55, 144
anti-racism 56, 57, 144
anxiety
  about ageing 168
  about immigration 88–9
anziani see older adults

Apple iPhone 86, 90
apps 14, 89–98, 105, 157
  alarm clock 91
  for allotments 95
  attitudes to 95–6
  calendar 91
  health 113–16, Fig. 6.1, 105n
  maps 84, 91
  mindfulness 36
  organising 96
  plant-identifier 94
  step-tracking 115
  translation 84, 124
  travel 91–3, Fig. 5.8
  weather 91
Apulia 17, 44, 75, 131
Arabic (language) 131
ASSA (Anthropology of Smartphones and Smart Ageing project) 83, 119
  and app usage 89
  fieldsites 35, 101, 166
asylum seekers viii, 24, 48, 118, 136
audio messages 98
Auser (Associazione per l'invecchiamento attivo) 24, 118
Australia 37, 87, 132, 135
autonomy 61–2, 62, 76–8, 164–6
  and privacy viii–ix, 71–5, 104
  and surveillance 168
âwâra (wanderer(s)) 138
awareness, and awakenings 143–8, 156, 167

badanti see care workers
balance *see equilibrio*
Bangladesh 45
Barati, Ashraf 136
becoming, processes of 157
beekeeping 34, 50
Behind Venice Luxury: A Hazara in Italy (film) 136
belonging, sense of vi, x, 9, 10, 18, 39, 78, 96, 129, 134–9, 161, 165
Berlusconi, Silvio 89
bicycle clubs 48
Bologna 11
book clubs 48
books and encyclopaedias 145–7
Brazil viii, 35
bridge generation 37–9
'Brothers of Italy' party 60n
Buddhism 36

182

Bulgaria 70
bullying 104
  online 101

Çağlar, Ayşe 15
Çağlar, Ayşe, and Nina Glick Schiller 15
Calabria 44
calendar, app 91
Cameroon 118
Campoli del Monte Taburno 69–70
capitalism 144
care, caregivers 27–30, 36, 37
  and communication 118–23
care workers (*badanti*) 29, 30–1, 33, 115
  migrant 31
Casa, Vittoria 87
case di ringhiera (apartment buildings) 8, 13, 72–5, Fig. 4.2
  window shutters Fig. 4.1
Catholicism 61, 143, 144, 146, 154
  and Christianity 148–9
  nuns 59n
  and role of *nonna* 68
  shifting role of 148
CD-ROMs 146, 147
Central Asia 136
charities, charitable work viii, 23, 24, 75, 108, 118, 126
childcare, by grandparents 65–6, 67–9, 87
China 44
  ASSA fieldsites in 101
Chinese communities 18n
choirs ix, 54–5, 56, 143, 166
  women's multigenerational viii, 13, 54–5, 58
Christianity 145, 146, 149
  see also Catholicism
Chrome 90, 91
citizenship, social citizenship vii, 129, 131, 133–5, 138–9, 161, 162, 165
Civenti, Graziella 72
classes, Italian language 13
climate change 49
Cocco, Roberta 5
cohousing movement 164
collective living (co-living) 164
commonality, domains of 16
communication and 2G activism 134–5
  visual 98–101, 163
  voice messages 54
  see also emojis; memes; stickers
communications, online 90
community
  activity groups 87
  breakfasts 13
  community spirit 57–8
Como 7
companionship 43, 81–105, 155, 168–9
computers 146
  personal or desktop 90
contradictions ix, xi, 22, 83, 105, 154–7, 163, 169
Corriere della Sera 97
couples, married 27
Covid-19 pandemic 125, 105n, 106n
  and digital technologies 109–10, 125–6
  and isolation 71

lockdowns 25, 109
  and role of *nonna* 79n
crafting of lives 105
Croatia 70

Dari language 135, 138
Das, Veena 43
dating apps 36
day-care centres, state-run 32
Denmark 117
depression 121
diaspora studies 15
digital literacy 24, 115
digital technology 144
  and health 109–11
dinner parties 64
discrimination vii, x, 133, 144, 165
  against LGBTQ people 64
  against migrants x, 10, 119, 134, 153, 165
  ageist 35
  ethnic 76
  gender 122
  regional 16
disinformation 88–9, 101, Fig. 5.4
diversity, hyper-diversity 8, 9, 15
divorce 27, 70
doctors, attitudes to 111–13, 119–20
Dominican Republic 45
dromology 158n
Duque, Marilia 35

Ecuador 31
education 94, 145, 151, 152, 156, 167
Egypt 4, 13, 17, 38, 44, 45, 52, 74, 84, 96, 118, 124, 130–1, 132, 163
El-Tayeb, Fatima 133
Electronic Clinical Record (CCE) 110
email 83, 91, 110
'Emergency' (NGO) 120
emic perspective 20n
Emilia-Romagna 109, 111
emojis 54, 55, 97, 101, 148
entanglements, ethical vii, xi, 39, 155, 156, 157, 161
entrepreneurialism 136, 167
environment, environmentalism 48–50, 56, 144
equilibrio (equilibrium/balance) ix, 61, 148, 151, 156, 157, 163
ethnicity, fictive x
ethnography, urban digital vi, 162
ethnonationalism 17
'EU: Ageing well in the information society' (campaign) 23
EU citizens
Europe, Hazara immigration to 135
European Health Insurance Card (EHIC) 108
European Union (EU) 23, 108, 117
  'Active Ageing' vision 165
exercise classes 48, 52
exhibitions 50
existential conditions 138, 155
existential object xi, 157, 168–9
existential questions vii, 43, 46

Facchini, Carla 29
Facebook 38, 84, 101
　and allotments 50
　and community spirit 57–8, 59
　education and local history pages 95
　and environmental activism 49
　and fake news 88–9, Fig. 5.4
　familiarity of 119
　Messenger 89, 91, 96
　NoLo Social District group 11, 56–8
　sharing photos 93
　sharing recipes 93
　and sociability 74
　transnational communities and 137
　use by older people 87
　use by women 122
　Via Padova groups 56
'fake news' 82, 88–9, 124–5, Fig. 5.4
families
　activities for 48
　lack of communication within 147
　nuclear and extended 63–4, 64–6
　transnational 155
　values of 143
family and home ix, 26, 37–9, 40, 47
Fascism 45, 89, 144
feminism 56, 144
Ferragosto (public holiday) 45
file sharing 137
film clubs 48
film portrait of Milan 149, Fig. 8.1
film-making 129, 136–7, 138, 139
Five Star Movement 87
folklore 68
food and cooking 38
　recipes 93
　and role of grandmothers 69
　tutorial Fig. 5.10
Foot, John 64, 71, 74
foreigners (*stranieri*) and Italians 9, 16–17
frailty 24, 39, 115
　control of 22
　equated with ageing vii–viii, 21, 40, 157, 166
France 87
friendship 52, 71–2, 74, 164
future, uncertainty about 18, 32, 38, 40–1

Garvey, Pauline 35
gender 65, 162
　discrimination 122
　normative constructions of 148
generational, cross-generational
Germany 87
GiraNoLo walking group 12
The Global Smartphone 90, 153, 169
Goffman, Erving 156, 41n
Google 119
　and information on health ix–x, 123–5
Google Maps 14
Google Translate 54, 124
grandchildren 29
　photos of 14
grandparents vii, 23, 32, 61
　childcare by 65–6, 67–9, 87
　grandmothers, groups 56

nonna (grandmother), role of 65–9, 70, 78, 79n
Grey Panthers 25, 116
Gulf states 135

Hafez 137
Hazara x, 12, 17, 129, 135–8, 151–4
　and poetry 137–8
Hazāragi language 135
Hazarajat 135
health
　and digital technology ix–x, 109–11, 118, 166
　googling for information on ix–x, 123–5
　health and care 107–26, 134, 166
　holistic 121
　maternal and infant 119
　start-ups and initiatives 114, 117
　see also frailty
health apps 113–16, 166, Fig. 6.1, 105n
　most used Fig. 5.9
health tourism 108
hipsters 10
history, local 94
holidays 44–5
　public 45, 54
holistic health remedies 121
home (*casa*) 64–6, 169
hormone replacement therapy (HRT) 121
horticulture 9, 48
hospitality 70
housing, co-living arrangements 164
human chain 57
human rights 136

identity
　notions and practices of x, 10, 16–17, 129, 133–9
　Salvini on 130–1
Iezzi, Vincent, *More Coffee with Nonna* 67–8
immigration, policies on 31
'In my school no one is a foreigner' (mural) 9, Fig. 1.5
Indonesia 44, 52
inequalities, socio-economic vii, 36, 59, 126, 133, 139, 144, 164
'information age' 144–6, 167
Instagram 49, 51, 87, 101
integration 54
intergenerational relationships 16, 37–9, 78, 132
International Women's Day 54
International Workers' Day 45, 54, 57
internet 146
interviews 13–14, 162, Fig. 1.9
iPhone 86, 90
Ipsos 87
Iran 135, 136, 138
Ireland viii, 35, 70
isolation and loneliness 59, 71
'Italianness' 17, 70, 131, 132, 134, 148
Italy
　business hours 45
　economic crisis (2008) 2, 3, 33
　far right in 130–1
　Fascism in 45

general election (2018) 60n
median age 83
migration 2–3
Ministry of Health 125
national healthcare system ix, 23, 107–9
National Liberation Day 45, 55
Nazi occupation of 45
Northern League party 131
politics 69–70
population 1
post-war economic boom 144, 148
resistance movement 50, 55
smartphone penetration in 87
telecoms market 3, 86
tourism 69

Japan 115
   ASSA fieldsites in 101
Jews 18n
Jones, Tobias, *The Dark Heart of Italy* 148–9
jus sanguinis 134
jus soli 134, 165

kinship 63–4
   categories 70
   models ix, 71
   non-biological 64, 72, 77
   patterns 63
knitting 26, 84, 96
Kuruvilla, Gabriela, *Milano, fin qui tutto bene* 46–7

Lamb, Sarah 23
landline phones 77, 90, 102–3
language barriers x, 121
language classes 26, 47–8, 52, 58, 75–6, 96, 121, 166
   tensions in 54
laptop computers 90
Lazio 68
LG 90
LGBTQ people
   discrimination against 64
   households 64
Liberation Day 54
liberation theology 144
Libya, fake news on migrants from 88
life course 152
life expectancy 65
Liguria 44
Line (app) 101
living alone (*vivere da sola/o*) 65, 70–1, 77
'Living and carrying out research in the neighbourhood' (film) 15, Fig. 1.9
Locatelli, Paolo 110
location 15, 107, 109, 126, 157
Lombardy 54, 107, 108
   regional healthcare services in ix, 108–9, 113, 115
lullabies 68

McKay, Deirdre 96
male workers, and sociability 56
Malta 70
maps, apps 84, 91
marches 49, 56
material culture 94
meaning-making 157–8
meditation app 28, 115
Meloni, Giorgia 60n
memes 161, Fig. 5.11–13
   on extent of smartphone use 82, Fig. 5.2
   and friendship and affection 98–101, 148Fig. 5.11, Fig. 5.13
   sharing of 99, Fig. 5.12
menopause 121–2
menstruation 122, 147
mental health 153
mHealth 111, 113, 114, 115, 116, 126, 165
Middle East 136
middle-aged people, as smartphone uses 83
migration, migrants 24, 48, 69–70, 153
   and anti-immigrant rhetoric 88–9, Fig. 5.4
   from Egypt 4, 13, 17, 38, 44, 45, 52, 74, 84, 96, 118, 124, 130–1, 132, 163
   from Libya 88
   from Peru 4, 8–9, 17, 30, 31, 44, 45, 47, 52
   from Philippines 4, 17, 44, 45, 96–7
   and healthcare 119–20
   national 16, 37, 156
   and NGOs viii, 118–19, 133
   transnational 37, 144, 59n
   see also 'second generation'
migration studies 15, 133
Milan
   Bosco Verticale 4, Fig. 1.2
   character of 163
   Chinese, Somalian and Jewish communities in 18n
   City Council (*Comune di Milano*) 49
   digital innovation 5
   Digital Transformation and Civic Services 5
   Digital Week 4
   Fashion and Design weeks 4
   fieldsite 5–15
   film portrait of 149, Fig. 8.1
   Gratosoglio district 130
   Hazara community 12, 17, 129, 135–8
   Istituto Nazionale dei Tumori 108
   location Fig. 1.1
   metro 81, Fig. 5.1
   migrants to 64
   Milano Centrale station 44
   Navigli (canal system) 44
   Ospedale Niguarda 108
   Peruvians in 47
   photographs of 44
   Piazza Morbegno 10, Fig. 1.6
   Piazzale Loreto 7, 8, 51, Fig. 1.4
   Pirelli Tower 4
   Politecnico di Milano, School of Management, Digital Innovation in Healthcare Observatory 110–11
   population 3–4
   Porta Nuova complex 5
   La Scala opera house 4
   as 'smart city' 5, 36, 104
   space and place in 46–8
   urban redevelopment 50
   Via Padova 8, 10, 46–7, 51, 52, 56, 58, 97, 134
      street parade 57, Fig. 3.4

Viale Monza 10, 44
weather in 43–4
Wi-Fi in 86
zones 5–7, Fig. 1.3
Milano-Bicocca, University of 3
Miller, Daniel 35
mindfulness app 36
misinformation 88–9, Fig. 5.4
mobile health 27, 36
mobile network providers 86
mobile phones 103
mobilities 142–3, 155–6
  transnational, and well-being 150–4
Moldova 31
money 33, 36, 120, 130, 136
Monsutti, Alessandro 138, 153
moral assemblages 154
Morocco 44, 45, 118
mothers, motherhood 26, 27, 32–3, 51–2, 53
  mother-daughter relationships 29–30, 67, 71–2, 77, 164
  role of 68, 75, 84, 98, 122, 132, 150
  and work 37, 68, 147
multi-ethnic households 64
multi-scalar networks 8, 15
multiculturalism 15
multigenerational households xi, 64, 77, 139, 162, 164
music 10, 131, 137
  festivals 12, 130–1
  on YouTube 28, 47, 93, 137, 143, 151
Mussolini, Benito 7, 50, 76
'My smartphone' (film) 85, Fig. 5.3

Naples 131
neoliberalism 144, 127n
'new Italians' 129
NGOs viii, 13, 24, 26, 48, 49, 54, 86, 108, 118, 120, 121, 133, 134
'no-mobile-phone phobia' 87
NoLo (North of Loreto) 7–9, Fig. 1.8
  activities 48–56
  Centro multiculturale 50–3, 58, 161, Fig. 9.1
  character of 150, 163–5132
  concept of 11–12
  diversity 57, Fig. 3.4
  everyday life in 43–59
  Facebook groups 56–7
  fringe festival 12
  gentrification of 8, 10
  healthcare in 118–23
  introduction to (film) 11, Fig. 1.7
  negative perceptions of 8, 46, 57, 58
NoLo Pride 12
nonna, role of 65–9, 70, 78, 79n

objectification 106n
older adults (*anziani*) vi, 21, 48
  in Afghanistan 152–3
  as 'differently young' 25
  feeling younger than actual age 21–2, 40, 157, 166
  health and physical issues 40
  negative views of smartphones 103
  smartphone use 87
  stereotypes about 168

'One day in NoLo' (film) 46, Fig. 3.1
'onlife' (as term) 141n

Pakistan 45, 52, 135
palazzi 8, 50, 73
  see also *case di ringhiera*
papacy 148
participant observation 16, 162
pension, old-age vii, 22, 33, 166
performances, public 50
Persian language 152
Peru 4, 8–9, 17, 30, 31, 44, 45, 47, 52
'Peruvianness' 8–9
Pessoa, Fernando 143
pharmacies 110, 112, 121
Philadelphia 67
Philippines 4, 17, 44, 45, 96–7
photography 14, 44, 102, 106n
  archives 15
  sharing 53–4
Piedmont 44
Pieta, Barbara 23, 25
Pink Floyd 89
poetry 129, 137–8, 139
Poland 31
political justice vii, x, 137, 139, 154
politics
  discourse 8, 16, 132, 138
  engagement with viii, 54, 55–6, 57–8, 59, 76, 95, 139, 154, 166
  and fake news 88
  identity and 9, 130–1, 134, 139
  and migration 135–7
  Nonna and 69–70
  poetry and 138
  and populism 145
  public holidays 45
  and retirement 36
  and 'second generation' 133
  and use of smartphone 87, 95–8
popular culture x
populism 145
post-traumatic stress disorder (PTSD) 108, 153
posters, information 120–1
Pride 57
privacy 61–2
  and autonomy viii–ix, 71–5, 104
public and private lives 75–7

Quatriglio, Costanza 136

racism 59, 76, 89, 133, 144
radio 77
Radio NoLo 12
Ramadan 93, 130
rapping, in Arabic 131
refugees viii, 24, 48, 69–70, 136
relationships, smartphones and 36, 84
religion xi, 39, 67, 68, 154, 155
  religious holidays 45, 54
  see also Catholicism; Christianity
La Repubblica 69, 87, 89
research participants 17–18
  observation of 16, 162
retirement 22, 33–7

groups for retired people viii
and in-family care 132
money, time and financial precarity 35–7, 40
official age for vii, 33, 166
and sociality viii, 55
time and freedom in 33–5, 40, 166
'Retirement and activities' (film) 33, Fig. 2.1
retirement or nursing homes (case di riposo)
    and care homes (case di cura) 32–3
rituals and routines 45–6, 58
Rocco e i suoi fratelli (Rocco and his brothers)
    75
Roma people 76
Romania 31, 70

'sacrificial child' 30
Safari (search engine) 90, 91
saints' days 45
Sala, Giuseppe 'Beppe' 51
Salutile (app) 113
Salvini, Matteo 69, 70, 88, 130–1
same-sex civil unions 64
Samsung 90
    Galaxy 86
'sandwich generation' 27–8
SanNolo music festival 12
Sanremo Music Festival 12, 130–1
Sardinia 112
Sartre, Jean-Paul 160n
'scalable sociality' 80n
Scandinavia 164
Screen Ecology 90
screensavers 14
search engines 90
'second generation' 17, 129, 132, 133–5, 139,
    165
Second Vatican Council 159n
Second World War 6, 64, 67, 73, 107
self-justification xi
self-sufficiency 23, 116, 165
    and digital technologies 116–18
Sembra mio figlio (film) 136–7, 138
separation and divorce 27, 70
sewing groups viii, 13, 24, 48, 52, 53, 55, 56,
    161, Fig. 3.3, Fig. 9.1
sexism 35
sexuality vi, 64, 147
Shakespeare, William 169
Sicily 17, 44, 131
single-person households 70–1
Skype 25
Slovenia 70
smart city (as concept) 5, 36, 104
smartphones
    addiction to ix, x, 81–2, 86–7, 104, 139
    age of users 82–3
    combined with landline receiver 102, Fig.
        5.14
    compared with Wi-Fi use 84–5
    as constant companions ix, xi, 43, 81–105,
        155, 168–9
    discourses about 14–15, 17
    as existential objects xi, 157, 157–8, 168–9
    and grandparenting 67
    and intergenerational care 37, 151
    loss and theft of 105

as material objects 14, 105
and mobility 143
monitoring usage 163
as objects of research 14–15
and opportunities for income 36
penetration in Italy 86
personalising 96, 102–4, 105
positive and negative views of 84, 86–7,
    102–4, 146
and relationships 36, 84
ringtones 52
and searches for information 84
and social participation 47, 59, 78, 84, 87–8
as 'Transportal Home' 64, 153–4, 169
ubiquity of use 82, 84, Fig. 5.2
use by older people 87, 90–3
use in language classes 54
use in NoLo 90, Fig. 5.5–7
usefulness (utility) of 23, 44, 84, 87, 102–3,
    116
Snapchat 101
sociability 161–2
    and *case di ringhiera* 73–5
    and co-living 164
    male co-worker 56
'social availability' viii, 61–78, 169
social benefits vii, 166
social change 16, 64, 132
'social death' 27, 156
social exclusion 76, 139, 144
social justice vii, x, 57, 64, 136, 139, 144, 165
social media 48, 56–8, 87, 101, 126, 157
    Hazara and 137, 153, 153–4
    and second-generation activism 134, 139
social relationships 48
    and separation and divorced 70
social spaces 51
'Social Street' 11–12, 59, 60n
social welfare 24, 148
sociality ix, 17, 64
    and autonomy 62, 76–8, 164–5
    scalable 80n
    value of 161
    WhatsApp and 97
'*Soldi*' song 130–1
Somalian refugees 18n
Soviet Union 135
SSN (*Servizio Sanitario Nazionale*) 23
step-tracking app 115
stickers 14, 101
'successful aging' movements (US) 22–3
surveillance ix, 101, 105, 125
    and autonomy 168
    and public health and safety 110
surveillance capitalism 18, 74
'symbolic violence' 59n

tablets 90
taboos 147
    social 122
Taliban 135, 136, 151
Tanzania 52, 118
technophobia 103
Telegram 96, 119, 137, 151, 106n
television 47, 76, 77, 97, 130, 147
Tilley, Christopher 15

TIM Telecom Italia 86
time 18, 32, 33
   experience of 43, 44–5
   and freedom 34–6
   smartphone and 8, 44, 84, 102
   structuring of ix, 44–6
   use of 43, 58, 63, 90
togetherness 122, 165
tracking 168
translation, apps 84, 124
translocality x
transnational care collectives 159n
transnationalism x, 15, 16, 37–9, 132, 163, 166, 169
   communities 137
   and families 155
   see also migration, migrants
'Transportal Home' 64, 153–4, 169
travel
   apps 91–3, Fig. 5.8
   holidays 44
Turco, Livia 134
Tuscany 109
Twitter 70, 87, 131

Ukraine 31
United Kingdom 135
United States of America 37, 87
   Hazara immigration to 135
University of the Third Age 24
urban digital ethnography 12–15, 15
usefulness
   of apps 95
   as citizen 23, 34–5, 58, 152–3, 166
   of googling 123
   of smartphones 23, 44, 87, 102–3, 116
   of WhatsApp 97
utility (as concept) 23, 39, 87, 166

vaccination records 127n
Valentine's day tour 50
Vatican 148
Venice 89, 136
Venice City Award 136
Vertovec, Steven 8
Viber 96, 119, 137, 151
Visconti, Luchino 75
visual communication 98–101, 163
Vodafone Italia 86
voice calls 91, 101
voice messages 54
volunteers, volunteering viii, 54, 166, 167

Wahidi, Amin 136
walking tour groups 12, 50–1, 56, 115
weather 43–4
   apps 91
WeChat 101
well-being 152, 153
WhatsApp 15, 58, 84, 96–8, 124
   and allotments 50, 96
   apartment building groups 96, 97, 164
   and audio messages 98
   choir group 55, 166
   and community 59

culture- and identity-linked groups 96
education and local history groups 95
and environmental concerns 49
and fake news 124–5
and family communications 30, 96, 98, 150–1, 163
groups 38, 49, 52, 53–4, 77, 135, 148, 151, 161
gym classes 96
and health 110, 111, 112, 121, 122, 125
Italian language lessons 96
knitting groups 96
memes 98–101, 161, Fig. 5.11–13
photographs 53–4, 67
popularity of 89, 91, 96, 119
positive and negative views on 97–8, 101
sharing photos 93
sharing recipes 93
and sociability 74, 161
and social availability ix, 62
transnational communities and 137
tutorials in 25
use by doctors 110
use by middle-aged people 83
use by older people 97, 111
use by women 122
uses of 23, 67, 96
video calls, visual communication 98–101, 163
voice calling 91, 101
Wi-Fi 84–5, 86, 104, 124, 146
Wikipedia 90
   app 146
Wind Tre 86
window shutters viii, 61–3, 77, 78, Fig. 4.1
women
   as caregivers 28, 31
   choirs 54–5, 166
   groups for 121
   health of 120–2, Fig. 6.2
   older 55–6
   roles in care and social work 118
   and sexism in workplace 35
   social group meeting 118–19
   social support for 13
   use of WhatsApp 122
Woolf, Virginia 169
World Expo (Milan, 2015) 5
World Health Organisation 24

xenophobia 59, 89

yoga 9, 24
young adults vi, x, 17, 48, 129–39
   as 'digital natives' 82, 86
YouTube 28, 47, 90
   documentaries 152
   and poetry 137, 151
   as source of music 28, 47, 93, 137, 143, 151

Zigon, Jarrett 154
Zontini, Elisabetta 37
Zoom 25
Zumba classes 52

Lightning Source UK Ltd.
Milton Keynes UK
UKHW020257280521
384484UK00003B/42